# Children Who
# Don't Want to Live

Israel Orbach

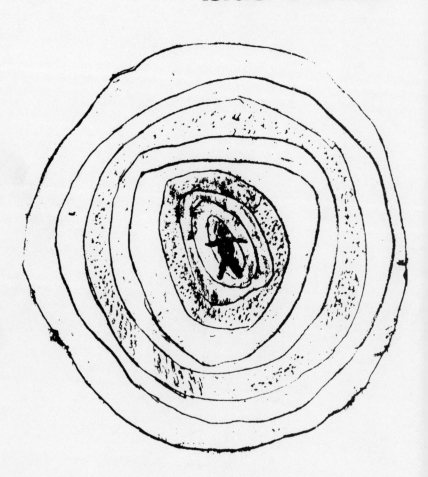

# Children Who Don't Want to Live

## Understanding and Treating the Suicidal Child

Jossey-Bass Publishers

San Francisco   •   London   •   1989

CHILDREN WHO DON'T WANT TO LIVE
*Understanding and Treating the Suicidal Child*
by Israel Orbach

Copyright © 1988 by: Jossey-Bass Inc., Publishers
350 Sansome Street
San Francisco, California 94104
&
Jossey-Bass Limited
28 Banner Street
London EC1Y 8QE

**Library of Congress Cataloging-in-Publication Data**

Orbach, Israel, date.
  Children who don't want to live.

  (The Jossey-Bass social and behavioral science series)
  Bibliography: p.
  Includes index.
  1. Children—Suicidal behavior. I. Title.
II. Series.
RJ506.S9073  1988      618.92′858445      87-46338
ISBN 1-55542-076-1 (alk. paper)

Manufactured in the United States of America

The paper in this book meets the guidelines for
permanence and durability of the Committee on
Production Guidelines for Book Longevity of the
Council on Library Resources.

JACKET ART BY TEN-YEAR-OLD SUICIDAL GIRL
DESIGN BY WILLI BAUM

FIRST EDITION
  *First printing: April 1988*
  *Second printing: April 1989*

*Code 8810*

The Jossey-Bass
Social and Behavioral Science Series

# Contents

# Preface

In the last few decades, the child has become a central focus in the study of psychology and other disciplines. But in spite of much research, there still exists a wishful fantasy that young children are somehow protected from the extreme anguish and pain that adults may experience. In particular, psychologists and others have tended to ignore a very critical problem—that of childhood self-destruction and suicidal behavior. Although child suicide is no longer a debatable phenomenon and although documentations of suicidal behavior in children date back to the turn of the century, many still find it hard to believe that children as young as five or six can sincerely wish to die—and that some actually do commit suicide.

Some of the similarities in suicidal behavior among adults and children are astonishing. Both display common patterns of development, beginning with intolerable pressure and a depressed attitude and culminating in the suicide act. It is commonly but mistakenly believed that, unlike adults, most suicidal children do not comprehend the meaning of death or the relationship between their actions and the possible lethal outcome. In most cases, it is exactly because children *do* understand the meaning of death that they wish to die. At the same time, child suicidal behavior has unique characteristics and dynamics, in contrast to adult self-destruction. However, a comprehensive conceptual approach to this phenomenon—and its treatment and prevention—is still sadly lacking.

One purpose of *Children Who Don't Want to Live* is to integrate current theoretical, empirical, and clinical knowledge about different manifestations of child suicide. The discussions are accompanied by and illustrated with case histories of suicidal children and their families. However, this book goes far beyond a simple integration of current knowledge. It formulates unique dynamics and processes of childhood suicide that are grounded in special life circumstances; and it tries to distinguish this behavior from adult suicide and from other pathological behavior by introducing the concept of the "unresolvable problem." Suicidal children, it alleges, are trapped by their families into impossible situations, not always detectable on the surface, and are faced with a narrow range of possible solutions or are prevented from adopting any other solution except suicidal behavior. From this perspective, suicidal behavior in children is not merely attention-seeking or manipulative behavior but something far more significant.

The conceptual perspective of the "unresolvable problem" is then integrated, along with other theoretical formulations and empirical findings, into a comprehensive phenomenological model. This integrative model has specific implications for evaluating and treating various phenomena of self-destruction in children. Thus, the reader is equipped with knowledge, a conceptual outlook, and a set of practical tools to approach the problem at hand.

## Overview of the Contents

Chapter One begins with two case descriptions of young girls who attempted suicide and then presents an initial theoretical outline. This material gives the reader an experiential base for understanding child suicide. Chapter Two deals with definitions and theories of adult suicide and their applicability to childhood suicide. Chapter Three describes the suicidal behavior of children as it appears in everyday life, its various manifestations and psychological meaning. Chapters Four and Five explore possible links between self-destruction and personality characteristics and between suicide and life circumstances. Chapter Six extensively analyzes the development of the death concept and shows how children cope with death under various conditions, such as when encountering death, when suffering from a severe illness, and specifically when facing suicidal urges. Chapter Seven delineates some of the possible family processes involved in childhood suicide. An in-depth case study of an adolescent's suicide is presented in Chapter Eight; it reveals the day-to-day manifestations of the family's lifestyle and the possible origins, in childhood, of this adolescent's death.

After the extensive presentation and analysis of data, clinical vignettes, and various processes in the preceding chapters, Chapter Nine turns to various conceptualizations that are unique to self-destruction in young children, including the "unresolvable problem" theory. This discussion culminates, in Chapter Ten, in the presentation of an integrative phenomenological model. Chapter Eleven focuses on the critical issues of diagnosis and treatment.

This book, which was first published in Hebrew in April 1987, is written for a wide range of people from the helping and health professions—including psychologists, psychiatrists, sociologists, social workers, physicians, nurses, educators, and school personnel. In addition, I believe that anyone who cares about children will be deeply interested in this book.

Although the subject matter is often painful, there is much that is hopeful in these pages. By understanding the underlying reasons for and processes of child suicide, we will be better able to recognize signs of suicidal behavior and help children solve their "unresolvable problems." The ultimate goal of this book is, of course, to prevent the problems from becoming unresolvable in the first place.

I would like to acknowledge the assistance of Michael Hoffman and the Schnitzer Foundation at Bar-Ilan University in the writing of this book.

*Flushing, New York*                                     ISRAEL ORBACH
*February 1988*

# The Author

Israel Orbach is currently senior clinical psychologist at the Adolescent Suicide Clinic of Albert Einstein School of Medicine, Yeshiva University, New York. He is on leave as associate professor from Bar-Ilan University in Israel from 1987 to 1989.

Orbach received his B.A. degree in psychology from Bar-Ilan University in 1968 and his M.A. and Ph.D. degrees in clinical psychology from the Ferkauf School at Yeshiva University in 1971 and 1974, respectively. He received his clinical training at Albert Einstein School of Medicine. He has been a visiting professor at the University of California, Los Angeles, and other universities.

Orbach has been engaged in clinical work on suicide for thirteen years. He has also developed several suicide prevention programs, conducted research, and published extensively in this area.

# Children Who
# Don't Want to Live

# 1

# Children Who
# Don't Want to Live:
# Two Cases

One does not go unguided into the dark night of children who no longer want to live. My first guide was Rina. When I met her, she was seven years old and suspected of being retarded. As the new school psychologist, I was supposed to assess the case. Initially frightened about what was going to happen, Rina slowly warmed up, took off her cap, and unzipped the heavy winter coat that seemed to swallow her up. My journey into the world of child suicide had begun. Rina asked if she could use some paper and crayons that I had set aside. When I nodded yes, she drew two parallel lines for a road, which quickly filled with cars. She then drew a little girl on one curb and a woman on the other. Satisfied with her efforts, she asked me if I knew what the drawing was about. When I hesitated, unwilling to hazard a guess, she went on herself: "This little girl wants to get run over."

This was the first time that a young child had ever hinted to me about suicide. After my first astonishment passed, I asked her why the child wanted to be run over. Rina's answer was straightforward if indignant: "Because this woman wants her dead." Now completely shocked, I asked her to explain why the woman would want such a thing. Her reply: "That's just the question. Why does the lady want her run over?" As I sat in silent bewilderment, Rina's eyes filled with tears and she repeated in despair: "Why does she want the girl to die?" I started to

1

probe further, but Rina brought me to journey's end: "I have to go now, but I'll be back again." Then she left the room.

Rina, as I later learned, was the oldest daughter in a family composed of a mother who had been hospitalized as a paranoid in a string of mental institutions, a father who was a simple unskilled worker, and two siblings who had both been diagnosed as retarded.

Rina's problems had started three days after her birth, when she was brought home from the maternity ward. After one glance, her mother had insisted that Rina was not really her daughter, that there had been a mix-up at the hospital. Nevertheless, no one but the mother was allowed to touch her.

A relationship of dependence and destruction sprang up between mother and child. Once, when Rina had started to learn reading and writing, she proudly showed off her skills. Her mother's retort was "What do you think you are, better than the rest of us or something?" That may have been the moment when Rina first began to play the role of a retarded child, in order to resemble her siblings and regain her mother's love.

Often, Rina would appear at school with dark bruises. At first, she tried to hide them from me in our meetings. Only later did she feel free to show her awesome collection of welts and scratches. All were a product of unpredictable punishments, meted out for no apparent reason by her mother. At times, Rina's mother would deny her food for a day or make her stand in the corner overnight. Once, she even locked Rina in a chicken coop. The girl seemed to be an easy target for fits of maternal anger, fright, or frustration.

Over time, I found out that Rina had woven an intricate net of suicidal plans and games for many months. She had often tried running into traffic in order to be run over. Her fatal tendencies got to be such an open secret that teachers were afraid to take her out on school trips. On one occasion, she was actually hit by a car and suffered minor injuries. The warm attention that she received from the medical staff constituted almost her first contact with affection.

I was aided in therapy with Rina by one of her school counselors, Mira. Our goal was to give Rina a heavy dose of "improved parenting." During the one or two hours a week that we saw her, we tried to provide warmth, love, acceptance, security, and boundaries. Rina was more than willing to adopt us as substitute parents. She even demanded that we take her home with us. She pushed us to display our love. She was furious at other children in treatment, even to the point of hitting them. All in all, Rina tested our abilities and patience to their end and derived great pleasure from her newfound powers.

During the first months, our relationship with Rina was on a straightforward, give-and-take basis. We gave and Rina took —hungrily, passionately, without end. It was as if we had to make up for debts long overdue. The therapy only served to make everything more obvious and pressing. It removed her façade of quiet self-containment. Rina demanded without inhibition and with considerable vehemence. Any refusal was met with a storm of anger and epithets.

Rina had much to teach us about therapy with children who don't want to live. This was a course that no university could provide. For example, if Mira or I did not pass one of her loyalty tests, Rina would run to the window, hop on a chair, and threaten to plunge from the third floor. She would closely follow our every reaction. At the outset, we tended to discount her attempts as no more than "attention getters." Only later did we begin to fathom the depth of her seriousness. She was acting out the message "If you don't love me, there is no life." We therapists treated these incidents in a way that ran counter to standard textbooks. One of us would take her off the chair. Then we would hug her and tell her that we wouldn't let her hurt herself. Rina enjoyed this response no end and sometimes found it hard to hide her glee when she would threaten to jump to her death. Not unexpectedly, our treatment only increased the initial rate of these threats.

Sometimes, Rina's death games became more bizarre. For example, she would enter the room angry and surly, shut up within herself. Then she would whip out a metal pin and try to stick it into a socket to electrocute herself. One winter day, she tried to throw herself on an electric stove. This behavior went beyond attention seeking to express anger, protest, and despair.

She wanted to kill herself in order to share death with the whole world. This pattern often appeared after a night of abuse by her mother, as her father stood by helplessly. It reached the point that Rina once came in, sat down, and burst into tears. "I want to die. I can't take it any longer." These suicidal acts were no mere attention-seeking ploys but represented a serious struggle between life and death.

The death games came to an end suddenly one day, after the following interchange. I had asked her, "Rina, have you ever seen someone dead?" "Yes." "What does it mean to die?" "To die is like sleeping." "And what happens to someone who dies?" "They take him to the hospital." "And then what do they do?" "They take care of him and they give him medicine." "And then?" "He goes home." "When did you see someone dead?" "Once on the sidewalk." "Have you ever seen a dead dog?" At this, Rina paled; her features seemed diminished. She was silent. "What happens to a dog that dies?" I continued. She turned to me with a look of panic: "They bury him?" At that, she called upon her familiar refrain whenever anxiety ran rampant: "I have to go now. I'll come back later." It was as if Rina had suddenly grasped a connection between her suicide attempts and death, a link she had been unaware of before. It seemed that Rina simply had not associated her knowledge of death in animals or people with her suicide games.

From then on, Rina stopped using suicide games. She began to express her death wishes verbally—in direct, open expression of her distress. She began to disclose and defuse the contents of her home life. Therapy with Rina did not necessarily become less trying, but at least it had taken a new course. It was as if her anxieties over death had reined in her impulsive acting out and brought to the surface new coping processes.

After a year and a half of therapy, Rina was placed in a boarding school by court order. The legal confrontation with the parents paved the way for us to contact them and help them get the aid they desperately needed. Rina's life took a dramatic turn for the better. The sadomasochism between mother and child fell off substantially. As if in a fairy tale, the girl who was once thought retarded bloomed into one of the outstanding students in her class.

The reasons for Rina's suicidal behavior seem obvious: extreme rejection by a mentally ill mother, physical and mental abuse, a massive attack on her identity, and estrangement from her family. In other cases, however, the dynamics of and reasons for self-destructive behavior are not so easily identified. Lily was ten years old and the youngest in her family when she walked into the therapy room following an attempt to hang herself. Her father had returned early from work and had found her standing on the dining table trying to attach a rope to the chandelier. Lily insisted that she was "just playing" and did not mean to harm herself. Lily's parents also assured me that she had not intended to kill herself. They were positive that her behavior was merely an attention-seeking tactic. However, they could not imagine why she would feel the need for such maneuvers. At school, she was a good student, had many friends, and was engaged in numerous extracurricular activities.

Throughout this session, Lily shrank in her chair as if she wanted to disappear. Whenever her parents turned to her for a response, she bashfully nodded her head, agreeing with everything. Whenever I asked her a question, she would first examine her parents' expressions and then would nod or shake her head or simply shrug her shoulders.

In the next few sessions, I saw Lily alone. She appeared to be very uneasy and signaled that she wished she were not in the therapy room. Later, when she became more comfortable, she disclosed that at times she felt as if she would rather not be alive. She had often thought of killing herself but was afraid to do so. She sounded very sad and desperate but could not come up with any specific reason for her feelings. In a lifeless, detached voice, she revealed that, on the day her father surprised her, she had attempted to hang herself, but she was not sure then that she really wanted to die. She also mentioned that, on the previous night, she had heard a news report on television about a young girl who hanged herself.

In the course of the therapeutic meetings, she started to verbalize some of her feelings more concretely: "There is no room for me at home. There is not enough space. Wherever I go, I am driven out by somebody." She related that she shared a room with her older sister but was forced to leave whenever her

sister entertained friends. Her older brother would not let her
stay in his room for even five minutes, and she could not watch
her favorite shows on television because it disturbed her father.

Such complaints can by no means be considered reasons
for suicide. Nevertheless, they reflect a sense of rejection. This
feeling indeed surfaced after a number of meetings with Lily
and with different members of her family. As was revealed later,
Lily's mother did not welcome her pregnancy with Lily. She
had planned to go back to school and begin a long-sought career
for herself as an interior decorator. The father categorically rejected the idea of an abortion. He also had very rigid ideas
about the roles of husbands and wives in family life: the man is
the provider, and the woman is the emotional supporter and
educator. He insisted on having more children. The mother gave
in, and Lily was born as a symbol and reminder of the deep parental conflict. The mother's frustrations grew as her authoritarian husband pushed her to her duties in the kitchen, crushing
her dreams about a career of her own. Whenever she asked the
children to help with household work, the father would accuse
her of interfering with their homework. He was especially adamant about Lily, whom he regarded as the most intelligent in
the family. He constantly urged her to get on with her schooling
and would cut short any of her initiatives to help her mother,
encouraging her to do "more important" work. The mother's
anger took the form of a passive resentment toward Lily. She
admitted that she had had difficulties in touching Lily when she
was a baby. When it was suggested to her that unconsciously she
held Lily responsible for her frustrations, she agreed. Inciden-
tally, as was later found out, Lily had made her suicide attempt
one day after a serious quarrel between the parents.

How can Lily's suicidal behavior be understood? What is
there in the family dynamics and processes that led her to the
suicidal gestures? What traces did these dynamics and other
events leave in Lily's emotional experiences and mind that urged
her to choose such "games"? Are such life circumstances or personality characteristics unique to the formation of suicidal tendencies rather than to other types of disturbances? Moreover, to
what extent does this ten-year-old girl share the inner experi-

ences of a suicidal adult? Can childhood suicide be understood by the same psychological principles as adult suicide? Do children like Rina and Lily know the meaning of death, and do they associate their own suicidal behavior with death?

The major concern of this book is to deal with these and other critical questions. The answers are sought in various areas: in theories of adult suicide and their appropriateness for understanding child suicide; in studies of the meaning of children's suicidal behavior; and in an in-depth examination of research on personality characteristics—such as depression, weak ego functioning, and lack of self-control—that might contribute to child suicide. We will then examine the life circumstances of suicidal children, including issues such as loss, abuse, family characteristics, and academic pressure. In addition, since we cannot understand suicidal behavior without knowing how the concept of death develops in children, we will attempt to answer the critical question of children's comprehension of death. Specifically, how do attitudes toward death and knowledge about death become a part of the suicidal process itself?

A central hypothesis evolves from our examination of clinical data, theoretical issues, and research—namely, that self-destructive tendencies in children, and to some degree in adolescents, are strongly linked to familial processes rather than to personality factors. The suicidal tendency may originate in early childhood, when the youngster is strongly attached to his or her family, although the act itself may not materialize until later in life. Some of the possible family processes are elaborated theoretically and are also demonstrated in a case study of a bereaved family trying to discover what led a seventeen-year-old girl to commit suicide.

Following the groundwork and discussions of the various issues, the focus of the book turns to efforts to explain suicide and suicidal behavior in children such as Rina and Lily. A number of theories of childhood suicide are provided under several models. The psychoanalytic model explores, for example, the roles of loss and guilt in adult suicide and their implications for children. Another model emphasizes the role of the family in the suicidal process. A third model views suicidal behavior as an outcome of specific gradual developmental processes. Other models of suicide in the young include a multidynamic theory, a biochemical model, and models based on systematic research.

Critical analysis of the various models gives rise to a new concept, which, I believe, explains the unique dynamics of childhood suicide. This is the concept of the unresolvable problem. Although this concept does not contradict other explanations, its integration into other theoretical concepts allows one to determine when an event or a process such as divorce or rejection may turn out to be lethal and when it will produce less harmful effects. The unresolvable problem is actually a complex and disguised family problem, which appears on the surface as a problem for the child only. The child is pressured to resolve a problem that is unresolvable by its very nature or that is beyond the child's capability. At the same time, the youngster's attempts to resolve the problem are blocked. He cannot use new approaches; yet he cannot avoid dealing with the problem. The persistence of the unresolvable problem, on the one hand, and the continuous pressures to resolve it, on the other hand, eventually lead to suicidal wishes.

An unresolvable problem can be identified in Lily's case. Lily was pressured to resolve a longstanding problem between her parents. She was used as an outlet for her mother's hostility against her father. She was also used by the father to express his contempt for his wife. The parents refused to acknowledge such feelings against each other; at the same time, they kept involving her in their hostile exchanges and did not let her avoid the conflict. Lily was caught in the cross fire. Thus, an impossible situation—or an unresolvable problem—was created for Lily.

The concept of the unresolvable problem and other valid theoretical concepts and research data give rise, in turn, to a wider theoretical model—the phenomenological model. The premise of this model is that self-destructive behavior is a multi-determined end result of conflicting forces. Four such forces are distinguished and elaborated in the form of attitudes toward life and death: attraction to life, repulsion by life, attraction to death, and repulsion by death. Each of these attitudes can be regarded as a complex mixture of cognitive concepts, emotional

stress, and motivational tendencies. The various attitudinal clus-
ters are developed and affected by numerous dynamics that can
cause or increase suicidal behavior. Although such opposing
forces exist in all children, they form a unique constellation in
suicidal children and increase the danger of self-destructive behavior. This model is elaborated and its explanatory value is
demonstrated through case presentations and experimental
studies. The model is also applied to diagnosis, prediction, and
therapeutic strategies to be used with suicidal children.

The last questions dealt with in this book concern diagnosis and therapy with suicidal children. Even the brief case
studies of Rina and Lily make it clear that both evaluation and
therapy should take place within the family context. Such complicated processes as the unresolvable problem, destructive relationships, and other dynamics cannot be assessed or treated
without the participation of the entire family.

This chapter has introduced the theoretical issues and
views for understanding child suicide and its treatment. In
Chapter Two, we review some theories of adult suicide as a
background for investigating and understanding childhood suicide and suicidal behavior.

# 2

# Adult Suicide:
# What Can It Tell Us
# About Suicide Among Children?

The topic of child suicide is a new addition to a field that has historically focused mainly on adults and their self-destructive behavior. Theoretical discussion of child suicide has in many cases been no more than a spin-off from theories oriented toward adults. This adult perspective has colored both the definition and the conceptual analysis of suicide. It has at times increased our understanding of suicide, although in other instances it has short-circuited creative efforts. In any event, this adult literature on definitions and theory can help us understand some historical roots of current approaches to child suicide and evaluate their relevance to self-destruction at an early age.

### Definitions of Suicide

At the outset, suicide appears clear, obvious. As Shneidman (1985) puts it, there is a dead person, a gun in his hand, a hole in his head, and a letter lying open on the table. Shneidman also offers a less concrete definition of suicide as an act of self-inflicted intentional cessation. Yet these definitions still leave a number of questions unanswered. Are suicide and attempted suicide the same, differing only in degree? Should an act be called suicide only when it results in death, or is intent sufficient? Does suicide require a single act, or does it include gradual processes of self-destruction as well? Are acts of self-sacrifice for the sake of a cause or a belief basically the same as a suicide?

At first glance, these questions seem academic and philosophical, but they have many immediate psychological implications for those involved. Labeling an act as suicide alters the effects of treatment and intervention. Let us look at a case of an older man, a chemist in charge of analyzing a potent hallucinogenic drug. Although acquainted with the drug's influence, he unthinkingly dipped his finger into the material and tasted it. After a few minutes, he began to drive home, despite waves of blurred vision, dizziness, befuddlement, and panic. A fatal crash was inches away. When he arrived home, he threw himself on the bed, burst into tears, and called for his long-deceased mother.

When the chemist replayed the events and the experience in a therapeutic session, he said: "I see now that actually I tried to commit suicide." At the time, he had been despondent and depressed over his recent divorce from his wife, which he saw as an echo of his early separation from his mother. How should we classify this case? This chemist's behavior was not consciously motivated, lacked any clear intent of self-destruction, but nevertheless nearly resulted in a fatal crash. Should his actions be seen as suicide, accident, or just stupidity or thoughtlessness? Is therapy required or just a good dressing down?

The range of human self-destruction poses questions even to the most hard-boiled professionals. For example, there are cases of people who execute two acts of self-destruction in a row within a short time interval. In these cases, only the second attempt seems to evoke the label of suicide. A young man of nineteen, an outpatient in a psychological clinic, cut his wrists one night while the whole family was in the house. He was taken to the hospital and treated. He stayed overnight under close medical observation and underwent psychiatric evaluation the next day. Since the suicide attempt was considered "not serious," he was left the next night without any supervision. He was even given a bit of a dressing down. Toward morning, he went up to the seventh floor of the hospital and jumped to his death.

This case illustrates the risk of overemphasizing the severity of outcomes when defining suicide. At times, searching for theoretical hairs to split leads to unintentional neglect of the person, his world of experiences, and his attitude toward life and death.

Smith (1984) reports another case that challenges an overstrict emphasis on intent. A twenty-one-year-old athlete, a popular and successful student, wrote a suicide note after breaking up with his girlfriend. He then climbed a scenic university tower, jumped, and was fatally injured. Yet his final words, "Don't let me die, I don't want to die," raise doubts about the depth of his intent. Despite the actual implementation of a plan made and executed with full awareness and consciousness, his resolve is unclear.

This definitional issue regarding the role of severity and intent has paralleled theoretical discussions regarding the degree to which those who attempt suicide and those who complete the act are similar or different. One approach has been to make a basic differentiation between the two patterns on the basis of the personalities and motives involved. "Attempters" are thought to be manipulative, vocal, and dependent individuals who only behave as if they are going to commit suicide. They never reach the edge despite repeated behaviors in that direction. The "suicidal" are seen as depressed or mentally ill individuals who are motivated by self-destructive tendencies. They are not likely to use scare tactics but, rather, mean to carry out their plan. If they are saved, it is only because of extraordinary circumstances.

Another distinction between those attempting and those completing suicide revolves around life circumstances rather than personalities. Those who actually commit suicide are thought to face intolerable life situations involving unresolvable conflicts. Those who only attempt suicide face lesser anguish, which may still be defused. The suicide attempt is seen as an instrument toward this end.

A more flexible approach is taken by Shneidman (1985), who emphasizes the existential experiences surrounding attempted and actual suicide. People who commit suicide feel helpless and hopeless. For them, life is permeated by anguish and frustration. Their aim is to resolve an intolerable dilemma through oblivion. Their basic conflict, then, is between existence and obliteration. Their thought is colored by dichotomous thinking and distorted concepts of the world. In contrast, those who merely attempt suicide feel pain resulting from a fear of abandonment. Their aim is to find relief from this pain. The basic conflict here is between the wish to live and avoid pain and the wish to die. The thinking pattern is characterized by obsession and many distortions in perception. Shneidman's approach does not categorically distinguish between acts of suicide and attempts at suicide. Indeed, it is one of the few to consider the possibility of a continuum of self-destructive behavior. This process may start with nonfatal acts, such as thoughts, wishes, threats, or attempts, and slowly reach the peak of the process with fatal suicide actions.

Among children, the definitional vagaries regarding intent and severity become further amplified. Moreover, some psychoanalysts assert unequivocally that children under the age of twelve are incapable of suicide. The arguments are varied and impressive: "Children are incapable of the guilt or destructive terror needed for suicide." "They don't understand the concept of death." "They couldn't carry it out even if they wanted to, since they can't deal with the complexities of planning." The phenomenological approach offers a potential way of cutting through these definitional webs. Its notion of a developmental continuum and its emphasis on the internal world of the child seem directly relevant to the problems posed by child suicide. These concerns are developed further throughout this book.

### Theories of Adult Suicide

Theories of adult suicide are many and varied, making it preferable to review them in an eclectic fashion. Two of the approaches discussed here—those of Freud and Durkheim—were chosen because of their historical centrality in the field. The others were chosen because of their unique emphases. Shneidman's work focuses on phenomenological concepts, Smith's on a modern mix of phenomenology and psychoanalysis. Maris ad-

dresses life circumstances from the vantage point of existentialism and the research literature.

*Psychoanalytic Theory.* Application of psychoanalytic
theory to suicide has undergone twists and turns paralleling the
history of the theory itself. When Freud ([1927] 1953) began
to add concepts such as the death instinct to his theory, his
views on suicide broadened. Freud's disciples further extended
the domain of analysis. Thus, the resulting theory combines a
rich brew of ideas, such as Thanatos, libido, id, ego, superego,
and identification. These are then mixed with experiences of
loss and primitive yearnings for the mother and for rebirth.

According to psychoanalytic theory, suicide is a highly
convoluted process related to depression and pathological
mourning. It has its origins in an ambivalent love-hate reaction
toward someone lost through death, separation, or rejection.
Yet identification with the parental figure and simple emotional dependence prevent any overt expression of anger. Rather,
the anger is turned inward and takes the form of sadistic self-
punishment. As Shneidman puts it, suicide is murder turned
180 degrees. In Freud's terminology, the superego "punishes"
the ego subconsciously with guilt and creates an unconscious
impulse to die. Thus, the redirection of aggression inward re-
lieves guilt over aggressive thoughts and opens the way for reunion with the loved person.

Fenichel (1945), one of Freud's followers, argues that
suicide is a symbolic murder of the loved-hated person. It also
has psychosexual and erotic aspects. Unconscious desire for reunion with a lost loved one is viewed as an attempt to actualize
primary erotic wishes. In this context, it is interesting to note
that a study of terminally ill women (Weller, Florian, and Tenenbaum, forthcoming) found that their image of death was characterized by references to sexuality and that they pictured death
as masculine. Some psychoanalytic researchers (Van Hellmuth,
1965) attribute to children a similar tendency to view death as
an omnipotent figure who arouses attraction and repulsion.

A slightly different view of suicide is offered by one of
the more recent transformations of the psychoanalytic approach:
object relations theory. This theory bases personality develop-

ment on the internalization of parental figures, both in positive and negative terms. The arena of development is shifted from the psychoanalytic focus on the eternal conflicts between life and death, or sex and aggression, to issues of separation and individuation. In normal development, the child gradually severs the close bonds linking parent and child and creates a distinctly separate, independent personality. According to the theory of object relations, suicide represents the adamant refusal to separate, to untie the primary symbiotic knot. It stops maturation, which would eventually result in distance from the parental source of security, love, and support. Paradoxically, death becomes the basis for creating an eternal relationship. The act of suicide is triggered when there is a threat from the environment of disattachment and separation. It is especially likely when the person's sources of nurturance, love, and security are less than satisfactory.

A quirk of most psychoanalytic theories is the ability to interpret a phenomenon and its opposite with the same concepts, or to use contradicting notions to arrive at the same conclusions. For example, some theorists use object relations concepts to arrive at suicide from a contrary route (Richman, 1978). They regard self-murder as an escape hatch from the family framework rather than as a means of maintaining the bond. Moreover, the psychoanalytic concepts and principles used to explain suicide are essentially identical to those used to explain all other forms of behavior—pathological and normal. Thus, these concepts do not permit prediction of potential suicides and are incapable of distinguishing suicidal individuals from those with other ailments. Nonetheless, the phenomena noted in these theories often do appear in case histories of those with suicidal tendencies.

*Durkheim's Sociological Approach.* At the turn of the century, Durkheim laid the cornerstone of a sociological theory of suicide that continues to stand to this day. In his pioneering volume, Durkheim ([1897] 1951) outlined a general social model applicable to a range of phenomena. Suicide forms only one example in its analytic scope. According to Durkheim, destructive behavior is a result of the type of control that society exerts over the individual and the relationship between the individual and society. He presents three kinds of relationships that are likely to lead to different types of suicide.

First, society may exert control over the individual through norms, values, and rituals. Certain societies leave no freedom for the individual—even to the point of dictating suicide as a specific norm. In Japan, for example, suicide by harakiri or in kamikaze planes was regarded as appropriate and noble. At times, the individual was trapped into the suicidal act and had no alternative. Durkheim refers to this type of suicide as altruistic suicide.

A second type of suicide arises in a society where there is an absence of control over the individual. This situation occurs in alienated groups with little sense of social or cultural belonging. One of the results is a feeling of isolation and lack of support, which leads to suicide. In the United States, for example, those people who are not connected to others through social institutions such as the church or marriage have higher suicide rates. This type of suicide is called egotistical.

Durkheim's third type of suicide, the anomic, arises in social situations where a sudden crisis has destroyed the few links the person had to his environment. This crisis typically involves a loss of status, work, companionship, or love. It is accompanied by feelings of alienation from society. Even purportedly positive shifts, such as becoming rich overnight or receiving an unexpected job opportunity, can unbalance the person and shake up his or her usual habits and social relations.

*Shneidman's Phenomenological Approach.* More recent analyses have focused on the drama of suicide itself, through research, observation, and encounters with people who have considered suicide. Shneidman (1982), for example, puts himself in the very midst of the death by visiting the scene of events and the morgues and by talking to the most meaningful people in the suicide's life. These untraditional methods give entrance to the inner world of the person standing on the brink of death.

Shneidman views suicide from three experiential vantage points: lifestyle, emotional inner world, and thought patterns. The suicidal lifestyle is characterized by hostility toward the self and others. The suicidal person does not love himself, is persistently pessimistic, and cannot enjoy himself or those surrounding him. He is in continual conflict with his environment. He changes jobs often, exposes himself to failures, and tends to argue with everyone. This is a person who is always setting goals that are difficult to achieve and thus is never satisfied.

The emotional state of a person who commits suicide or has suicidal tendencies is a state of constant uneasiness or perturbation, of never-ceasing disturbance. It is a stirring combination of guilt, fear, shame, uncertainty, and vulnerability. The person feels trapped, caged, rejected, and enraged. He slides often into helplessness and hopelessness. There is no escape from the internal uproar. This emotional state is manifested in many forms, from regression and introversion to externalized, continuous, exhausting action. A woman on the verge of committing suicide expressed her kaleidoscopic inner experience in the following sentences: "I'm not worth anything, I can't stand myself. . . . I'm different from everyone else, so I don't deserve to live. . . . I have no bonds with anyone, so what is there to live for? I haven't done anything in my life and never will. I don't see how all this is going to help. So what if I'm a good mother? It doesn't help my children. I only infect them, so what good is it? . . . The songs I write won't interest anyone anyhow. Everyone loves me but for no reason, I don't deserve it. I can't even smile to myself in the mirror. I stay in bed and stink. I have no energy to get up. Nothing interests me. I don't love anyone, they simply pity me."

Shneidman believes that a suicidal person also displays characteristic ways of thought. Central to these is the dichotomous perception of events in terms of black or white, yes or no, "suitable" or "unsuitable." The world is divided in two, with no shades of in-between and no other options. Acts are either good or bad; no love means hate; incomplete success is complete failure; if life isn't perfect, I'd rather die. Shneidman claims that the dichotomy is expressed in the recurrent use of *always, never, forever,* or *only.* The use of dichotomous thought makes one's options narrower and narrower. The suicide begins displaying tunnel vision, a very focused perception lacking background and context. Dichotomous thought is accompanied by logical errors and mistakes in simple induction and deduction. It blunts one's ability to differentiate between the important and the incidental. A depressed woman in the throes of an internal conflict over suicide described the process thus: "It's like walking on the mountain top with a rocky trail supporting you from both sides. Slowly the path leads down to the ground, and the walls on either side get higher and higher. Suddenly the trail plunges into the ground, around and around, with no way out. You're afraid to walk up the sides and leave the path, take a new step. Where could you get the energy for such a move? Instead, you sink into your own whirlpool."

All these patterns are thought to peak at the time of the suicidal act. Shneidman (1982) quotes a woman who described her experiences in the last moments before she jumped from a fifth floor but miraculously did not die. She was in a hospital, following a prior suicide attempt from which she had been saved. With complete detachment, she left her room, walked up the stairs, and climbed onto a railing of the roof. Her mind was in a complete fog; she had no thoughts or feelings. The only thing she saw was the point from which to jump. Once she got there, her mind remained a complete blank. With such thought processes, it is easy to see the invidious attraction of suicide once the idea arises.

Personality patterns such as these do not come about overnight. They coalesce over a lifetime, along with basic coping styles. The suicidal are thought to have a tendency toward rigidity and a pessimistic outlook. They are uncompromising and find it hard to tolerate vagueness or unclarity. They always tend to exit or retreat when frustrated, even to the point where they simply walk away from life.

But suicide is more than just running away. Behind every suicide, Shneidman believes, there is an aspiration that ordinary means cannot attain. Suicide is an attempt to achieve the goal in one fell swoop. People who write suicide notes often give instructions to those left behind them. There is an intimation that the soon to be dead will actually remain nearby to witness the execution of their instructions.

Shneidman's approach can be seen most clearly in a detailed case history. A fifty-five-year-old man, who had worked for years as a successful engineer at a large company, committed suicide after suffering from a prolonged depression. He was famous and respected, a good family man with two children. Somewhat compulsive, he leaned heavily on logic, for emotionality seemed to him contemptible, a sign of weakness. Excellence was the linchpin of his life. His parents—regimental, rigid, pedantic, almost ritualistic—had taught him that success was the only way to receive recognition and love.

He had come to therapy after three years of deep depression, which had begun when a new administrator made organizational changes that substantially lowered his status at work. All at once, his life started to crumble. He felt that he had become old, wasted, miserable, superfluous, and useless. In his thinking and his conversations, he compulsively emphasized his worthlessness and his experience of bodily and mental deterioration. He longed for his glorious past and dismissed any notion that he could ever flourish again, since neither his present employer nor any other employer would appreciate his talents.

Despite a disbelief in psychological treatment, he followed his doctor's orders to seek help. Therapeutic communication was alien to him. Yet after approximately three months of therapy, he felt some relief. He even stopped taking the medication he had believed in so strongly for the past three years. And then, despite many admonitions, he cut off therapy.

Four months later, he returned, beaten down a second time. It was surprising, since a renewed job hunt with professional assistance had turned up a position whose perquisites surpassed those he had received earlier. Nonetheless, he remained despondent and pessimistic because he was afraid that he would again prove a "failure."

The second bout of therapy ran the same course as the first. After an initial wave of improvement, he stopped therapy. And then, three months later, he called to make another appointment. It was just before the contract at his new place of work was to be signed. On the day of the signing itself, he killed himself with sleeping pills. With the act of suicide, this gloomy and beaten man rehabilitated a destroyed reputation and image, while sidestepping the risk of another loss. In this perspective, there is only a slight difference between suicide due to personal problems and that based on heroic self-sacrifice. This gloomy man, like the kamikaze of World War II or the protest suicides by priests in Vietnam, aspired to reach an important goal through drastic means. These rehabilitative aspects of suicide can also arise in less fatal attempts.

The instrumental role of suicide can be seen in the case of a soldier whose initial attempt at suicide was classed as a non-lethal act of manipulation, a means of avoiding hazardous duty. After the soldier attempted suicide a second time, in-depth examination revealed that his purpose was not to shirk responsibility but, rather, to rehabilitate a torn relationship with a respected officer, an apparent father figure. This, then, was the hidden, unfulfilled need and aspiration: to regain love and respect. When the relationship began to improve, the suicidal attempts ceased. Yet if the soldier's underlying purpose had been misread, one of the attempts undoubtedly would have succeeded.

As this case illustrates, there is often a dynamic link between those attempting and those completing suicide. In both completed and attempted suicides, there is an underlying need to be satisfied. If the attempt does not satisfy the need, it may develop into a completed suicide. Shneidman's notions offer a basis for positing the existence of a continuum of destructive action. This notion will be addressed in further detail throughout the book, because of its relevance to child suicide.

*Theory of the Vulnerable Personality—Smith.* Smith's (1983) starting point is a modern psychoanalytic mix of object relations and phenomenology. He uses two elementary concepts to explain suicide: ego vulnerability and the demolished life fantasy. Ego vulnerability refers to the internal organization of the individual's forces for coping with reality and the problems of disappointments, losses, frustrations, and anxieties. Certain factors make one more vulnerable: high social demands, limited emotional expression, and a view of death as a serious option for resolving problems. Others include rigidity in problem solving, an immature sexual identity, and an exaggerated emphasis on one particular aspect of the personality to the exclusion of others.

The life fantasy is defined as the manner in which the individual prefers to satisfy basic needs for love and self-esteem. Most people are forced to revise their fantasies after experiences of frustration. Without such compromise, a person is vulnerable to repeated frustrations and disappointments. Yet when a life dream is suddenly upset by the loss of a relationship, status, or esteem, one is overtaken by uncontrollable anger. The self-image deteriorates, and a feeling of internal decomposition arises. These experiences accelerate toward suicide those who are unable to reach new equilibrium and compromise.

*Theory of the Suicidal Career—Maris.* Maris's (1981) approach arises from an interesting mix of existentialism and empirical research. It starts with the notion that all people share basic themes in life: work, love, mortality, illnesses, and uncertainty about the future. Yet the specific exigencies of human existence vary from person to person and society to society. In Maris's opinion, one's particular existential status is the main element in determining suicide. Suicide is the result of an inability or a refusal to accept the conditions of one's life. Most people do not countenance suicide; instead, they develop various alternative means for solving problems—alternatives such as religion, art, work, love, sex, familial relations, entertainment, money, alcohol, drugs, and denial. Those who are unwilling to accept life as it is differ from fellow sufferers of life's travail in signal points. First, they cannot find—or refuse to seek—effective alternatives to suicide. Suicide seems ever more available, understandable, and acceptable. Second, because of physical, genetic, or psychological shortcomings, these people are simply not built to cope with life's difficulties. Their tolerance threshold is very low, and their efforts at adjustment have repeatedly failed. Finally, there is the issue of their suicidal career: even the nonsuicidal coping methods that they adopt (alcoholism, isolation, violence, drugs, risk taking) are steps toward a fatality postponed.

In Maris's view, suicide is directed at goals of escape, attack, and change. The suicidal person seeks to escape from pain or from hopeless situations brought about by old age, failure, dissatisfaction, or disease. Suicide also includes elements of attack. It is often chosen as an aggressive move against another person or an institution. Its motives of revenge or manipulation have a logic all their own. Alongside these goals is that of change in self or the life situation. These goal orientations make suicide a rational choice, even if it is not always premeditated.

## Summary

Of the theories reviewed here, some, such as Durkheim's or the early psychoanalytic formulations, have little applicability to children. The classical psychoanalytic approach even goes so far as to exclude the possibility of suicide in childhood. Somewhat more relevant are the works of Smith and Maris, yet even they use concepts demanding extensive life histories and a well-formed reasoning process and personality. For example, Maris talks about bouts with failure and frustration stretching over spans greater than a child's lifetime. Of greatest relevance are the works of Shneidman, since they forgo the analysis of structure and history to emphasize the immediacy of phenomenological experience. Although his particular formulations about adults may not always jibe with those regarding children, the questions he poses and the tools he offers for seeking their answers can be applied to child suicide as well. In many of the following chapters, an attempt will be made to adapt Shneidman's perspective to childhood.

# 3

# Suicide Among Children:
# Attempts, Threats,
# and Messages

For many reasons, most of them understandable, adults prefer to believe that children do not commit suicide. It seems inconceivable that children could become so desperate and suffer so much at their young age that they would choose death over life. Guilt and anxiety make us blind to the truth, even when it cries out to us. We are also blinded by false perceptions about childhood. One such perception is that childhood is a carefree, happy time. Another is that children lack the cunning and intrigue necessary for the act of suicide. Finally, there is the more sophisticated notion that children's personality structure does not permit the passionate emotional processes that might fuel self-destruction. Possibly all these perceptions account for the curious conclusion of the United States county coroner quoted by Rosenthal and Rosenthal (1984). He stated that any death of a child under the age of fourteen should be regarded as accidental, even when a suicide note is left behind.

A recent case illustrates the dramatic proportions of denial in the face of glaring truth. A nine-year-old boy's body was found charred under a shed in his grandfather's yard. Investigation showed that the fire had been deliberately ignited with a flammable liquid. For weeks before the fire, the boy had been acting strangely. Under severe emotional pressure, he had deteriorated to the point of losing contact with reality. Moreover, he had told his friends that he was tired of living and that he was going away to another country soon. In parting from his friends, he gave away some of his most precious possessions as gifts. Drawings from his last few weeks expressed an obsession with death. He drew pictures of graveyards and of people hanging from trees, and he filled page after page with tombstone crosses. One gets the impression that the boy had first attempted to sublimate his death through drawing before acting it out. In spite of the massive evidence of suicide, the shocked parents refused to accept the verdict. Their strenuous request that the cause of death be filed as accidental was eventually accepted by the police.

Child suicide is uncommon, but it definitely exists. One recent press report details the bizarre death of a ten-and-a-half-year-old girl who was found hanging from the handle of the kitchen freezer. Shortly before she was discovered, she had asked her uncle to tie a dead man's knot in a rope for her. The strange position she assumed assures us of her intentions: she hanged herself sitting down. At any moment, she could have prevented strangulation simply by getting up. The manner of her death gives mute testimony to her will and determination to die. Rosenthal and Rosenthal (1984) reported one of the youngest cases of suicidal behavior. They described a two-and-a-half-year-old girl who swallowed aspirin and was found unconscious after a few hours. At the time, the girl's mother was hospitalized for severe back pain, after a long period of depression. Following this almost lethal incident, the girl was brought for psychotherapy. In the playroom, she displayed aggressive, hyperactive behavior and engaged in compulsive games around the subject of death. She "force-fed" her doll aspirin and then asked her therapist to save it. She explained that the doll had to take the aspirin because "she should die today." She played for many hours with ambulances and bandages; she pretended to be dead by lying on the floor with a blanket covering her face; and she continuously verbalized ideas about death and dying.

In this case description, one can delineate many characteristics that are used to identify suicide in adults: a compulsive interest in death, a lethal act, and a diffuse awareness of the possible final outcome. One can see definite signs of intentionality and can identify a particular event that may serve as the immediate motivating force behind the destructive behavior.

Yet in the case of this two-and-a-half-year-old girl, as in other cases of child suicide, an uncertainty remains about the child's understanding of death itself. Although this particular young girl made a verbal connection between swallowing pills and dying, she still seemed to believe that her doll would be saved or revived by the doctors. Can we say, then, that this child and others like her want to die in the "true" sense of the word? Although later chapters address more fully the question of children's knowledge of death, suffice it to say that children from the ages of seven and up have an adequate, if tenuous, understanding of many critical aspects of death.

One of the difficulties in accepting child suicide is that the acts are easily mistaken for accidents—particularly since most children do not leave suicide notes (Motto, 1985). The causes of death themselves involve an element of chance: traffic accidents, falls from high places, fatalities in handling guns, or drowning. The potential for accidental death, when joined with concerns regarding children's understanding and intentionality, makes it easy to misread the signs.

This definitional problem overshadows any serious attempt to assess the dimensions of child suicide. Furthermore, most statistics are limited to adolescents between fifteen and nineteen, where suicide is the second or third most frequent cause of death (Holinger and Offer, 1984); statistics concerning younger age groups are only infrequently reported. The limited data concerning frequency of suicide in the young are to be found at the Division of Vital Statistics, National Center for Health Statistics. In 1955, according to these statistics, the suicide rate for ages ten to fourteen was 0.3 cases per hundred thousand population. In 1979, it had more than doubled to 0.8 cases for each hundred thousand. If this trend continues through the next century, the rate will be 1.8 cases for every hundred thousand children by 2001. Significant sex differences appear in the suicide rate of children, just as in that of adults. In 1979, the United States rate for boys was 1.1 cases per one hundred thousand, versus 0.5 for girls (Holinger and Offer, 1984).

The Division of Vital Statistics does not provide information on suicide among children under the age of ten. In England documentation covers even very young children, but reports for 1962–1968 indicate an absence of any deaths. However, reports by various centers and clinics throughout the United States present a much graver situation, at least concerning suicide attempts. One report concludes that 10 percent of the children brought into the psychiatric emergency wards during the year 1960 displayed suicidal symptoms (Mattson, Seese, and Hawkins, 1969).

The submerged part of the iceberg can be detected in a study by Pfeffer, Conte, Plutchik, and Jerrett (1980) of thirty-one children with emotional problems who were admitted to a psychiatric clinic in the Bronx, New York. A full third of the group displayed symptoms of suicidal behavior. This study suggests that the true dimensions of suicidal behavior may go beyond those few unfortunates whose destructive goals are reached. In dealing with threats and suicide attempts, figures are exponentially higher but less certain. About 120,000 children are thought to be hospitalized every year because of suicide attempts in the United States (Rosenthal and Rosenthal, 1984). The question arises, of course, as to how much weight should be given to attempts and to what degree they are indeed related to suicide.

## Actual Versus Attempted Suicide in Children

From a definitional standpoint, suicide attempts by children and actual suicides can be treated as different points on a common developmental continuum. An apparently harmless suicide threat can eventually turn into a lethal act completed over time. In-depth inspection shows that both the seemingly insignificant attempts and actual suicides by children have their common roots in the same destructive processes. Indeed, research demonstrates that a good way to evaluate suicide risk is to note the number of previous suicide attempts.

One can often discern a process whereby, slowly and tentatively, the child approaches the brink of death. The process starts with a harmless attempt, by which children can assess the effect it has on their surroundings. At the same time, this attempt represents a test of their ability to cope with their fear of death. A second attempt often follows the first—especially if there is only a minimal response from the social environment. This second attempt is a little more bold and dangerous, and has more serious consequences. It is as if the child were having a highly restrained and well-controlled tête-à-tête with death.

It seems that the first attempt minimizes the anxiety around death to a certain extent and sets the stage for the more hazardous act that follows. This step-by-step process accelerates when the response of the immediate surroundings falls below children's expectations. Indeed, a failed attempt often leads to a degeneration of the situation. In some cases, the attempt even brings on attacks of vituperation: "Next time, try from the sixth floor. You can't kill yourself from the second." Although that is not their purpose, such responses can spur the child on to more fatal attempts.

Indirect empirical support can also be garnered for the view of suicidal threats and actual attempts as part of a continuum. For example, Marx and Heller (1977) found a basic similarity between the personalities of those who attempt suicide and of those who fulfill their intention. Clinical evidence also demonstrates the steady, step-by-step approach to the brink of death, as illustrated in two letters written by a ten-year-old boy who threatened suicide. In the first, he wrote: "If only I had the courage, I would have jumped a long time ago. I'm tired of it all. I'm tired of always being blamed. If I had the guts, I would be rid of all of you. Then you would have peace and quiet and could finally say 'we're rid of him.' If only I wasn't afraid." The child's parents remained indifferent to his threat. To discourage further behavior of this sort, they told him that they really didn't care. His second letter was soon to follow: "To my family. I think it would be very frightening to jump from the fifth floor. I'll be in the air and then I'll crash and die. . . . You might think I'm crazy but I've reached a final decision. I'm jumping. I've had it with you all. I know you'll be sad and so will my friends, so what?'' (This boy's drawing, in which he illustrates his plan, is shown in Figure 1.)

There is an obvious difference between the tones of the two letters. The first highlights the boy's fears about jumping and expresses anger toward his family. The main tenor appears to be getting attention. The second letter is also manipulative, but it has a more decisive tone and seems to be geared more toward providing the necessary zeal. In the second letter, the young boy comes one step closer to self-destruction.

At times, the very slow, gradual process of approach to suicide has its roots somewhere in earliest childhood and comes to lethal fruition in later years. For example, the parents of a nineteen-year-old student sought counseling after he had attempted suicide twice. In the course of a therapeutic session, the mother related that both she and her husband had had children from previous marriages. The suicidal son had been conceived in an attempt to bring the two families together. The father was very surprised to hear this, nineteen years later, since he himself had not really wanted another child at that point in his life. His son's birth had interfered with his own life and career. It was clear that the youth was supposed to have filled an important role that his father knew nothing about. Moreover, he was not even completely wanted. This situation greatly influenced his life.

When the mother was asked about suicide attempts at an earlier age, she showed me a picture that the boy had drawn at age six. The carefully preserved picture showed a large eye with crossbones drawn inside the pupil. Worms crawled up and down, and one gnawed at the eye. The picture reflected an air of a complete self-loss. It strongly suggested the presence of early destructive feelings, which reached expression only at a later period of stress. His parents had associated his suicide attempt with a recent rejection by the young woman he was in love with. Yet this rejection apparently did no more than join a long history of disappointments and rejections, dating back to the time his conception was first planned. This last event was only the final straw. All in all, this case appears to illustrate the gradual development of suicide from a stance of primary basic rejection.

Figure 1. A drawing by a ten-year-old boy, who describes his suicidal threat and the means he intends to use to complete his suicide.

Another perspective on the slow developmental approach to suicide can be seen in the long period of preparation found with some children and adults. They may cut out newspaper clippings on deaths and suicides or jot down in their diaries ideas about death many years before the act. Some collect the means for their destruction over months and years, pill by pill.

The major risk of self-destructive behavior at a very young age is not the immediate possibility of death but, rather, the emergence of a self-destructive personality. At a later period, the child may then carry out a complete suicide. The meaning of these destructive kernels can often be seen only at later times. For example, the increased rate of suicides among adolescents does not seem to arise simply from the sudden appearance of an intolerable life situation or the temporary emotional upsets that accompany this period of life. It seems more probable that those who choose to commit suicide in adolescence or young adulthood had the idea implanted at an early age. The stressful times of adolescence only trigger the hidden impulses.

The decision to live or die must be made at a certain stage in all normal developmental processes (S. Tiano, personal communication, 1986). Until adolescence, the child is entwined with her parents and their way of life. In adolescence, the child establishes a social and sexual identity of her own. Decisions about her way of life become mainly her own affair. Yet, in order to achieve this independence, the adolescent must pass through a very important personal stage: she must make the decision to live and later decide how to live. Decisions about life are not necessarily conscious or easy. The need to face their complexity may explain some of the morbid ideas and actions in this age group: risk taking, philosophizing about death, or romanticizing death. Although many adolescents deal with these issues without any disruption in day-to-day life, others test them out in reality by taking drugs or having close encounters with death. These adolescents seem to require a direct confrontation with the realization of their mortality.

For a few children, suicidal behavior may seem to be a rational solution to an intolerable life situation. In this context, a suicide attempt provides a one-shot temporary solution, almost a wiping out of the past in an attempt to begin again. Thus, the suicide attempt often is accompanied by feelings of great relief or mellow relaxation following extreme exhaustion. Despite the fear, shame, and guilt accompanying it, the suicide attempt acts as a safety valve for the release of internal pressures that have no other form of escape.

One bright ten-year-old boy expressed himself in the following manner after a number of suicide attempts: "I was like a loaded bomb. I felt that I was going to explode and then I would try to do something. Every time I tried to kill myself I felt a little better, almost relieved. After a while I would feel like a bomb inside and I would try to kill myself again. Finally I realized that it wasn't helping and then I really wanted to kill myself." In spite of this child's rich verbal abilities, one can see that he had no way of releasing intense feelings. It is no wonder that he chose to compare himself to a walking bomb. Suicide became his palliative absolution. Adolescents, like younger children, also may use suicide as an emotional outlet for internal and external inhibitions. Their release is expressed on the physical plane rather than the symbolic one.

The mental processes that take place can be seen more clearly through the life history of Rebecca, a sixteen-year-old girl who had been rejected by her parents since her birth. She had been an unplanned and unwanted child. As a very young child in nursery school, she developed a pattern of injury and loss whenever she felt rejected. She would suddenly disappear from school and arrive later at home, bruised and hurt. Her parents in their alarm usually reacted by further punishing her. The relationship between the father and daughter was one of silent, mutual vengefulness. Rebecca would retreat to a corner and plan her revenge against paternal rejection.

Like most children her age, Rebecca transferred the focus of her love outside the home. Attractive but socially rejected by boys, she began having sexual relations at a very young age without taking any precautions. Indeed, by the time she was in treatment, she already had undergone two abortions. Each abortion had been followed by a short period of depression and mourning before the pattern repeated itself. Pregnancy was her path of vengeance and release. As she herself said, rejection or a disappointing love affair often made her want to die, so she would decide to get pregnant. After successfully choosing her "victim," she would explain to her parents that her pregnancy was the result of rape. "After every abortion I'm sad but then I feel good and I want to start everything anew. I want to return to my studies and to get along with my parents but things just don't work out."

Rebecca's parents generally responded with great agitation and harsh physical punishment. Thus, the abortions resulted in no real change; and, despite Rebecca's hopes, things just got worse. Finally, Rebecca decided to put an end to her life in a direct fashion. She swallowed a large number of pills, but her courage failed her and at the last minute she ran in pain to tell her parents. As a result of her suicide attempt, Rebecca received treatment for the first time.

Although this particular case is complex, one can still identify the longed-for relief that is sought in the suicide attempts of youth. In the beginning, Rebecca sought catharsis in her pregnancy; when this emotional outlet dried up, she turned to alternate deadly means.

The most important aspect of a self-destructive act by children or adolescents is the cry for help (Farberow and Shneidman, 1965). For a number of reasons, this cry is often disregarded. First of all, children do not know the real reason for their distress and, as a result, latch on to seemingly inconsequential happenings. "I didn't get a present," "You love my sister more than me," "I don't feel good and I don't know why," "You didn't come to my school celebration." Since these explanations are clearly of little importance, one is hard put to seriously accept the child's suicide attempt or threat. In addition, cries for help often are seen as attempts to get attention. Many of the suicide attempts made by children are viewed as nothing more than emotional blackmail. Children are thought to derive pleasure from their parents' worry and the fact that their demands are immediately met. This view of the children's underlying motives is a misguided assessment of what is happening. Even if there is an element of emotional blackmail, the child clearly has decided that she can fulfill her needs only by taking drastic measures. Unfortunately, the blind response to the "extortionist" behavior without in-depth examination of its roots does not help the problem. Rather, it often makes matters worse because the real problems thereby become even more distant.

Some of these issues were played out by Nathan, a twelve-year-old boy whose mother remarried after his father had been dead for many years. Nathan was rebellious, hard to please, and difficult to understand. Nathan's mother wanted to solve the friction with her son by sending him to a boarding school. His angry response to this suggestion was to climb out on a fourth-floor porch banister and hang by his hands while he threatened to jump. Even if Nathan did not intend to carry out his suicidal threats, there is a clear message here—a cry for help. His threats of punishment relate to a complicated and perverse relationship with his mother and not just to the background of friction emanating from the beginning of adolescence. Over and above the fact that Nathan suffered a loss at a very young age, there is a background of rejection that is very basic and not circumstantial or a reaction to a passing behavior.

The fear of drastic change in the immediate future also may lead to self-destructive behavior. Such changes are often viewed as threats to the entire cast of life, endangering status, self-esteem, and relations to others. The suicidal child sees even minor changes as demands for all-encompassing accommodations beyond his capacity. Fourteen-year-old Sammy displayed this fear even when fortune seemed to knock at his family's door. Sammy had two parents who were blind, and he often used this fact to assuage his deep feelings of inferiority when faced with failure. Moreover, he enjoyed the special treatment afforded him when he declared their handicap. At home, Sammy took over and manipulated things his way. No wonder that Sammy was less than delighted when he learned that an operation might return his mother's vision. Outraged, and professing his fear that his mother would leave the family when her sight was restored, he tried to persuade her not to have the operation. The mother proceeded with the operation, criticizing Sammy's selfishness. Overwhelmed with anxiety about the changes yet to transpire, Sammy tried to take his own life.

## Means of Suicide and Attempts by Children

What are the means of suicide employed by children? Not quiet and hidden, but violent and aggressive, as a summary by Pfeffer (1981b) indicates. She describes a nine-year-old boy who tried to hang himself, an eight-year-old girl who declared her intent to jump through a bathroom window, a boy of nine who tried to get run over, a girl of nine who tried to stab herself with a knife, and a six-year-old boy who tried to strangle himself. Another study (Paulson, Stone, and Sposto, 1978) found that a group of depressed children with suicidal tendencies had explored such drastic and aggressive measures as stabbing with a knife, burning with hot water, jumping from a high building, running into a moving car, and setting themselves on fire. Similarly violent means of death are cited in studies of children hospitalized for suicide. In one case, 65 percent of the sample had chosen violent means (Pfeffer, Conte, Plutchik, and Jerrett, 1979).

The notion that children choose violent deaths is further confirmed by a study of twenty-six children under twelve years old who had actually tried to commit suicide (Rosenthal and Rosenthal, 1984). Over 31 percent ran into moving cars, 19 percent tried to jump from a high place, 13 percent tried to throw themselves down a staircase, 6 percent either stabbed themselves or cut their wrists, 6 percent tried to burn themselves. Only 25 percent tried to commit suicide by taking an overdose—a relatively nonviolent method of suicide. When the suicide was a second attempt, even more violent measures were employed.

Overall, there appears to be a similarity between the suicidal means used by adults and youngsters. Both groups tend to use aggressive rather than peaceful methods of killing themselves (Neubower, 1986; Frederick, 1985; Barraclough, 1973).

One is tempted to ask whether the method a child selects is linked in any way to his or her age or personality. Unfortunately, the sparsity of studies regarding different means of suicide used by children prevents the drawing of any conclusions. At present, the child's selection seems to be related to the availability of different means. Since access to weapons is limited and hanging oneself is a bit complicated, these means are less frequent. The child's eventual choice appears dictated by simplicity: running into a moving car, jumping from a high place, or swallowing pills.

## Children's Messages About Suicide

Messages concerning death among the young include death wishes and suicide threats; displays of pathological curiosity regarding death; repeated games dealing with death and suicide; and, more obliquely, drawings, songs, and stories of destruction. All these constitute messages about the child's emotional state. In their early manifestations, they may be no more than hints of problems and difficulties that the child is encountering; yet, when they fall on deaf ears or do not receive an appropriate response, they can gradually become part of the suicidal process.

*Death Wishes and Suicide Threats.* The mode of communication often reflects the child's personality. An active child might express a suicide wish in an angry outburst: "I wish I were dead. Who needs this kind of life?" These were the words chosen by twelve-year-old Joey, who said them as he bashed his head against a wall. Although he made his threat after he had had a seemingly harmless and meaningless fight with his parents, it was not the first or last time he voiced such phrases, embodying a wish, a declaration, and a threat. Such words fit his general profile of hyperactivity, restlessness, and low frustration tolerance and were consistent with the general family tendency to shout and to employ strong emotional expressions. In contrast to Joey, ten-year-old Gideon was a quiet, reserved child. The first time the idea of suicide came to him, he was immersed in silence and solitude. "One evening I was lying alone on my bed in my room. No one was in the house and I was alone. I was very sad. I have no friends. My sister always nags me. I was unhappy and I was terribly bored. I felt that my heart was empty and then I thought to myself that maybe I ought to die. I don't

enjoy anything anyhow." This silent suicide wish was the beginning of a destructive process that culminated in a number of
serious attempts.

Death wishes are particularly meaningful among children
who have experienced the loss of a close loved one at an early
age. The wishes are often combined with a great longing for the
deceased and accompanied by fantasies of death as heaven or
the continuation of life under "improved conditions." When
death wishes are linked to longings, they are more dangerous because they add greater momentum to the suicide process—especially when the wishes persist over a long period of time and are
seen as an imaginary escape from dealing with present pain and
loss.

A rare and extreme example is presented by thirteen-and-
a-half-year-old Abe, who lost both parents through heart attacks
over a half-year span. He frequently spoke of his desire to be
with his parents, even though he was taken care of very lovingly
by his older brother's family. Despite his outward self-confidence, he was a sensitive and vulnerable child. The smallest conflict, frustration, or rejection aroused his wish to die. In his
imagination, Abe saw himself living with his parents after death.
"Everything is as usual but I'm together with them." Abe's wish
for death, in the form of a better life, occupied his mind constantly, although he claimed not to believe in life after death.

Suicide threats and wishes are essentially different forms
of the same type of communication, of which the direct verbal
threat is the clearest expression. Such statements as "I'm going
to kill myself," "I'm going to commit suicide," "I'm going to
jump into the street" are so direct and threatening that parents
are unable to take them at face value. The common defensive
responses to such directness range from "Stop talking nonsense"
to the seemingly provocative "All right, so do it." Parents use
this language to convince themselves and the child that such
statements are not serious.

In many cases, suicide threats are disguised, becoming
clear only after an actual attempt has been made. The statement
"There's no meaning to life, I get nothing out of it" might appear to be a fairly clear and direct message; yet the emphasis is

placed on the lack of meaning in life rather than the intent to commit suicide. Not surprisingly, this oblique declaration leads to arguments over the meaning of life rather than the issue of death. Questions about death are usually interpreted by parents as evidence of the child's mental maturity and his philosophical tendency to ponder existential questions. One nine-year-old boy continually turned to his parents with the question "Why is life worth living?" His mother's attempts to answer him did not satisfy him, nor did those of his teacher or his neighbors. The boy then began to rephrase his question, in order to state his intent more clearly: "Give me reasons why I should live." Once again, everyone tried to convince him that life was worth living, but with no success. Only after a visit to the graveyard, when he said "I wish I was under that stone," did the parents begin to get nervous. They finally realized that they were not dealing with an exceptionally bright child's philosophical questions concerning life but were facing a very threatening message.

A bolder form of suicide threat is the suicide note. Children's notes are different in their aim from those written by adults. Children usually write such notes in an attempt to test the response of those surrounding them. In contrast, adults write a letter just before they carry out a suicide attempt. Even so, the clear message behind such letters by children should not be ignored.

In spite of their clarity, suicide notes often cover up issues that the child does not dare to express in words because of his fear of his family's reactions. These hints can be understood only after close examination. Otherwise, the thrust of the message is likely to be overshadowed by the threat itself. For example, one eleven-year-old boy with learning and social difficulties was under great pressure from his parents. He wrote a suicide note and then proceeded to busy himself with the contents of the medicine cabinet. When his parents found him out, he directed their attention to his note on the table: "To whom it may concern, To all the family, I'm doing it because of school." Although the words "To whom it may concern" had been crossed out and replaced by "To all the family," they offered greater insight into the boy's suicidal motives than the reference

"because of school." They reflected the child's unbearable sense
of alienation and loneliness. Only by going beyond the more
overt message of school could one discover the true message
contained in the note.

Children's farewell messages, like written notes, require
attention to both their overt and their latent contents. Fare-
wells before committing suicide often do not sound like final
goodbyes. At worst, they appear to be an attempt to get a reaction from the environment. One common message is "I want to
give you my stamp collection. I don't need it anymore." Such a
message contains several levels of meaning. First, there is the
cognitive content: "I have no more interest in collecting stamps."
Second, there is the emotional content: "You are a very good
friend of mine and I want to give you my collection as a sign of
our closeness." Finally, there is the oblique threat: "I don't
need it anymore because I won't be around." Normally, one
hears the shallow cognitive level of the message or receives the
emotional communication of friendship and relates to it as a
compliment. Few hear the last, and most highly charged, level
of meaning, partly because of the casual, everyday context in
which the message appears. If the speaker were demonstrative-
ly sad, if he were to cry, the emotional meaning woven into the
message would be placed in bold relief. The lack of emotionality puts us off guard and dulls our sensitivity.

*Suicide Messages in Creative Activity.* Games, drawings,
songs, and stories are natural means of expression for children.
In suicide, both the messages and the medium are ways of ob-
taining relief. Games or drawings symbolically replace the act
itself. For onlookers, they may constitute a window through
which the child's inner experiences can be glimpsed.

The relationship between the symbolic expression and
the actual tendency toward suicide is hard to assess. To what
extent does the symbol actually replace the signified act? Clinical data suggest that the child's ability to express his or her
inner world in a creative manner temporarily postpones actual
death. However, artistic efforts do not completely avert the possibility of action. As such, an obsessive creative expression
around the subject of death and suicide should not be taken as

evidence of an immediate plan of action. However, it does indicate a cause for worry, though the danger itself may be manifested only in the distant future.

Let us look first at Dalia, whose interest in death became
apparent in the course of her therapy. Dalia was a seven-year-
old girl who was referred for adjustment difficulties rather than
suicidal tendencies. Dalia had no friends, felt rejected, and was
greatly confused about her sexual identity. Even brief observation revealed an obsessive preoccupation with death. In the
therapy playroom, Dalia would spend her entire time in the
sand box, burying little dolls and uncovering them. Her games
and drawings focused on death and birth (see Figure 2) and
often included such catastrophes as storms, fires, earthquakes,
or drownings. Outside of therapy, she was obsessed with death
and birth. She closely followed every birth or death of household pets and hovered over them constantly. The death of a
puppy or a kitten would cause her great anguish. She would
run from school or any other activity to see the dying animal.
Births made her happy, but death aroused an emotional storm
in her.

A more extreme example of obsessive death games and
the expression of suicide wishes can be seen in the behavior of
Mark, a twelve-year-old boy who showed signs of serious disturbances bordering on the psychotic. He attended a school for
emotionally disturbed children. His boundaries between fantasy
and reality were quite blurred. Outside of his home, he refused
to eat for fear of being poisoned; even at home, he watched
closely while food was being prepared. Sometimes he believed
that if he jumped from the window he would be able to fly and
would not fall. When we spoke of death, he said, in a statement
bordering on a question, "In the grave it's nice and warm, it's
like a bed, like a home." He was immediately so shocked by his
own words that he turned pale with anxiety.

When Mark was in therapy, his divorced mother met a
man and planned to marry him. She agreed with her new husband's desire to send Mark to boarding school. The boy became
very panicky and had attacks of restrained fury. He lacked the
ability to express his feelings properly. When the topic of board-

Figure 2. In this drawing, a seven-year-old girl describes her wishes for
death and rebirth. The tree represents a reflection of the self-image.
The branches look like two swords. And in the child's own words,
"A little girl is trapped in the bottom of the trunk waiting to be freed."

ing school was raised, his facial expressions were frozen and at times he seemed to be smiling. Later, his true feelings would be displayed in unexpected outbursts. More than anything, Mark was filled with an immense anger: anger about the early rejection by his father; anger toward the man who was coming to take away his mother; anger toward his mother, who disappointed him and was selfishly willing to let him go with such ease.

Mark found relief in death games and suicide wishes. In his death games, he called himself a "man of science." He made cruel experiments on animals, drowning cats and birds and drying them out to see if they came back to life. He would put goldfish into boiling water in order to see how long they would live. Sometimes he would throw puppies under passing cars. On occasion, this cruelty to animals was transferred to children, and he described how he would maltreat them. On other occasions, he would destroy property, starting fires in neighbors' yards and enjoying the sight of the destructive flames. A number of times, he tried to drown himself. He tried to "go swimming" in a lake when he did not know how to swim. His games were charged with meaning and provided relief from his feelings of destructive anger toward the world. This anger was slowly turned inward and displaced onto himself. Possessed by suicidal drives, Mark cautiously examined the boundaries of death and life and the point of no return. How far could he go and still turn back?

Sometimes, toying with death may be expressed in poetry. Thirteen-year-old Jack expressed his disturbances through writing and had notebooks filled with poems on death. Every page dealt in some way with death: mourning, eulogies, death wishes. Jack's writings had a philosophical, religious tone. He regarded himself as someone who was interested in death and its meaning. He devoted many hours of thought to the cruelty of the Germans, the Holocaust, and the different ways in which the victims were killed. Pictures of the Holocaust would freeze him in anguished paralysis. He "knew" that he must remember and continue to pass on the message that no one "really understood."

Jack's father had become gravely ill, and he could not deal with the anxiety over his father's fate. He panicked and began to entertain ideas of suicide as an escape from his anxieties. His deep and somewhat bizarre interest in death contained both the fear of the expected death of his fatally ill father and his own suicidal wishes.

*Pathological Interest in Death.* Not every manifestation of interest in death is evidence of self-destructive tendencies. Games about death, interest in death, and creative expressions of concern about death may all be seen in children who have no suicidal tendencies. Questions concerning death are a normal part of development from ages two to eight, although they may be formulated in various ways and at different levels of abstraction. This interest usually comes about as a result of contact with death, which leads to both curiosity and fear. When children turn to their parents with questions, they usually focus around such things as "Who died? Will you die? Will I die?" The questions tap a fear of separation, which is understandable and natural. However, many parents make the natural mistake of calming the children by promising them that neither they nor the children will die. With time, as anxiety abates, the children begin to realize that they and their parents will not live forever.

Normal death games often take place after a tragic event in the neighborhood or family. War or a similar mass catastrophe can also be a trigger. These games generally start with great force and only slowly abate after the event. It is not unusual to see a group of children aged eight or nine pretending to be at a funeral. In a similar fashion, most parents are acquainted with the death rituals children insist on having when a loved pet or someone else's pet dies. These games help children deal with and confront death.

What, then, are earmarks separating normal and abnormal preoccupation with death? First, normal preoccupation with death is temporary and follows some tragic event. Second, normal interest in the subject usually appears in group fashion, in games involving a number of children. Third, the emotional charge accompanying such games and drawings is usually subdued and passing. It rarely is combined with serious emotional problems or pathological signs in other areas of behavior. Normal interest in death stands in sharp contrast to a pathological obsession with the subject. The pathologically disturbed child

displays a constant fascination with death. His or her interests
are expressed privately and furtively, with great emotional involvement. This interest does not follow some traumatic event
but, rather, accompanies long-term emotional difficulties, such
as depression, loss, or an extended family crisis. As such, the
differences are usually striking to laypersons and clinicians
alike.

## Patterns of Development of Suicidal Behavior

In general, the data indicate that child suicide exists but
is rare in children under the age of fifteen. However, other forms
of self-destructive behavior seem more widespread. One danger
of early self-destructive behavior may be the creation of suicidal
tendencies, which come to be expressed in a more lethal form
during life crises at later ages. Thus, early self-destructive behavior can be seen as part of a gradual process, leading to suicide,
which may continue over a number of months or years. Although
it may be latent for years, it eventually bursts through in an
overt manner.

Overall, the similarity between self-destructive behavior
in children and in adults is striking. Both display common patterns of development:

1. intolerable pressure (frustration, rejection, unresolvable
   problems, loss, family confusion)
2. a depressed attitude (sorrow, despair, uselessness, hopelessness, anxiety, and alienation)
3. initial attempts at adjustment and coping (isolation, manipulation, surrender, aggression, rebellion, or a search for substitutes that satisfy needs)
4. accumulated frustrations and the wearing down of emotional strength
5. appearance of the idea of suicide
6. attempts to adjust through self-destructive means (insignificant or serious suicide attempts, signals of despair, obsessive concern with death, overt threats, and perception of
   death as attractive)
7. environment's responses to self-destructiveness (shock, guilt,

alterations in relationships, escalation of pressures on the child, punishment, neglect)
8. a resulting confirmation of the child's pessimistic view of life and of the idea that suicide is the only solution
9. continuing accumulation of new frustrations, leading to the ultimate act of self-destruction

This pattern, of course, is an approximation. Not all the stages are found in every case or arise in this exact order; yet some of them are present in every suicide or attempted suicide. In later chapters, these stages will be illustrated by case studies.

# 4

# Children at Risk:
# Exploring the Links
# to Personality Traits

One approach to research on suicide has been to elucidate personality traits of those with self-destructive inclinations. Unfortunately, most studies of personality traits have a number of methodological defects (for example, in definitions of "suicidal" and in the selection of comparison groups). In spite of such shortcomings, one can still outline some basic conclusive findings. This chapter illustrates the research complexities and summarizes much of the current knowledge in the field.

## Depression in Children

Depression is widely agreed to be characteristic of adults who commit suicide. Thus, one avenue of research has been to seek an analogous role for depression in children's suicide. The question arises, of course, as to whether such an analogy is justified. Among adults, depression involves multiple emotional states and feelings: lack of self-worth, guilt, pessimism, and hopelessness. Depression has been associated with varying dynamics: the real or symbolic loss of a loved one, as well as injury to one's self, status, or possessions; guilt and self-deprecation, including a failure to fulfill excessively high self-expectations or, as psychoanalysts put it, the demands of a rigid superego; and the internalization of aggression meant for others.

In adults, the depressed state subsumes a great range of symptoms: despair, sorrow, apathy, loss of pleasure, lack of initiative, retarded motor responses, sleeping difficulties, bodily aches, loss of appetite, and feelings of worthlessness, hopelessness, and helplessness. Often, depression appears to involve a willful relinquishment of control or even interest. Clearly, the great diversity in one's experience of depression precludes its simple description. Yet the oppressive strength of the experience is succinctly reflected in the words of one victim: "It's like being in a deep narrow hole with a whirlpool at the bottom that pulls you down. The walls of the hole are slick; there is no way to grasp hold. You can hear the voices of the people who are standing on top, but you just don't have the strength to get out."

Professionals in the not too distant past often questioned whether young children were actually capable of truly experiencing a depressive state (Rie, 1966). Many of those who negated the possibility tended to deny the existence of child suicide. But researchers now have come to accept the notion of depression in very young children, just as they have come to accept the existence of suicide in these age groups.

In discussing childhood depression, we need to consider two separate questions. First, how do young children experience the state of depression? Second, is childhood depression indeed related to child suicide? Must a child be depressed in order to commit suicide?

Bowlby (1980) argues that depression in adults and children has its base in early childhood. He believes that it occurs when the young child experiences a loss without the opportunity for relief found in mourning. Spitz's (1965) observations of young children and babies suggested to Bowlby and his followers that depression evolves in three stages following loss: (1) protest of loss; (2) despair; (3) apathy, isolation, and regression. By focusing on early loss, Bowlby has tended to downplay some of the Freudian dynamics often cited in depression—for example, a rigid superego that "absorbs" and "regulates" depression, as well as the theme of internalization of aggression. In their place, Bowlby highlights a dynamic of loss and mourning, which has common developmental roots for child and adult alike.

Bemporad (1978) is another student of childhood depression whose developmental view tends to avoid Freudian concepts. Bemporad assumes that depression includes a number of elements that can be found at all ages: sorrowful mood, delayed spontaneity, stable negative self-image, negative expectations for the future, and guilt feelings related to some internal conflict. However, Bemporad argues, it is difficult to speak of true depression in early infancy. Although maternal separation or lack of stimulation may produce signs of retreat and introversion, this state is highly transitory and can be easily reversed the minute conditions are improved. During early childhood (ages two to four), one can begin to discern early forms of depression in a general inhibition of response accompanied by sadness. This type of pattern often arises from parental subjugation of the child's spontaneity and self-expression or in the depressed atmosphere of a home where parents are depressed. Yet here, too, it is difficult to talk of a stable depressive state. Certain elements, such as guilt, are absent; others, such as negative self-esteem, have not yet formed or solidified.

During middle childhood (ages five and six), as the self-image begins to be formed, a more complete type of depression, involving negative self-esteem, can occur. Moreover, the child now has a broader understanding of reality, so that reactions to loss and frustration are stronger and feelings of failure more vivid. The ever-widening gap between parental expectations and the desire for self-expression offers fertile grounds for sadness and one's first experience of worthlessness. Yet these feelings must still be seen as transitory and dependent on immediate circumstances. Children have the ability to defend themselves against such feelings by self-distraction. This technique is particularly useful since children at this age lack a clear sense of future and do not display guilt associated with an ongoing focus on internal conflicts. In this light, it is difficult to speak about the existence of adult forms of depression.

In Bemporad's view, the nature of depression begins to change substantially when the child reaches school age. This change is rooted in the definite internalization of parental value systems, the stabilization of conscious self-awareness, and an extended comprehension of the external world. The child forms a complete system of beliefs and expectations about himself, so that he blames himself for any failure in self-expression or social graces and therefore can give way to prolonged reactions of sorrow and depression. One's sorrowful moods are no longer a transitory response to a punitive, inhibiting, or unfulfilling environment but, rather, a stable reaction to the attribution of failure and frustration to one's self. Therefore, the child no longer is reassured by protective parents' attempts to soften these feelings of suffering and frustration. Bemporad emphasizes the role of self-attribution of failure in the school-age child's depression. The experience of internal conflict solidifies and becomes a permanent source of dissatisfaction and lack of pleasure. Yet, for this very reason, depression at this age differs from that of later periods. The depressed child, because of his limited perception of time, does not display the adult's inclination toward hopelessness. As a result, there is a greater likelihood that the elementary school child's depressed outlook can be changed.

In adolescence, Bemporad believes, development has progressed to such a stage that depression reaches its adult proportions. Intellectual processes have matured to an adult level and allow a full measure of self-representation, self-judgment, time perception, and feelings of internal conflict. Moreover, adolescence is known to be bound up with emotional crises and self-doubt. The parents put increasing pressure on the youth to make the most of opportunities and acquire new skills. Any failure is totally attributed to personal fault. Here one sees a rich brew of accumulated frustration, which repeatedly damages self-esteem and engenders feelings of guilt when the youth contrasts what she has accomplished with what she desires to accomplish. Thus, Bemporad argues that adolescents can and do feel real depression.

Unfortunately, Bemporad's developmental analysis of qualitative changes in depression over childhood has not been applied to diagnosis of the malady. From a simple diagnostic viewpoint, most clinicians tend to employ similar symptomatology for identifying depression in children and adults alike. These symptoms include behaviors such as loss of appetite or weight, sleep disturbances, retarded motor activity, apathy in everyday life, changes in mood, feelings of worthlessness, difficulties in concentration, and thoughts about death. Other symptoms include social withdrawal, pessimism, and frequent crying. These symptoms are used for the assessment of depression in children and in adults.

The difficulty in identifying depression in childhood is heightened by a phenomenon that some call hidden or "masked" depression (Toolan, 1975). That is, young children, in order to defend themselves against the painful experience of depression itself, react by channeling the depressive behavior into acting out, distractions, and various forms of escape. Similarly, young adolescents often express depression through delinquent behavior, general uneasiness, or the inability to deal with solitude. Other adolescents turn to drugs, alcohol, or intensified sexual activity or cling to their peer group for support. Other signs of masked depression are excessive separation anxiety, desire to run away from home, feelings of being unwanted and misunderstood, general disquiet, isolating oneself in one's room, aggression, unwillingness to participate in mutual family activities or plans, neglect of outward appearance, sensitivity to rejection, and antisocial behavior. These substitutes make the experience of depression easier to deal with.

Because "masked" depression includes the entire range of problems encountered with children, critics of the theory (Lefkowitz and Burton, 1978; Kovacs and Beck, 1977a; Carlson and Cantwell, 1980; Puig-Antich, 1985) allege that it does not enable one to differentiate between depression and the various other problems. In addition, the numerous diagnostic approaches and methods of evaluating depression (Jaffe, 1987; Kovacs and Beck, 1977a; Puig-Antich, Chambers, and Tabrizi, 1983; Petti, 1978; Kazdin, 1981; Weinberg, 1972) further contribute to the confusion. Nevertheless, the concept of masked depression has a strong appeal because it emphasizes the defensive character of substitutive behaviors and symptoms in alleviating the painful experience of being depressed. As such, it has important theoretical and practical implications for suicide in children. Depression is no doubt a potent risk factor.

However, researchers have questioned whether children must be depressed in order to become suicidal. Not surprisingly, measurement issues have clouded the answer to this question as well. One of the most important criteria for clinically determining depression is the obsessive dealing with death and death wishes. Yet the tautological use of the same characteristic for both conditions is apparent. For example, a boy who is constantly preoccupied with thoughts of death and death wishes is immediately diagnosed as being depressed. Yet this same behavior serves as the basis for a diagnosis of having suicidal tendencies.

Methodology often dictates final conclusions regarding the role of depression in suicide. Those using strict criteria (that is, reliable objective measures and severe symptoms such as loss of weight or social withdrawal) find little support for the necessity of depression, whereas those who use broad diagnostic considerations (that is, impressionistic criteria and relatively slight symptoms such as sadness or mood changes) reach opposite conclusions. In one study, where children with suicidal tendencies were compared to those without them, depression was evaluated on the basis of general clinical impressions (Pfeffer, Conte, Plutchik, and Jerrett, 1979). The result: the suicidal were found to be more depressed, particularly in regard to hopelessness and worthlessness. Nonetheless, those suicidal children who were demonstrably diagnosed as more self-destructive were not necessarily more depressed. In another study, where a number of measures for depression were used, children who were more depressed on one measure were not necessarily more depressed on another (Rosenthal and Rosenthal, 1984).

Yet many researchers—despite the inconsistencies in their data—still conclude that depression is a striking characteristic of suicidal individuals (Otto, 1977; Pfeffer, Zuckerman, Plutchik, and Mizruchi, 1984; Pfeffer, Plutchik, and Mizruchi, 1983). As the criteria become more stringent, the role of depression appears more limited. Carlson and her colleagues (Carlson and Cantwell, 1979, 1980; Carlson and Orbach, 1982) performed a highly developed set of studies. In her summary, Carlson (1983) notes that relatively few of the suicidal displayed severe signs of depression. In most cases, the reason for their hospitalization was the suicidal act rather than depression. Therefore, Carlson concludes, although depression may exacerbate self-destruction, it is by no means a necessary element. A similar conclusion is suggested by Kosky (1983), who used very strict criteria to determine depression in suicidal children.

Some researchers (Kazdin and others, 1983) suggest that phenomena related to depression, but not part and parcel with it, may provide the dynamic link to suicide. Particular attention has been given to the role of hopelessness. Children hospitalized as psychiatric patients were assessed on the following dimensions: hopelessness, depression, and various forms of self-destructive behavior. Depression was measured meticulously with the use of four different tools. Hopelessness had a strong correlation with all but one measure of depression. Suicidal children felt hopelessness to a greater extent than children suffering from other disturbances but were not more depressed and did not feel a greater degree of worthlessness.

The evident conclusion of this study is that hopelessness and not depression is the critical element in self-destructive behavior. Hopelessness is one aspect of many in depression. It is possible that the reported technical and theoretical connection between depression and suicide is a result of the overlapping of these two variables through the common denominator of hopelessness and not the other elements of depression. From the clinical point of view, we can assume that as long as a depressed person has not lost all hope for change in the near or distant future, that person will not reach the point of attempting suicide. The work of Kazdin and his associates is also important because they have developed a methodological approach that can differentiate among the many elements and dynamics of different people with different levels of motivation for suicide.

Another interesting recent finding (M. J. Rotheram, personal communication, 1986) related to the issue at hand shows that suicidal youngsters cannot derive pleasure out of everyday life. They lack the capacity for enjoyment. This characteristic also is found in depressed adults. The inability to derive enjoyment from life may be yet another link between depression and suicide.

In attempting to summarize the empirical data on depression and suicide, one is impressed by the complexity of the findings and the range of methodological and theoretical approaches employed. This variety has no doubt contributed in part to basic inconsistencies in the findings reported. Those problems have been complicated by overlapping behavior, a tautological factor that tends to inflate estimates of their interrelationship. Overall, the findings suggest that depression and suicide are interconnected but that depression is by no means a necessary antecedent to self-destruction. At most, depression appears to heighten the risk of suicide. Furthermore, preliminary research suggests that this exacerbating effect of depression may be attributable to more limited facets of the phenomenon, such as feelings of hopelessness, rather than to the entire collage of dynamics involved in a depressive state.

## Serious Psychopathology

Are those who attempt suicide emotionally ill? Is the act of suicide a sign of emotional deterioration, a serious impairment of judgment, or a pathological loss of drive control? Such notions have a central place in the theoretical works of Ackerly (1967), who has greatly influenced the study of child suicide. As we will see in Chapter Nine, Ackerly argues that children who make serious suicide attempts suffer a serious deviation from reality and display internal deterioration. In Ackerly's view, suicide provides an escape from the total deterioration of self and from one's fear of a total loss of contact with reality. The descent from suicide threats to serious attempts is interpreted as evidence of ever-growing pathological disturbance. The child who actually attempts suicide has, in Ackerly's view, disintegrated into a general mental illness.

Ackerly illustrates his views with the case of five-year-old George, who was hospitalized because of repeated attempts to strangle himself. He related to the doctors that he was sad because his mother did not love him and that he had no father because his parents were divorced. George wanted to die, he said, because his mother told him that there would soon be a world war and he didn't want to die in it. In particular, he was afraid of being run over by a tank.

George's distorted thought pattern seemed clear evidence of psychosis to Ackerly. Yet review of the particulars makes the diagnosis less clear. A look at George's family history shows that he was two years old when his mother divorced his father on the grounds of cruelty. George's mother had herself tried repeatedly to commit suicide following deep depressions. She admitted that she did not love George, partly because he was born out of wedlock; and she had beaten him numerous times.

George had first tried suicide at age five, a half year after his younger brother was born. During this period, George was very difficult to discipline. He suffered from insomnia and feared that his father would come back and try to kill him. After his mother was placed in a hospital for the mentally ill, George was sent to an institution to await a foster home. It was then that George tried to commit suicide for the second time. Ackerly concluded that George was a psychotic who suffered from sexual conflicts and uncontrolled aggressive impulses, that his sense of reality was impaired, and that he had "bizarre" ideation.

After reading the case description, one is hard pressed to see the justification for concluding that George had a severe psychopathology. There is obviously some "strangeness" in the child's ideas of a world war. Yet George's case history surely indicates sufficient cause for him to kill himself without any need to adduce psychopathology, internal deterioration of the ego, or rebellious, aggressive impulses. The intolerable situations and processes in the external reality could easily have brought George to the brink of suicide without any internal deterioration. Ackerly's conclusion that children who make dangerous suicide attempts are mentally ill seems overgeneralized and inexact. It definitely does not relate to the entire population of children who have ever attempted to end their lives.

Pfeffer, Conte, Plutchik, and Jerrett (1979) tried to examine Ackerly's supposition by testing the connection between degree of pathology and suicide. They also attempted to isolate mental features unique to suicidal children and to those suffering from severe pathology. Behind this search lay an attempt to understand the variables that lead to self-destructive behavior as opposed to other emotional disturbances. These researchers tested a group of fifty-eight children (aged six to twelve) who were in a psychiatric hospital. Evaluations of the extent of self-destructiveness and psychopathology were made by the children's therapists. The children's personality traits (including their coping mechanisms) and their perceptions of death also were assessed. The children hospitalized for suicidal tendencies had the following characteristics: depression, hopelessness, worthlessness, parental depression, obsessive dealings with death, and a perception of death as temporary and pleasant. In contrast, the characteristic pattern of children suffering from severe disturbances consisted of high levels of anxiety and aggression, obsessive preoccupation with failures in school, learning difficulties, fear of parental punishment, parental separation, difficulties with relatives and peers, and problems in ego functioning. The conclusion was that the emotional patterns of the suicidal and those with other psychopathologies can be differentiated. However, no clear conclusion can be drawn from this study with regard to suicide and severe pathology because the investigators did not use a control group of nonhospitalized suicidal children. Moreover, many of the variables in this study were based on impressions rather than on objective measures.

A clearer conclusion can be drawn from a study by Paulson, Stone, and Sposto (1978). Most of the suicidal children (aged four to twelve) in their sample did not suffer from any serious mental disturbances. Indeed, despite their difficult lives, they displayed impressive mental strengths. Kosky (1983) came to much the same conclusion. Similarly, Cohen-Sandler, Berman, and King (1982) categorically conclude that there is no pattern of symptoms of any kind characterizing children with suicidal tendencies. Although they may display various symptoms and emotional disturbances, these are in no way unique or uncommon.

One explanation for research findings linking psychopathology and suicide may be found in problems of circular thinking surrounding diagnosis. Attempted suicide usually is seen as a sign of a pathology. It necessitates preventive measures such as hospitalization for observation. However, hospitalization itself creates an impression of psychopathology. This error is more likely to be made by those with insufficient professional experience or when the evaluation is made closely after the attempted suicide (Carlson, 1983). As was noted earlier, similar problems of tautological thought appear in research dealing with suicide and depression. Another source of research error is the inconsistent use of different types of populations. Some have dealt with patients in psychiatric hospitals, while others have used public or private clinics.

Not only are most suicidal children free from severe pathologies but in many cases they display quite positive features (Orbach, 1981). Many are excellent pupils, the best in their class, with outstanding creative and athletic talents (Kosky, 1983). Many are popular and intelligent and maintain good relations with peers (Shaw and Scheklum, 1965). Some are even teachers or leaders of others. In addition, despite their intolerable pain, one sees among them strong and beautiful humanitarian qualities and a wealth of mental strength and function. For them, the act of suicide may be regarded as an adaptive act—as a last call for help, or as the only means of escape from internal pressures, or as a maneuver to create a positive change in life.

So it was with one young man who was introverted, lonely, and afraid. He had come for therapy because of problems relating to women. The young man had taken to shoring up his shaky self-confidence through antisocial acts of theft and lying. After therapy, he met and married a young woman. Nonetheless, he continued his antisocial behavior to the point where he felt he had lost control over it. As his depression increased, he decided to end his life. His suicide attempt was unsuccessful, but the relief and purification that he felt as a result fostered a major emotional change. The man finally was able to tell his wife of his problem behavior. Moreover, he began to gain control over these tendencies. Shneidman (1982) relates a similar case of a woman who decided to kill herself by jumping from a high building and was miraculously saved. After this attempt and a subsequent brief period of therapy, her personality changed almost from one extreme to the other. These cases illustrate some of the positive forces involved in suicide and refute the view that suicide is necessarily an expression of the decline toward pathology.

In sum, although children who display suicidal intent may frequently be disturbed, the vast majority do not display any striking signs of mental regression. Emotional disturbances and pathology may increase the risk of suicide, but they are by no means necessary preconditions. This conclusion has, of course, practical implications for prevention and treatment.

Those who are experiencing suicidal impulses for the first time often believe that such impulses are a sign of mental disturbance. This misperception, in and of itself, may bring them one step further toward such an act. Charlotte Ross (1985), one of the founders of suicide prevention programs for children of school age, has made the misperception of abnormality one focus of her intervention efforts. A central principle in her work is that feelings of despair, depression, hopelessness, and thoughts of death are not necessarily signs of mental illness. Rather, they are common, even normal, feelings that almost every person experiences at one point or another.

### Self-Control

One of the well-known myths concerning suicide among children is that it is a spontaneous, unpremeditated action. In this view, children kill themselves impulsively on the spur of the moment. Therefore, destructive behavior is often associated with traits such as impulsivity, hyperactivity, and uncontrolled aggression. In other words, suicidal children lack self-control.

Two cases of destructive behavior reflect the polar opposites of this issue of self-control. First, there is the case of Simon, who slowly translated his suicidal wishes into actions. Simon was a quiet boy, very reserved, slow, and withdrawn. Only on occasion would he cry and express his pain. Even this he did in a controlled manner. He was considered a "good" boy, although many would characterize him as depressed. He planned his suicide step by step. He took into consideration all possible reactions, planned how to communicate his messages, and continuously listened to the feedback from his environment. He planned first to speak to his parents about "how it wasn't worth living." If there was no response, he planned to mix paint with water to make a poison, drink the concoction, and only afterward tell his parents what he had done. If he did not die and no meaningful changes took place, he intended to start swallowing pills. He would first take small doses and then larger ones. If that did not work either, he would jump from the roof. Simon was faithful to his plan and followed it step by step until his parents understood the seriousness of his intentions.

Eleven-year-old Sammy presents the other side of the coin regarding self-control. Sammy was always flighty and vocal and had frequent physical confrontations and outbursts of anger. His mood was mercurial. Sometimes he was a "wonderful child"; at other times, he was impossible, nagging, aggressive, and hostile. He was a creature of impulse. During one of his many fights with members of the family, his mother slapped him for being insolent. After being momentarily shocked, he screamed, "Enough, I want to die." He grabbed a chair, placed it by a fourth-floor window, and opened the shutters. His sixteen-year-old brother struggled to take him off the chair and fought with him on the floor. Sammy screamed, kicked, hit, bit, and banged his head on the floor. He finally burst into tears and only then quieted down.

As Simon and Sammy demonstrate, children with strikingly different levels of self-control can display suicidal tendencies. However, it is still worth investigating whether a substantial portion of the children with suicidal tendencies manifest a lack of self-control.

At first glance, a good case can be made for impulsivity and suicide. An impressionistic study (Haider, 1968) of hospitalized children reveals that the most common diagnosis of children and adolescents exhibiting self-destructive behavior involves personality or behavioral disturbances. Most are defined as immature, impulsive, and oversensitive, with a tendency to hostility and aggressiveness. Another study (Green, 1968) portrays suicidal children as impulsive and aggressive, with a history of parental violence.

One of the clearest portrayals of impulsivity and aggression as a central dynamic in child suicide appears in an early finding (Shaw and Scheklum, 1965). All the suicidal children in this sample had impulsive personalities, and their suicidal behavior was impulsive. The researchers found that suicide was frequently a punitive response to some inconsequential parental act and formed part of a more general impulsive and aggressive stance toward the surroundings. The children's behavior before their suicide attempts often seemed to be relaxed and calm. The investigators described the suicide as the result of a sudden uncontrolled impulse, sometimes having no apparent reason. The extreme position taken in this study is seen in the assertion that some children attempt suicide as easily as if they were pouring a glass of water to drink.

In reading the early studies on self-control, one can differentiate between two views regarding the role of impulsivity in suicide. The first is of impulsivity as a general personality trait among children with suicidal inclinations. The second is of a sudden suicidal act that occurs without any reason or warning among children who are not necessarily impulsive. As we shall see, the notion that suicide occurs without any reason reflects no more than a lack of awareness regarding the child's deterioration or the difficulties he faces.

In contrast to early clinical impressions, systematic research suggests that impulsivity has only a limited importance for an understanding of suicide in children. In one comparison between suicidal children and a group of children with emotional disturbances (Kosky, 1983), it was found that the suicidal children did not differ from the others in impulsivity. Furthermore, there were no histories of gross antisocial behavior. Indeed, most of these children were fairly quiet and polite. A similar study (Connell, 1963) concludes that only 17 percent of the children who committed suicide in England during a given period exhibited uncontrolled antisocial behavior before their deaths.

The work of Cohen-Sandler, Berman, and King (1982) probably offers the greatest backing for the view that impulsivity is not a prerequisite in child suicide. These researchers systematically compared children who had attempted suicide with depressed children and those with other disturbances. Suicidal children were in no way more impulsive or lacking in discipline. "Impulsive" behavior, such as stealing, running away from home, and angry outbursts, was no more prevalent among the suicidal children than among the other children.

Another aspect of self-control sometimes linked to suicide is aggression. Yet the notion of overt aggression among the suicidal stands in direct contradiction to the hypothesis that suicide involves the internalization of aggression. Further, it is in conflict with the notion that the suicidal are depressed, since depression is the polar opposite of active aggression. One study (Pfeffer, Plutchik, and Mizruchi, 1983) demonstrated that some suicidal children are aggressive and some are not. Those who are aggressive have impaired ego functioning and tend to identify with impulsive and aggressive parents. Those who lack aggressiveness have proper ego functioning but are depressed as a result of pressure from their surroundings; moreover, these children tend to identify with suicidal or depressed parents.

The possibility that depression and aggression may combine in suicide has been pursued in a number of other studies (Puig-Antich, 1982; Chiles, Miller, and Cox, 1980; Breed, 1970; Shaffer and Fisher, 1981; Amir, 1973). The findings suggest that the idea of suicide as either the complete externalization or the complete internalization of aggression is too simplistic.

In general, the literature on self-control and aggression resists glib generalizations. On the one hand, it is clear that suicidal children are not necessarily lacking in self-control. Neither are they characterized by extreme hyperactive or aggressive behavior. Indeed, some of the suicidal are actually restrained and quiet. Nonetheless, in a number of cases, these factors appear to contribute to the broader pattern of dynamics.

### Cognitive Rigidity and Flexibility

Adults who try to commit suicide lack flexibility (Shneidman, 1982), a finding that raises interest in this multifaceted dimension among children and adolescents. One facet of flexibility is the ability to look at a given situation from new perspectives or to find new solutions to a problem when the old ones fail. Another facet of flexibility is the ability to go beyond dichotomous, black-or-white thinking. According to some researchers, suicidal individuals rigidly cling to extremely negative views of themselves and the world. Some cognitive features contributing to this extreme negativism include (1) overgeneralization, the tendency to arrive at conclusions on the basis of a single incident and generalize to a broader range of events; (2) arbitrary deduction, the tendency to draw conclusions without proper supportive evidence; (3) selective conceptualization, the tendency to perceive a situation on the basis of partial and irrelevant aspects; and (4) negative exaggeration and positive understatement, the combined tendencies to overstate the importance of a negative event and to belittle positive ones (Beck, Rush, Show, and Emery, 1979).

These cognitive processes seem to hasten a decline toward feelings of hopelessness and, at the same time, to curtail one's ability to find solutions. Hope for change is slowly drained away as the range of possible action becomes constricted. The deadly effect of these thought patterns is illustrated in one patient's words: "I have two fantasies, one where everything is fine and the other where it always gets worse. Every day gets harder with less options available. It's like a tunnel that gets more and more narrow until there is nothing left and nothing for me to do but commit suicide." Shneidman (1982) calls this phenomenon "tunnel vision."

The importance of flexibility in contrast to rigidity is elucidated at a philosophical level by humanistic psychologists, who stress the importance of an ability to renew, to vary one's self-expression, and to change. Creation and procreation arise through the revelation of the possibilities in the world and ourselves. The depressed and suicidal diminish this experience by their inability, and sometimes stubborn unwillingness, to change. As such, they suffer a reduction and total negation of self.

These philosophical notions have come to be grounded in hard fact. A systematic study by Schotte and Clum (1982) supports the hypothesis that rigid people who are exposed to pressures from their environment become more easily depressed than flexible people and eventually turn to self-destructive behavior. Students with rigid thinking were shown to be more preoccupied with thoughts of suicide than were colleagues who had more flexible thought processes. However, it is possible that thoughts of suicide and feelings of hopelessness are the causes rather than the results of rigid thinking. The suicidal person, it might be argued, clings to the known and is afraid to throw away the old in order to find new resolutions. Thus, further research is needed to assess the specific causal pattern linking rigidity and suicide in adults.

The few works on young children's thought patterns and their relationship to depression and suicide are often only suggestive (Jaffe, Feshbach, and Feshbach, 1983). For example, in one study (Leon, Kendall, and Garber, 1980), children who were depressed tended to attribute positive events to external causes and negative events to their own acts. Only one study (Orbach, Rosenheim, and Hary, 1987) has addressed the issue of flexibility directly. It contrasted three groups of children: suicidal children, normal children, and children suffering from a malignant disease (such as leukemia). In this study, the children were requested to solve an imaginary problem relating to life and death in the form of a discussion over the desirability of changing a living being to an inanimate object. After the children gave their own views, they were asked to guess what answers other children might give. It was assumed that an understanding of other points of view indicates a greater flexibility. The results showed that all the suicidal children were less flexible than the others, even though their IQ level was similar to that of the other groups. Moreover, in this suicidal group, there was a high correlation between attraction to death and rigidity of thought. This correlation did not arise in the other two groups. Interestingly, there was no association between intellectual capacity and rigidity.

Although it is still too soon to conclude that rigid thinking is a characteristic found in all suicidal children, this research does point to the lethal role of cognitive rigidity. Moreover, it suggests that rigidity is a mediating factor in the link between stressful circumstances and suicidal tendencies. Clearly, not all stressful events lead to rigidity or suicide. For example, the leukemic children in this study expressed some of the greatest stresses imaginable yet did not show any fatal attraction to death. When thoughts of suicide arise in reaction to stress, however, cognitive rigidity may turn the idea of death into a single, all-encompassing solution for one's problems (Shneidman, 1982). Further research is required to assess the clinical and diagnostic value of this proposal.

An inflexible cognitive approach also makes it difficult for the individual to solve everyday life problems. Orbach, Bar-Yosef, and Dror (1987) have demonstrated that suicidal individuals lack a strategy for problem solving and therefore adopt drastic but ineffective solutions. It is reasonable to assume that such individuals will tend to feel frustrated, hopeless, and helpless.

Some of the problems of rigid thought are demonstrated in the case of a twelve-year-old boy who came for treatment because of a compulsive interest in death. Throughout every meeting, he would return to the single refrain "Nothing helps, nobody can help me, nothing can change things." At first, it seemed that his statements were a camouflaged attempt at leading me to the source of his distress through a game of "Hot and Cold." If I strayed from his problems, his protestations that nothing would help grew louder. Yet later it appeared that his cries reflected a basic unwillingness to alter his perceptions of self and the world around him. Despite the obvious impact of therapy and his enjoyment of the process, he held on stubbornly to his negativistic stance.

### Suggestibility and Oversensitivity

Early research on hereditary elements in suicide involved studies of identical twins raised separately. To date, these studies have yielded little substantive evidence of a direct genetic source for suicide. Subsequent interest has turned to familial and social elements in place of genetic ones. Nevertheless, certain biologically based personality traits seem to appear frequently in those with suicidal tendencies. These traits include suggestibility and oversensitivity.

Suggestibility refers to one's openness to external influences—that is, one's willingness to relinquish self-control to external authority. Suggestible people blend into the roaring crowd with great emotional enthusiasm. Moreover, they are easily swayed by the views and rational arguments of authoritative figures. For suggestible people, a chain reaction can be set in motion by reports of a suicide. Phillips and Carstensen (1986) found a relationship between media reports of an initial suicide and a general subsequent increase in the suicide rate. It seems that publicity about one suicide induces others to commit suicide. Although not all the work on chain reactions is so supportive, it appears that news media attention to the person who commits a fatal act greatly influences people in distress, especially adolescents and children. The suicide of a well-known and influential figure is especially likely to start a chain reaction. These social stars are sources of identification for people in great emotional distress who are easily influenced. Their act lends legitimacy to suicide and conveys the impression that it is acceptable. Identification amplifies feelings of pessimism: If such a strong person was unable to find a better way of solving his problem, what can the weak do?

The problem of suggestibility is simplified with children. By nature, they are more exposed than adults to the process of latent influence. Shaw and Scheklum (1965) argue that they are therefore particularly vulnerable to continuous covert messages that they are unwanted and that it would be better if they killed themselves. In their sensitivity and despair, suicidal children receive the messages clearly and act upon them. But despite the intuitive logic of suggestibility as an element in child suicide, not all research supports the assumption that people with suicidal tendencies are more suggestible than others. Thus, its centrality is still uncertain.

Another constitutional trait that has been linked to suicide is oversensitivity. Some theoreticians (Hussain and Vandiver, 1984) describe the suicidal child as having a high level of sensitivity to his or her surroundings and a low threshold for frustration. Any minor frustration is experienced as a major disruption and gives rise to a disproportionate reaction. This inappropriate response elicits, in turn, an angry reaction from the environment. This reaction prompts another reaction from the child, which leads to another reaction from the environment, and so on. The accumulation of tension within the household is thought to lead to a suicide attempt. However, there is no real evidence to support the idea that oversensitivity is either unique to or characteristic of children with suicidal inclinations.

### Masochistic and Obsessive Tendencies

Masochistic tendencies are considered by some (Cohen-Sandler, Berman, and King, 1982) to be a central personality trait in child suicide. Masochistic children tend to commit acts of nonfatal self-mutilation—banging their heads against a wall, biting themselves, pulling hairs, or scratching and cutting their bodies. One five-year-old suicidal boy exhibited masochistic behavior by riding his tricycle at demonic speeds into a wall. He crashed over and over again, claiming that it was pleasurable to strike the wall with force and then fall injured to the ground.

It is hypothesized that children who display masochistic behavior have very high thresholds for physical pain. Rosenthal and Rosenthal (1984) report that children with self-inflicted injuries hardly ever cry when brought into emergency rooms for treatment; they seem to lack sensitivity to pain. Similar descriptions have been given by bereaved parents of children who had committed suicide. This oblivion to physical pain, combined with an oversensitivity to emotional pressures, may lead some suicidal children to self-destructive behavior. However, further research is needed to assess this hypothesis.

An additional characteristic of the suicidal individual is an obsessive preoccupation with death in various forms. This preoccupation can be reflected in thoughts of suicide, great curiosity about death, fear of dying, or exaggerated concern for the well-being of family members. At other times, it is expressed in concern over body parts or phobias for lethal diseases. All these varying and opposing facets can appear separately or together in different combinations. An obsessive preoccupation with death probably is part of the broader entity of suicide per se, rather than a distinctive external cause. As such, preoccupation with death is not necessarily an antecedent part of the personality of children with suicidal tendencies but, rather, a product of that personality.

## Sex and Age Differences

Can one identify sex differences in suicidal personalities and behaviors at different ages? The study most relevant to this question (Hussain and Vandiver, 1984) involved three different groups of suicidal children ranging in age from four and a half to fifteen. Among children four and a half to eight years of age, the boys were generally characterized as hyperactive, aggressive, and unruly. The suicidal girls were equally undisciplined but showed less hyperactivity and aggression. Both boys and girls expressed their suicidal intent by running into traffic. Suicidal boys and girls in the second group, aged nine to eleven, displayed similar qualities of passivity and anxiety. Sex differences reappeared in the last age group, composed of children twelve to fifteen years old. Boys were emotionally inhibited and tended toward acting out their mixed moods of aggression and depression. The girls were introverted without the added element of acting out. In general, the boys appeared to be more aggressive, while the girls were more inwardly oriented. However, this characteristic appears to be a reflection of general cultural differences between the sexes. It does not seem to say anything unique about suicidal children.

## Summary

Overall, the attempt to find a personality pattern underlying suicidal tendencies has yielded few fruits. In spite of cherished beliefs and theories, none of the traits commonly used to characterize suicidal children has received full empirical support in the research conducted. Indeed, the findings are at best inconsistent and indicate that children with varying and often opposing personality traits can reach the one-way street of self-destructive behavior and suicide attempts.

It does seem valid to conclude that children with suicidal

inclinations display some aspects of depressive reactions, such as inclement moods, sorrow, despair, hopelessness, and dissatisfaction; however, this depressive symptomatology generally arises as a reaction to events occurring just prior to the suicidal attempt. Suicidal children also are obsessively preoccupied with the subject of death in all its different forms and show a tendency toward rigidity in thinking. Yet at this point, the images of the suicidal diverge. Some can be aggressive; others, completely unaggressive. Some reflect serious emotional disturbances, but this is not a necessary element. A few manifest good self-control and proper personality functioning, whereas others are impulsive and antisocial. Some of the children are isolated, while others have good or at least bearable social relations.

This diversity suggests that suicidal tendencies are not caused by personality traits alone. Rather, a few traits—such as depression, preoccupation with death, and low frustration threshold—appear to function as risk elements. When combined with other properties, these traits increase the likelihood of escape through suicide. It is also possible that the search for a personality pattern is useless because there is actually more than one pattern leading to the same consequence. The data presented here are insufficient to reveal a comprehensive picture of the different personality patterns and what unifies them.

The question that remains to be dealt with is why some children become suicidal and what differentiates them from children with other emotional disturbances. Why do children with the same personality traits "choose" suicide instead of nonsuicidal depression, antisocial behavior, or psychosis? At present, we cannot point to the dynamics distinguishing between suicidal tendencies and other disturbances.

Most of the studies referred to in this chapter focused on a search for pathologies or personality traits representing defective functioning. As a result, certain aspects of functioning that might shed some light were ignored. For example, practically no attention has been given to the ways in which suicidal children confront problems. How do they resolve conflicts? How do they organize their reactions or respond to difficulties? What happens to them when their first attempt to bring about change fails? Do they give up, persist, abstain, raise or lower their expectations? One's ways of dealing with life might ultimately lead to a rejection of one's whole life. Therefore, these elements clearly warrant investigation.

Another unexplored subject concerns the expectations of the children themselves and their ability to compromise. High expectations that are unachievable, accompanied by an inability to compromise, seem to invite frustration and dissatisfaction. Repeated experiences of this sort are likely to leave a lasting impression of hopelessness and helplessness, which are heavily weighted elements in the process of suicide. The picture will become clearer when we move on to an examination of the special life situations that suicidal children find themselves in.

# 5

# Suicidal Behavior
# as a Response to
# Life Circumstances

Are there special conditions that lead adults and children down the road to self-destruction? What experiences can be so intolerable as to force a child to conclude that life is worthless or to see suicide as an "all-or-nothing" gamble that things will get better? What could bring children to "threaten" such drastic measures? These questions take on added weight when we recognize that most of the broad range of experience is shared by large groups of adults and children. Most of us have some understanding of pain, suffering, and even intolerable situations. Yet only a minority of us ever reach a point where we prefer death over life.

Obviously, one's life situation is a matter not of purely objective measurements but of subjective impressions. Therefore, we must look at children's experiences through their eyes. For example, large groups of children were separated from their families in London during the "Blitz" of World War II. We as adults might have expected that the terrors of war would be the central aspect of these children's experience. Yet, for most of the children, separation from their parents was the most heart-rending part of the war. We often tend to assess separation from a loved one in terms of the objective length of time involved. Yet clinical experience shows that a shorter separation is not always less anguish-laden than a long-term separation. Children often lack the ability and the experience to perceive time lapses, so that a separation of only a few days can seem an eternity.

Therefore, the need to understand the meaning of life strictly through the child's experience serves as an underlying point of reference throughout the following discussion.

## Reasons Children Give for Suicide

How do children explain their motives for killing themselves? In a study by Shaffer (1974), children who committed suicide had complained most frequently about disciplinary problems, fights with friends or parents, expulsion from school, or the presence of a mentally ill parent. Kosky (1983, p. 459) quotes the reasons given by young children from five to twelve years old for their suicidal behavior: "To be with my brother so that mother will love me like she loved him." "So that my father won't hit me anymore." "Everyone blames me." "I'm a bother to the whole family." "I'm sad and I'm angry." Paulson, Stone, and Sposto (1978, p. 235) found similar themes. One six-year-old boy claimed: "I want to die." An eleven-year-old: "No, no, it doesn't matter to anyone if I live or not." An eight-year-old challenged his parents: "You'll be glad when I die." A boy of ten said: "Everyone kills, everyone dies, there's no way out." Careful inspection of these words reveals the loss, rejection, and helplessness that the children feel and the complete absence of hope. Yet, when one delves further, one is troubled by the commonplaceness of the motives. We intuitively expect that when someone chooses the course of suicide, something extraordinary should occur—something that differs greatly from what most of us know as life's hardships.

In this chapter, we will try to examine in depth the experiences leading to suicide, in order to go beyond the apparent shallowness of reasons that children offer. We will also try to determine some of the complex processes that result in the subjective experience that one has no avenue of escape.

## The First Trauma

A 1985 study by Salk and his colleagues has created interest in the possibility that the seeds of self-destruction are sown at birth. The researchers hypothesized that suicide among adolescents may be related to the mother's difficulties during pregnancy and in giving birth. Data were collected from the medical files of fifty-two adolescents who had committed suicide; these data were then compared with data on nonsuicidal adolescents born in the same hospital at the same time. The data concerned medical supervision during the pregnancy, maternal illnesses, maternal age, family status, difficulties with the delivery, and the history of the birth. Three variables significantly differentiated the suicidal adolescents: (1) medical negligence during pregnancy, (2) chronic maternal illness, and (3) neonatal respiratory difficulties that persisted for an hour or more after birth. Over 60 percent of the suicidal adolescents suffered from one or more of these problems, compared with less than 20 percent of the control groups. It is ironic to note that, if they had not received medical and mechanical assistance, few of these infants would have survived.

The findings suggest a form of biological predestination: Children who avoid death with the aid of modern medicine may eventually find their way to death through other means. Disruptions in pregnancy may embed biological weakness, which makes adaptation to life and survival very difficult. Despite this work's fatalistic attraction, it lacks decisive facts that could lead to a definitive interpretation. Lacking are comparative data on adolescents with similar disturbances who did not commit suicide or on those who committed suicide but had no birth difficulties.

The complexities of the case allow many counterexplanations. It is possible that medical neglect during the pregnancy fostered maternal rejection of the baby even before it was born. Alternately, the respiratory difficulties during and after the birth may have hindered proper development and led to later rejection by the mother. In any case, it is clear that our understanding of suicide must go beyond biological experiences to more complex and interweaving social and emotional events. Central among these are those of loss and destruction.

## Loss and Suicide

*Empirical Findings.* When dealing with the topics of loss and separation, we must recognize that, by our very nature, we are bonded to one another. Our identity and our essence become meaningful through our relationships with other people. This symbolic umbilical cord is never severed, although the objects of our attachment may change. We have the wonderful flexibility to transfer our emotional relations from one object to another, from mothers and fathers to other people, and even to animals, inanimate objects, and symbols.

We charge our relationships with meaning and emotions. The experience of the relationship is internalized and adds new dimensions to our self-definition. New and old contacts are fueled by a basic childish need to be with another person. In this fashion, we nurture and are nurtured all in one. Loss—of a loved one, a job, social status, even a precious trifle—empties us, leaves us diminished. Moreover, it forces us to reevaluate ourselves and the world when we are still injured and in pain. The most concrete example is the loss of an arm or a leg. There are those who believe that the "phantom pain"—the pain of a limb that is no longer there—reflects not only neurological and physiological processes but also our absolute refusal to separate from the lost part. We relate to our damaged body in light of its past integrity and present anguish.

Most of us have the stamina to suffer pain and start again. Yet recovery from a significant loss is never complete. It remains in the background, occasionally coming forward.

How able are children to deal with loss? On the one hand, there are ample reasons to believe them vulnerable: their young and tender years, their dependence on others for love and satisfaction, and their general lack of skills. On the other hand, they are flexible, forget quickly, and can easily transfer their love from one object to another.

Dorpat, Jackson, and Ripley (1965) studied the relationship between loss and suicidal tendencies by comparing attempted and completed suicide in adults. Case histories were used to determine whether these adults had experienced a loss that had led to disintegration of the family unit, what had caused the loss (for example, divorce, death of parents, personal desire to leave home), and at what age the loss occurred. Loss and separation resulting from parental death were highest among those who committed suicide; among those who only attempted, home life was generally disrupted by other causes. Over 45 percent of those who committed suicide had experienced a parent's death at an early age; in contrast, only 21 percent of those who made fairly harmless attempts had suffered the loss of a parent at a young age. Most of the individuals in both groups were threatened with another separation shortly before their suicidal act. The researchers concluded that early loss—particularly a loss brought about by death—contributes strongly to the formation of suicidal tendencies. The difficulty in accepting and dealing with the loss seems to be the basis for suicidal tendencies and depression (Levi, Fales, Stein, and Sharp, 1966).

The destructive impact of loss in early life on adolescents was brought home in another study (Stanley and Barter, 1970), in which the researchers contrasted age of loss among adolescents hospitalized for attempted suicide and those hospitalized for other reasons. Ninety percent of the suicidal adolescents had experienced loss before the age of twelve. Although most of the nonsuicidal adolescents had suffered some loss, only half had experienced it at a very young age. The importance of age was further highlighted by the absence of group differences in social adaptability, frequency of hospitalization, or numbers and types of losses.

In another study (Crook and Raskin, 1975), childhood parental loss was examined in suicidal adults and in nonsuicidal depressed adults. Here a critical distinction was found in the frequency of loss. Those who attempted suicide had experienced repeated losses through divorce, separation, and factors other than death. The notion of losses dating back to early ages also appeared in at least one empirical contrast of suicidal and nonsuicidal young children (Kosky, 1983). Here the suicidal were found to be beset by numerous separations. In over 80 percent of the cases, the suicidal had suffered at least one loss involving death or divorce. In contrast, only 20 percent of the nonsuicidal group had ever lost someone close to them. This finding confirms the impression that children who attempt suicide live in an atmosphere of loss under particularly tragic circumstances.

The finding of multiple losses through death, divorce, and other separations among the suicidal has fueled interest in the "broken home hypothesis." This hypothesis posits that the sudden breakup of a loving and protective family framework destroys children's secure base just as they are developing relations with people outside the home. The broken home shakes their faith in their ability to deal with life, satisfy their needs, and create a place outside the home.

In sum, empirical data indicate that suicide is related to multiple loss, at an early age, and often for tragic reasons. It is clear that the suicidal are no strangers to tragedy and family disruption. Nevertheless, a loss that leads to suicide must have some unique characteristics; otherwise, we would expect to find a higher rate of suicide in children.

*Reactions to the Loss of a Loved One.* To the bereaved child, a loss is devastating. It carries with it the entire range of reactions to sorrow (Worden, 1986): shock, apathy, anxiety, anger, fury, guilt, blame, and exhaustion, along with feelings of loneliness, yearning, and helplessness, and a slipping grasp of reality. There are severe physical changes, hallucinations, nightmares, uneasiness, sleep difficulties, and obsessive preoccupation with the loved person. The child searches for the loved person in every corner, obsessively reconstructing the last moments with the person and clinging to that person's possessions. At times also, there can be a paradoxical experience of relief.

Grollman (1967) describes in simple terms the broad range of reactions to privation in children. One of the most common is a regression to a very childlike state. The child's security is set asunder when she is deprived of the special love relationship. Also destabilized is the unique manner in which she was accustomed to having her needs met and receiving love. The void once filled by love and security is now filled with fear. No wonder, then, that the child retreats into primitive patterns of security. She may start sucking her thumb again, wet her bed at night, or even wet during the day. This regression may also be expressed through crying, whining, clinging, and demands for attention.

Another common reaction is to disregard the entire episode. A five-year-old girl or boy may act as if nothing has happened and may even deny that any loss has occurred. Relatives may regard this reaction as a sign of emotional strength or as evidence that the child "doesn't understand" the event. Neither view is true. Rather, the young child is distancing herself from the blow because the pain is too great to bear. The game of "things as usual" is proof of insulation from pain and mourning and forms the basis for pathological mourning and the encapsulation of pain. It is likely to have serious consequences for future relationships and attachments.

Another common response to loss is on a psychosomatic level: loss of appetite, sleep disturbances, feelings of suffocation, and breathing difficulties. All are expressions of general anxiety. Sometimes the child, much the same as an adult, feels symptoms that the loved one underwent just before death. He may feel chest pains, claustrophobia, palpitations, or other similar symptoms. All reflect the child's fear of his own death.

Every death brings home the realization that we all must die at some time. Fear arises as well for the well-being of the surviving parent, who is now the only anchor left to the child. He becomes terrified that he will be left alone and without protection.

Guilt is another reaction that appears even among the very young. Among adults, guilt over the death of a loved one is almost axiomatic and has been well documented in cases following war and tragedy. One's own survival is perceived to be at the expense of those who died: "If only I had acted differently, then maybe . . ." The guilt becomes stronger when there is even the slightest shred of reality to the feeling of responsibility.

Children tend to take on guilt because of their magical thinking. Angry thoughts and improper behavior are perceived as possible causes of death: "Father died because I was bad." Some figures of speech unintentionally foster a nucleus of guilt: "I swear this child is going to kill me." Even apparently disconnected remarks may serve as the focus for the self-attribution of blame. Grollman (1967) describes a girl whose parents told her that in order to live she had to eat her cereal. One day, she did not eat her cereal, and her father died that day. She immediately connected the two events and took all the blame upon herself. She then waited for her punishment for being the cause of death.

Along with feelings of guilt, there are contrary feelings of anger, which are part and parcel of mourning. Children more than anyone else perceive death as a voluntary separation and are hostile toward the deceased. The orphan who experiences loss as abandonment is furious with the betrayal. Even a short-term separation is known to be accompanied by anger. A child who runs to his father returning from an extended trip may turn away at the last minute for his mother's arms. He may act aloof or simply go about business as if he had nothing to do with this happy occasion. The renewal of the bond takes place gradually over time.

At times, mourning responses within the family assume completely opposite forms. Scharl (1961) describes the therapy of two sisters referred after their father's death in a car accident. The wide variations in their responses seemed to result from a mixture of differing ages, personalities, and patterns of relationship at the time of death. The case history also offers insight into suicidal processes resulting from a loss.

Eight-and-a-half-year-old Linda was the older of the two sisters. Her relations with her father had been very aloof, since she rejected any of his displays of emotion. She was very independent but tended to be quarrelsome and less than satisfied. Her father's death did not seem to affect her at all. In fact, she seemed to be quite the opposite of mournful. She became more independent, initiating, and cooperative and less moody. Yet her insistent refusal to speak of her father's death led to her being referred to therapy.

The therapist saw Linda as frightened and overattached to her mother. In her therapy, Linda repeatedly expressed anger over her younger sister's childishness and lack of responsibility. In the playroom, she occupied herself with death games, expressing death wishes and aggression toward her surroundings and her pets at home. She took apart and broke her toys, frequently "killing" them. She could take or reject responsibility for their death interchangeably.

In discussions, Linda threatened to kill anyone who didn't love her but was demonstrably appalled by her own words. She was also overcome with fright when two of her pets died, and she quickly absolved herself of all responsibility for their deaths.

The subsequent death of her mother's father exacerbated Linda's condition. She became very accident prone and frequently hurt herself. One day, she related that her guinea pig had killed himself by jumping over the side of the box he was in but that it was entirely her fault. She then pulled herself together and explained that she would get other pets and since she was a big girl she shouldn't cry.

Linda's younger sister was, at five and a half, a "daddy's girl." She was full of vitality, loved to adorn herself and to admire herself in the mirror, and made great efforts to be liked by others and to squeeze compliments from them. She was the "perfect" child who could do no wrong.

The expression of her mourning was open and direct: "If daddy has died, then there's no point in living." Yet, even at the first therapeutic session, she had no trouble separating from her mother. She made acquaintances with everyone at the clinic and enchanted them all. The little girl showered her love on everyone and even paid herself compliments. These social behaviors were very blatant in the therapy itself. There was a display of flattery toward her therapist, whom she asked to be a second mother. She enjoyed the games and expressed her pleasure in them.

The young girl believed that her father was alive and would one day come home. Yet, with the death of the next relative, she became frightened of people in the halls. In the playroom, she clung to the therapist and asked if she could take off her clothes and be fed like a baby. Although she was very aggressive to the toys, her relationship with the therapist became much stronger and closer. At a closing session before a vacation break, she presented the therapist with a peach and said, "If I don't return in the fall, I'll kill myself because I love you so much."

The two girls displayed two opposite reactions to bereavement. The older one attempted to escape toward maturity and initiative, interspersed with intermittent expressions of anger and fury and an undercurrent of guilt. She also strove for a better position in the family at the expense of her envied younger sister. The younger sister adhered to previous patterns of behavior, in which she attempted to gain love by showering love on those around her. In both cases, we see how repeated loss leads to a regression to the haven of childish and primitive patterns involving the hesitant denial of death, as well as signs of self-destructive thoughts.

*Impact of Loss on Suicidal Behavior.* How, exactly, does loss lead to suicide? There are a number of theories. One involves the notion of "attachment behavior." Bowlby (1969, 1973), after an in-depth study, proposed that attachment to a mother figure is a hereditary, biologically rooted instinct that has been molded by the process of evolution. The infant's attachment to the mother reflects primitive fears of predators and strangers and dependent needs for prenatal nurturance and protection. Attachment theory argues that man and animal alike have a basic fear of being abandoned, which accompanies them all their lives.

Other theories emphasize primarily the infant's basic needs. Since the mother fulfills these needs at the beginning of life, the child begins to see the mother as the main source of satisfaction. In this manner, the mother gains such an unchallenged value that she takes on greater import than the needs themselves. There is a growing longing for the mother herself, a process that sets the stage for later personality development.

Whatever the basis for attachment, most theorists agree that the child learns to preserve the relationship with the protecting figure and to transfer this relationship to other social figures as well. Separation immediately causes anxiety, sorrow, and anguish. The response to separation differs little between the young of either animals or humans.

Bowlby (1973) has described definite stages in the separation response during the days, weeks, and months following loss. The first stage is one of protest, pain, crying, longing, and the anxious search for renewed contact. These responses are accompanied by hostility toward the environment, aggression, and angry lack of cooperation. The second stage is one of apathy and despair, involving surrender and introversion. In the third stage, there is a disengagement from the protective figure and an emotional distancing from others. At this point, the child wants and needs a replacement for the protective figure.

Bowlby found that children separated from their mothers for long periods of time were willing to establish new relationships only when they were sure that these relationships would be more secure than the last.

In this light, the yearning for the dead reflects the biologically rooted longing for one's attachment figures. At times, however, this natural impulse may become distorted into a suicidal desire for a reunion with the dead through one's own death.

A number of factors contribute to the growth of suicidal tendencies after loss: the nature of the relationship with the deceased, the relative security of the bond, and the availability and form of additional social bonds. Was the relationship with the deceased exclusive? Did it involve overdependence or excessive anxiety? Did the child believe that this was the only relationship that would provide security? How ready or available are alternate attachment figures? To what extent are the child's attachment needs taken into account? How flexible and accommodating is the child?

These matters are illustrated by the case history of twelve-year-old Michael, whose parents both died of heart attacks in a half-year span when he was eleven. Michael, the youngest child, was lovingly taken in by his oldest brother's family. In spite of the family's warm contacts, the loss of both parents had left an indelible mark.

Michael's pattern of dealing with his tragedy followed previous habits of coping. When I first met Michael after the loss as a pupil in school, he seemed to be a happy and well-adjusted child. He was active, self-initiating, and a natural leader. He even disciplined other children and successfully gained the sympathy of teachers and classmates alike with his charm. Yet the scars left by the tragedy were apparent. He lacked patience and was often overbearing, vengeful, angry, and introverted. He was also vulnerable to the point that at times he would come to school in a state of tension and depression. At times, the tension would rise so disproportionately that he got into fights with his friends or suddenly left school. Finally, he began to contemplate suicide and told others of his plans.

Michael developed a style of coping with his loss that was

rooted in his personality and early behavior. He strove for complete control in all situations. He never allowed himself to be
caught off guard by any development, especially when dealing
with people. He had to set the tone and pace. This coping style
was partly a result of Michael's need to be loved by everyone.
He felt threatened by the realization that the world could survive without him. His double loss had convinced him that he
had to take control. The pattern blended well with his family's
unconditional support. Any attempt at restriction caused bouts
of anger and depression, during which he would isolate himself,
get into fights, or simply run away.

   He formed a detailed suicide plan just in case he decided
that life was no longer worth living. During difficult spells, he
would discourse on death and its meaning. Crying whenever he
spoke of his parents. Michael imagined that he would join them
and continue living with them "up there." But despite his plans
for suicidal action, one got the impression that they boded little
danger. Most were no more than expressions of his longing and
yearning for his parents. Yet it is likely that, without the massive support of his surroundings and his own mettle, Michael
would have acted on his impulses.

   Death wishes arise not only as a result of a loss but also in
the face of impending loss. Suicidal threats and wishes are often
a response to threatened relations between parents and children
or to the possible loss of contact with a loved one. For example,
one nine-year-old girl who followed her brother's long and painful bout with cancer began speaking of her own desire to kill
herself if he died. Coping with day-to-day deterioration had
exacted a heavy price from the girl's whole family. The atmosphere was heavy with impending death; everyone's life was organized around the dying child. The situation elicited a medley
of feelings: fear, the desire to speed up the process, guilt, the desire to stop the process, dependent clinging to and at the same
time distancing from the afflicted family member. Like the
other family members, the young girl submerged her own needs
to face her brother's tragedy. Yet she lost contact with her parents at a time when she most needed them. She began to feel
waves of resentment toward her parents and brother. Her jeal-

ousy fueled simultaneous wishes for death and fear of parental loss. Thus, her threat of suicide was partly an attempt to cling to her helpless parents in their hour of pain.

A similar situation arose with a twelve-and-a-half-year-old girl who tried to commit suicide by swallowing sleeping pills. Her mother was in deep mourning for an oldest son who had died a few years before. When called on at home, the mother—dressed in black—was sitting in the drawing room under a large picture of the deceased. The daughter frankly admitted that in her own suicide attempt she hoped to get her mother to finally speak to her. She was no less frank over her jealousy of a dead brother whom she actually never knew. The attempted suicide was a call to a mother lost behind walls of depression.

Pathological mourning deviates from more normal mourning processes (Bowlby, 1980). Normal mourning begins with a conscious recognition of the loss, which develops into an experience of pain and bereavement, followed by adjustment to the new reality and the establishment of other relations. In pathological mourning, there is an initial refusal to accept the loss. This refusal may be expressed through denial, emotional disengagement, or various rationalizations. On the other hand, there is a continuous yearning for the deceased and a magical hope that the person will one day return. Although these reactions are an acceptable part of the mourning process for a brief time, their continuation bodes ill.

Among children, the reaction of the environment can prevent the normal process of mourning. Some adults attempt to spare the children pain by keeping them away from various events and ceremonies, such as the burial or the memorial services. They tell the children that the dead person lives on, in a place far away. All these efforts prevent a discussion of the true loss and force the children into a stance of denial. By denying the opportunity for mourning, they only make final separation more difficult.

In pathological mourning, there is a situation of perpetual bereavement, in which the longing to renew bonds with the deceased brings the mourner closer to the idea of suicide. That was the plight of Judy, aged thirty, who came for treatment.

Orphaned from her mother at age fourteen, she felt lonely despite many friends. She was dissatisfied with her job and had had a prolonged but disappointing love affair with a married man. A chain smoker and a heavy drinker, she seemed a bitterly unhappy woman.

Judy's few happy memories from her childhood were centered on the blurred figure of her mother. One picture from her childhood was vivid: Her mother was walking to the corner store, and Judy was behind her on roller skates. The world seemed rosy, secure, and protected.

Judy's mother had died after a protracted bout with cancer, but Judy had no recollection of the period. She remembered only an open grave and an overwhelming desire to jump into it; her attempt was foiled by bystanders. Any further references to or questions about this period were met with resistance. For example, she refused to bring childhood photos to aid in recalling the blocked memories.

In the first year after her mother's death, her relationship with her father—which had previously been hostile and distant—deepened. She was grateful for her father's attention but lived in constant fear of being deserted again. As a result, she decided "never again to love anyone or become attached to anything." Unfortunately, her fears all too soon materialized: Judy's father remarried two years after her mother's death. That was the beginning of a traumatic relationship with her stepmother, which ended when Judy was thrown out of the house at age seventeen and told never to return. Despite this abrupt turn, Judy continued her relations with her father at a distance.

Judy continuously relived the pain of rejection and nurtured her anger. Whenever she was distressed, she turned to the picture of her mother. When she was lonely, she would pour her heart out to her mother's picture. This was her only source of comfort and gave her strength to go on. Her devotion to her mother became her sole source of personal gratification. Despite her many friends, no other relationship offered her meaningful support. In many ways, Judy had been left standing at her mother's grave at age fourteen and had never left.

In her woe, Judy was comforted by the thought that she

could always end her life. Although she never spoke of a belief in the hereafter or a desire to join her mother, the ideas could be discerned under her outer façade of rock-hard logic. She seemed prepared to attempt suicide at some future time.

Judy's lifestyle exemplifies pathological mourning. One can discern the perpetuation of pain and the refusal to replace one primary attachment with a substitute. In Judy's world view, no one is to be trusted, promises will always be broken, one will always be abandoned and deserted. When events refused to jibe with her view, she made them so, creating a wake of disappointment and abandonment. The sorrow locked inside her locked her out of the world.

Total denial of mourning, the opposite extreme from pathological mourning, can have an equally destructive impact on social relations. Feelings of emptiness and disquiet gradually fill one's life for no apparent reason. Newly formed relations seem to be pointless or are quickly terminated because of an apparent lack of compatibility. Those who deny their bereavement are in essence living a life of covert depression.

Rochlin (1959) discusses the processes mediating between loss and suicide in terms of the disintegration of self-esteem and the growth of helplessness. Relationships with people are the nurturant source of self-esteem. Warm relationships help one create a balance between the forces of love and hate that are present in everyone. The loss of such relationships pushes this delicate balance in the direction of negative expectations about the world and the self. The way is opened for the slide to self-hate and self-destruction. Guilt feelings further exacerbate the imbalance, as do "unresolved reckonings with the deceased."

Daily life offers illustrations of the growth of self-hate among those who have suffered loss. Orphaned children often appear ashamed of their loss, as if it were their fault. The loss has shattered their self-esteem and given rise to these feelings of shame.

Judy's life story illustrates some aspects of Rochlin's assertions. One is impressed by her repeated exclamation that no one in the world is worth the effort involved in establishing a relationship. She included herself in that group of the rejected:

"I'm not worthy of anyone's effort either." Implicit in her words is the projection that she does not love herself and therefore no one else can either. Having lost her mother's love, as Rochlin would have it, she was no longer lovable, even to herself.

Beyond their wealth of love, parents serve as interlocutors in the frustrations and failures that are part of every child's life. Their loss can only intensify the friction of daily discomfitures. Without their restorative comfort, pains and failures take a heavier toll in one's esteem. The fires of self-hate and denigration are further stoked with the loss of parents' protective cloak.

Rochlin highlights a second process in loss—the formulation of helplessness. The loss of the parent figure presents a serious blow to children's natural feelings of omnipotence. Children evolve feelings of omnipotence as a protective counter to their inferior position in the world. These feelings are nurtured by the belief that the parents are omnipotent and invulnerable and offer unshakable protection. These intertwined beliefs about parents' and child's potency help the child develop internal equilibrium and optimism. Loss tears aside this rosy-colored veil of omnipotence. All at once, the child is exposed to the basic feelings of helplessness of all people against the inevitable encroachment of death—feelings of pessimism and the loss of any belief in personal power to change the course of events. This helplessness destroys one's vitality, stamina, and zest for life. The path to self-destruction is opened.

Rochlin's analysis of the role of loss can be supplemented by more general concerns regarding the centrality of identification in the course of child development. One's personality is based in large part on identification with parental figures and the internalization of their values and behavior. Thus, parental loss before identification is crystallized can leave a vacuum. In this perspective, self-destruction may reflect in part the desire to regain parts of one's identity that were lost with the dead parent.

Feelings of loss do not always require actual separation. At times, even the threat of loss or separation is sufficient to arouse suicidal feelings. For example, Rachel, who came for therapy at the age of eighteen, had not lost either of her parents; nevertheless, feelings of privation formed a major part of her internal experience. At the outset, Rachel had come for therapy because she "did not feel right inside." The world frightened her and seemed distorted. Streets seemed to be crooked, houses were on the verge of falling, and people's faces looked peculiar. Rachel's first sentences in therapy betrayed the crux of her problem: "I don't feel myself. I feel dead inside. I don't know who I am. I don't know if I am me or someone else." Rachel felt that her selfhood lacked a firm basis of reality and emotional experience. Because her sense of self was anchored in her bond with her mother, she was in a constant struggle for self-determination and dreaded any severing of this bond.

From the beginning, Rachel had always felt that she was born for her parents and that she owed them her life. Any attempt at self-expression, even something as simple as buying her own clothes, was accompanied by anxiety and guilt. Because of her parents' overpossessiveness and involvement in her life, Rachel felt incapable of doing anything alone. Even though she recognized that her overdependence on her parents was not desirable, she was frightened of being without their backing and presence.

Rachel's identity was based on the internalization of her parents. Yet this normal process took on a pathological form, since there was no differentiation between her own identity and the identity of her parents. One of Rachel's expressions exemplifies the essence of her problem in all its force: "When I look at my mother's back, I don't know if it's her or me." Although Rachel found this situation intolerable, the thought of change frightened her terribly. She became lost between the two poles of dependence and independence.

Some months after therapy had begun, Rachel was to be drafted into the army. For the first time, she would be separated from the family, and she expressed fears for herself and her parents. Suicide and death became an inseparable part of the paradoxical maze: to continue being dependent on her parents meant one form of death, but to be separated from them was another form. In this manner, thoughts of suicide became an expression of independence and separation from her parents.

Yet at the same time, death would allow her to run away from the demands of independence.

Death became a frightening and fascinating phenomenon for Rachel. The fact that she could make a decision to commit suicide, and that no one else could participate in or influence that decision, gave her a feeling of independence and relief. The idea of suicide stayed with Rachel for a very long time.

Rachel's case reflects the manner in which loss or the threat of loss can lead to suicidal thoughts or acts. The underlying key appears to be in the threats to the young person's growing sense of selfhood. This growth of self rests on identification with the parents, so that any disruption or distortion of the parental bond eventuates in a loss of identity. In this atmosphere, suicidal thoughts may serve as a path for coping with the reassertion of the threatened self.

*Divorce, Separation, and Suicide.* Divorce is far from being a definitive cause of suicide. In fact, the separation of divorce may even bring about an improvement in children's lives, as calm displaces an atmosphere of friction and arguments. Nonetheless, many cases of divorce are followed by a subsequent history of self-destruction. In particularly vindictive relationships, parents may use the children as pawns for blackmail against each other. A common guise is a custody fight "for the good of the children," which can become more threatening than the separation itself. The extreme conflicts of loyalty that are engendered arouse anxiety and a feeling of being trapped as children are called on to assume a responsibility that is foreign to them. No less painful is the misplaced guilt that children feel about their parents' separation. If they had truly been good, their parents never would have parted. This guilt is accompanied by anger toward the parents. The resulting fusion of guilt and anger can bring on destructive forces of self-hatred.

Estranged parents often attempt to use their children as means of heading off a divorce or bringing it on or as "go betweens." All these attempts are camouflaged and subtle. In each, the child is being asked to solve an unresolvable problem at great personal price. Eight-year-old Danny had to play such a destructive role when his father left home. The mother rallied the children against the father, using any means possible. During the parents' fights, they made Danny the mailman for notes between them. Each tried to win him over as part of a titanic fight over custody rights. Ultimately, each parent decided to call him by a different name. Whichever name he answered to presumably would disclose his loyalty. It is not difficult to guess how Danny must have felt when his answering one parent was seen as rejection of the other. He was torn in two by the conflict.

Danny's parents did not even allow him the illusion that they were fighting over love for him. They revealed to him their plans to send him to boarding school. Of course, they presented it as a place where he would have "peace of mind and be far away from all the goings on." Yet Danny could see that both parents were rejecting him.

Danny took refuge behind a suicide threat. He had no other respite from the anxiety, rejection, and threat. His fantasy was that his death would bring his parents back together and then he would return to them. He planned the suicide down to the last detail. When he told his teacher, he was referred to therapy.

Besides the tremendous pain revealed by Danny's case, one can see the use of a suicide threat as a tool to prevent the divorce. The child's helplessness and inability to cope force him to threaten suicide in an attempt to allay the catastrophe. Fortunately, such cases seem to involve little long-term risk of actual self-destruction.

One should not be misled into thinking that the formal trappings of divorce are prerequisite to their destructive power. Long-term separation without the legalities or formal recognition may also have the same effect. Nine-year-old Tim, for example, was brought to therapy because he displayed a compulsive interest in death. His father had been abroad for a prolonged period of time for "work reasons." His mother looked at the separation as a test of her strength of survival and her value as a person, a challenge agreed to by the husband. Not surprisingly, when the mother had difficulty with this challenge, she refused help from friends. The atmosphere at home became tense as the mother became more and more nervous, desperate, and demanding. It was at this point that Tim began speaking about the lack of meaning in life.

His mother began to send frantic letters to the father, saying that "the boy can't find a reason for living and I don't know what to tell him." In the course of trans-Atlantic calls, she encouraged Tim to ask his father why life was worth living. When the worried father returned, the whole family came for a joint therapeutic session. "Now," claimed the mother, "Tim will stop talking nonsense. He's so relaxed when his father is around. He simply can't do without his father."

In Tim's case, it is clear that suicide was his mother's lever for shifting an unbearable weight. Yet, in denying her difficulties, she unconsciously placed on Tim the responsibility of returning the father home. Unknowingly, the mother encouraged Tim to become problematic and thereby carry her own message and suicidal wishes.

As these examples demonstrate, divorce and separation are not in and of themselves the direct causes of suicidal behavior. Rather, in each case, there appear to be additional processes at work that push the child, bewildered by pain, to act out self-destruction. These processes involve attempts to resolve unresolvable problems, a topic articulated in Chapter Nine.

*Parental Suicide and Depression.* Parental suicide is one type of desertion that has no emotional parallel in its destructive force. The family and child are bombarded by the forces of guilt, shame, self-punishment, and depression. Moreover, the act of suicide points out to the child the deadly means for coping with this maelstrom of emotion. Small wonder that over one-fourth of the suicidal adolescents in a study by Teicher and Jacobs (1966) had parents who had committed suicide.

The suicide of a parent leaves few other options for coping. One fourteen-year-old whose father committed suicide after a prolonged period of depression refused to talk about it with anyone. He did not take part in any of the mourning rituals, preferring to go on with his usual activities at home and school. There was no noticeable change in his mood or work. He showed no discomfiture in front of his friends and even got better grades than usual. It was as if the tragic event had never happened and as if he had never had a father. These reactions were not an expression of their relationship. Rather, they reflected intense denial. Even after his mother convinced him to go for therapy, he denied all feelings regarding the father's suicide. He summed it up with: "Father was mentally ill." By putting the suicide on this basis, the boy emotionally distanced his father without dishonoring him.

Unfortunately, clinical experience has proved that such tactics are short-term displacements of emotional debts that must be paid. Behavioral disturbances become obvious with time as more and more mental energy is needed to continue the repression. Without proper help, there is an eventual crisis, which sprouts from an "unexpected" source. Among adults, crises take place months after the supposedly accidental death of a child. Among children, similar responses are seen to death in a parent or relative.

Suicide attempts or suicidal tendencies have no less impact than the completion of the act. The connection between a parent's suicidal tendencies and child suicide has been demonstrated through clinical observations (Orbach and Glaubman, 1979b) and research surveys (Pfeffer, Zuckerman, Plutchik, and Mizruchi, 1984). The case of ten-year-old David shows that latent suicidal wishes of parents can take on overt expression in their children. David was the second of three children in a middle-class family. The father, a free-lance craftsman, was an easygoing and likable man. Somewhat passive in his relationship with his wife, he left most of the decision making around the household to her. He became involved with his children's education only when it was demanded of him. David's mother was pretty, outgoing, and sociable. Vocal and slightly negativistic in her approach, she tended to be domineering.

An important part of the family history was the care given to David's older brother, who was blind. His parents were unable to reconcile themselves to his blindness. During the first years of his life, they invested limitless energies in trying to find a cure for the incurable.

David himself was a lackluster fifth grader with a low intellectual potential. Childish and vulnerable, he got along well with younger children but not with his peers. His dealings with adults were a source of dissatisfaction and continuous complaints. He had a low threshold for frustration and difficulty in dealing with failure. More than once, he had run home in tears because of a disappointment. David frequently clung to his teachers and aroused their maternal instincts.

The parents, who had unfulfilled desires for professional achievement, wanted David to become a prestigious professional such as a lawyer or doctor. The contradiction between his natural limitations and the constant pressures put on him made every failure a source of anxiety for him and a reason for punishment and rejection by his parents. The mother's ambivalent attitude toward David was reflected in everything she did.

David made a few suicide attempts that were not dangerous but brought him to therapy. Two of the attempts occurred after he had received disappointing grades in school. On one occasion, he ran outside in tears, screaming that he would kill himself in the street. His teacher ran after him and stopped him. He threw himself to the ground in a fury. Another time, he took a rope and tried to strangle himself in front of the children and the teacher. He frequently would leave notes on the door to his room: "I'll murder myself."

David started with individual treatment, which he thoroughly enjoyed. The quiet and accepting atmosphere, the concentrated attention, encouragement, lack of demands, and freedom of expression were a great help to him. As a result of the therapy, his general behavior was more relaxed and even his schoolwork improved. It seemed as though the perpetual emotional storm had calmed down. Then, without any warning, the mother declared that she was stopping the therapy: "It's a waste of time and doesn't help at all." At first glance, it seemed as though the mother was having difficulty in separating from David as he needed her less and less. During the attempts to convince the mother to allow David to continue therapy, she softened. She cried that she could not allow David to feel better than she did. She needed help no less than he did. The parents were then brought into the therapy. Concealed parts of David's life history and behavior were suddenly uncovered.

The mother had suffered frequent periods of depression since she was a child, and she had considered suicide more than once. Her father was a stern man who had hurt her often. She spoke of him with hostility and hatred. Her childhood dream had been to leave her parents' home and set up a glorious one of her own. She wanted more than anything else to be a good mother. About a year after she was married, she gave birth to a boy, who was born blind. She could not cope with this blow. The situation worsened when the doctors told her that, because of her health, she should not risk having more children. Her world collapsed. She saw herself as a failure as a mother and a wife. She decided to end her life in a very unique manner—by getting pregnant. She wanted to give birth to a healthy child and to die in the process. However, she successfully gave birth and remained very much alive. David was the son born out of these plans.

Although David had not killed his mother, the "suicide pact" between them was never undone, and the mother's suicidal tendencies found expression through her relations with David. Whenever David complained about something, the mother would react by saying, "So what, you want to kill yourself?" And when he finally began to make suicide threats, she would say: "So what, now we're supposed to have another child in your place?" During stormy arguments between them, she would offer him a knife and a hot iron and ask him which he wanted to use to kill himself. The mother herself needed the option of suicide in order to cope with the problems of life. Because of her difficulty in separating emotionally from David, she viewed her own death and David's death as interchangeable. David was a kind of mouthpiece for his mother's suicidal impulses. His overt expressions provided relief for her latent suicidal wishes.

The description of this case displays certain mediating processes between parental suicidal tendencies and child suicide. One is the encouragement of the children to carry out the parent's own tendencies. A second process is modeling. Children learn to deal with life's frustrations by running away and leaving the situation. They acquire an escapist style of coping, along with a pessimistic outlook on life. Death becomes a possible solution to problems. A third process occurs when a helpless and depressed parent creates a depressing atmosphere for the child's own actions.

Two additional processes that deserve attention are identification and introjection. Through identification, the child acquires his own identity by absorbing that of his parents. In the case of a suicidal parent, the child takes on the parent's pain, his manner of coping, and his self-destructive tendencies. This process becomes accelerated when there is a close dependency between the parent and the child. Introjection involves the child's tendency to relate toward himself in the same manner that his parents relate to him. For example, when the parents treat a child with anger, he is likely to turn upon himself with equal furor, as if he were indeed the source of blame. Through introjection, the child also can internalize parental rejection or guilt.

One final process in this regard is overparticipation. A depressed, pessimistic parent who dwells on thoughts of death is likely to reinforce these tendencies in her children. Such a parent tends to be too accepting of the child's difficulties, hopelessness, and failure to find alternatives. This parental overparticipation in the child's depression actually encourages suicidal action.

Findings from certain research studies support the validity of these ideas. Although a number of studies show that there is not much difference in parental pathology between families of suicidal children and those of nonsuicidal children except for depressive tendencies (Kosky, 1983), other studies claim that depressive and alcoholic parents are the dominant elements in the formation of suicidal tendencies in children (Carlson, 1983). Sometimes the parents may not necessarily be suicidal but have limited coping abilities and separation anxieties and therefore present a defective model for coping with life's problems.

## Child Abuse and Neglect

Child abuse and neglect have been revealed in a number of studies as high-risk factors in child suicide. The most comprehensive study in the area was conducted by Green (1968). One unique feature of his work is a clear distinction between neglect

per se and the combination of abuse and neglect together. Green
suggests that the powerful combination of emotional neglect
and physical violence eventuates in self-destructive behavior in
later years.

In Green's work, the neglected children were identified
on the basis of court decisions indicating that parents were
physically neglecting children by not adequately feeding them,
clothing them, or supplying medical attention. Yet in no case
did children in this group show signs of physical beatings. Abuse
was determined by court referrals of cases where a child was
continually beaten; Green assumed that this abuse was associated with a history of neglect. A third group consisted of normal children who served as contrast controls. This design permitted a differentiation of abuse and neglect versus neglect alone.

Green also employed clear criteria for determining self-
destructive behavior. These activities included the following:
biting, cutting, or burning self; pulling out hair; bashing head
against the wall; or attempting suicide. These behaviors were assessed through parents' reports or those of the child's guardian.
The findings were clear and straightforward. Although the majority of the children who were both abused and neglected displayed self-destructive behavior, almost none of the neglected
or normal groups did so. Green concluded that neglect and abuse
together promote the explosive tendency toward self-injury.

Accounts of child abuse are filled with pathos, since it is
well known that abused children cling strongly to their parents.
In their pain, bewilderment, and confusion, these children seek
security from their abusive parent because they lack any other
source of protection. An angry father may assault his six-year-
old daughter and swing at her as if she were a punching bag. Yet
a minute later, the little girl will cling to him and hug the hand
that beat her.

By what manner is abuse related to the development of
self-punitive tendencies and self-destruction? Abuse is terrifying. The body and soul are broken open, leaving no privacy.
Moreover, the beatings are often arbitrary and unexpected, occurring with little or no relation to the child's behavior. The
child feels a lack of any control or effective defense in the face

of the aggressive onslaught, feelings that lead to depression and self-hate. These feelings are strengthened by the child's recognition that she has lost her parents' love. When these factors are taken together, one sees a dynamic picture similar to that which appears with other forms of loss and separation related to suicide.

Abused children also internalize the anger and aggression of their violent and hateful parents. This internalization is aided by their low threshold for frustration. By way of imitation, children then take up behavioral patterns of aggression that they themselves suffered.

These analyses of the impact of abuse suggest that self-destructive tendencies may be instilled by punitive child-rearing techniques of less aversive quality. For example, Green (1968) claims that the seeds of self-destruction and self-hate are planted at a very young age through punitive upbringing and rigid toilet training. He argues that a combination of punishment and rejection by parents slowly instills in the young child a perception of himself as evil, ugly, and disgusting. Furthermore, future failures and rejections throughout the child's life are likely to evoke the same self-hate and self-anger. Clinical findings support Green's claims regarding punitive child rearing and the tendency toward self-destruction (Sabbath, 1969; Hendin, 1985).

Neglect appears to amplify the destructive impact of abuse. The parents' apathy creates a feeling of superfluity in the child. At the most simple and direct level, the child learns that she is an unwanted burden. In response, the child may retreat into herself in order to be a less visible bother. She learns to make herself disappear.

Many neglected and suicidal children were unplanned and unwanted accidents (Rosenthal and Rosenthal, 1984). The children's behavior seemed aimed at doing away with the superfluous burden for others while reducing their own personal feelings of pain and neglect. Rina, for example (whose case is discussed in Chapter One), suffered throughout her life from her mother's rejection of her almost immediately after she was born. She continued to feel that she did not belong anywhere, that she was always being "forced on others," and that special efforts were necessary to make her acceptable. These feelings arose in all situations, even during such ostensibly happy circumstances as her graduation from high school.

Some neglected children express their feeling of not belonging through their interpersonal relations. When young, they react hungrily to any display of affection, physically clinging to anyone willing to hold them or impulsively jumping into someone's lap. In view of this tendency, some investigators suggest that rejection and emotional neglect cause children to feel they have no control over creating close and gratifying relationships (Corder, 1974).

Another result of emotional neglect among suicidal children is their feeling of alienation from their families, who seem to be presenting a united front against them. Some investigators have used this issue of alienation as a way of linking self-destructive tendencies to parental rejection (Sabbath, 1969). This approach will be presented in Chapter Nine.

Although the loss of parental love and acceptance can contribute to suicide, their presence has important preventive functions. The protective, encouraging framework of the family offers the child comfort and strength in the face of life's disappointments and frustrations. In this view, familial support and protection serve as a psychological system that softens the blows and changes the negative self-image to a positive one. Support and love have both a healing and a preventive effect (Shaffer and Fisher, 1981).

Despite the attention given to neglect and rejection in suicide, research findings suggest that they are not central or unique factors. For example, Kosky (1983) found that parental neglect did not figure any more prominently in children's suicide than it did in other pathologies. Thus, neglect appears to be a risk element that takes on added importance as a function of additional familial, personal, and situational factors.

## Family Aggression

A discussion of aggression and neglect directed toward children leads, perforce, to the notion of a more general atmosphere of aggression at work in the family. At times, it seems reasonable to view children's suicides as aggressive attacks that take place in an aggressive family atmosphere. One clinical study of thirty-four suicidal children revealed that most of these children came from families dominated by brutality (Paulson, Stone, and Sposto, 1978). In these families, conflicts quickly flared into fights with knives, razors, and loaded weapons. The atmosphere was electric, charged with revenge and aggression in all directions, including the self. About 20 percent of the children had witnessed a murder within the family, while others had witnessed attempts on their siblings' lives. Threats with weapons, attempted strangulation, and poisoning were not infrequent occurrences.

Although it is unlikely that such levels of aggression arise in all families of the suicidal, it is easy to understand how such violence can lead to self-destructive behavior. This atmosphere reduces a child's ability to control impulses and reinforces a low threshold for frustration, which evokes aggression. Moreover, it lays the foundations for a depressive personality with guilt feelings and a sense of no escape. As one child in the families surveyed put it: "I'm a bad child and I want to die."

## Family Crises

Family crises are frequently cited in reports accompanying child suicide (Kosky, 1983)—crises such as death, divorce, separation, illness, fights, alcoholism, birth, weddings, and other transitions. The dominant reference is to negative crises. It is unlikely that all family crises lead to suicide. Otherwise, in light of the impressive parade of changes, transitions, and tragedies that befall everyone, we would expect suicide rates to be greater than they are. What, then, are the types of events that are particularly likely to increase the risk of suicide? One study (Orbach, 1981), where an attempt was made to define the essence of this crisis, concluded that the central feature of such crises is that they exact a price from all family members. For example, a major financial reversal affects the whole family. In some instances, it may bring about family unification and mutual support. But when the father takes to his bed with depression and the mother sinks into despair, the event can create unbearable living conditions for the child. In almost all family crises, the child is called on to participate in the family effort. These demands can sap the child's emotional energies and threaten his internal integrity. Finally, when demands go beyond the child's capabilities, he is likely to escape through thoughts of suicide.

The crisis in eleven-year-old Josh's family illustrates what can happen to a child during these periods. Josh's younger sister suffered from a rare blood disease. The devoted parents held back nothing in the search for a cure for her. Both parents made frequent trips to hospitals and doctors. Many times, the mother would be away from the house with the sick daughter. The father had to work overtime to carry the financial load. The atmosphere was tense and nervous; the family became more and more exhausted. Josh had to take the mother's role in running the house, cleaning, buying food, and cooking. Rewards for his efforts were few, since his parents were not around to praise his hard work or show him affection. Moreover, Josh's family was from a cultural background where the division between male and female roles was clear. In the normal run of events, such a gross overstepping of boundaries was quite unacceptable. Josh felt a threat to his integrity and his masculinity.

When Josh could not take any more, he went to the roof of his school and threatened to jump to his death. "What do they think, that I'm a woman?" Josh declared that he was willing to do any work, to stop his studies and devote himself to his beloved sister. He just could not bear the role of housewife, since it was a direct threat to his masculine identity. The young boy explained that if he jumped from the roof, his parents could collect financial compensation from the school for negligence. He imagined that the money would help extricate them from their financial difficulties and help find a cure for his sick sister.

At one level, Josh's story displays elements of altruistic self-sacrifice. At another level, it reveals an attempt to escape from a situation that is personally intolerable for the child. Shneidman (1985) has made the telling observation that behind every suicide there is an essential need and that the only way of gratifying this need, from a subjective point of view, is through death. This type of crisis—where overwhelming and threatening demands bring on feelings of hopelessness and despair—probably can be found in all cases of child suicide.

## Academic Pressures

One other aspect of family life that has been associated with suicide are familial pressures for success and high achievement. Children who have attempted suicide often point to failure at school as the reason for their desperate act. Yet brief review indicates that the picture is much more complex than that. Children and adolescents who attempt suicide are often found to be above average in their intelligence (Shaffer, 1974). At the very least, they are not lower in intelligence than other children of their age group. Therefore, failure must be seen as a problem of relative expectations. At times, an excellent student will tend to view a moderate and temporary drop in her achievements as a sign of total failure, especially if she has higher than average standards and her self-esteem is based primarily on her academic achievements. In such cases, the academic failure should be perceived not as a primary reason for suicide but, rather, as part of a broader problem.

First, academic failure may often be no more than a reflection of particular circumstances that have led simultaneously to reduced motivation and to suicidal wishes. Loss, separation, and divorce are all recognized causes of poor school performance; and they all can contribute directly to suicidal tendencies, irrespective of academic success or failure. In such situations, temporary setbacks at school are simply an additional source of discomfort and stress, exacerbating an already problematic condition.

Second, the compulsive striving for academic success often serves as a defense system against daily anxieties or less than rewarding relationships. The drive for success becomes a central source of gratification and self-love in the face of ongoing deprivation. For some, excellence becomes the wellspring for their personality and self-concept (Hendin, 1985). In this light, even the smallest drop in perceived performance, whatever its basis in reality, poses a threatening death blow. Without the shield of success, the child is left open and defenseless before the range of negative feelings she sought to leave behind.

A third facet of academic failure and suicide involves the parents and their pressure for excellence. Some parents view their children's lives as extensions of their own and their children's achievements as a reflection of their own self-worth. When these parents become disappointed with their own achievements, they are likely to place enormous pressures on their children. Overtly or covertly, they teach their children that they will gain love and respect only through success at school and that failure will lead to rejection. In this framework, the issue of academic success takes a back seat to a broader, more complex weave of interpersonal relationships.

Finally, academic failure or pressure for success may conceal problems of the family as a whole or those of a different member. With Tim, the child who served as a pawn in his mother's attempts to return her husband to the fold, academic problems reflected the parents' domestic problems. While his father was away, his mother felt driven to prove that she could cope with everything independently. As part of this effort, she applied tremendous pressure on Tim to excel, just as his own school progress had begun to flag. Tim was ill prepared to cope with the added stress of his mother's excessive expectations. Tim's mother applied a particularly destructive set of pressures. Whenever she went out, she would call home every twenty minutes to check up on him. If he had left his studies, she would have one of the other children bring him back from play. When she was home, she would sit for hours with Tim as he tried to do his homework. Strangely enough, she would accuse Tim of forcing her to sit with him because of his desire for undeserved attention. But no matter how hard Tim tried, he could not satisfy his mother's ever-growing demands, since they were only a disguise for other problems.

## Summary

A review of this chapter suggests that situations related to child suicide can be grouped into three basic categories. The first category subsumes conditions that lead directly to self-destruction. Striking examples include parental depression, suicidal tendencies, or actual suicide. The second category of circumstances includes those that lead to suicide through their destructive impact on intermediary factors of self-esteem, depression, and hopelessness. This category includes child abuse and neglect, divorce or separation of parents, the death of a loved one (especially a parent), and family crisis. The third category relates to situations that heighten the general atmosphere of stress but have no direct link to suicide. Here one may include family aggression, academic pressures, and excessive demands.

One overriding conclusion is that each of the life circumstances surveyed must be dealt with at more than face value. Not every instance of divorce or a parent's death will lead to self-destruction. Rather, there appear to be hidden underlying dynamics that give these events their destructive power. These conditions all share the common theme of a problem that the child must confront but is powerless to resolve. This hidden process seems to distinguish between life circumstances that are injurious and those that are lethal. Unresolvable problems are discussed at greater length in Chapter Nine.

# 6

# What Children Know
# and Feel About Death

What do children know of death? As we shall see, the answer is both "a great deal" and at times "surprisingly little." The problem is that children's views of life and death differ sharply from adult views. In order to enter the child's understanding of death, we must often lay aside our adult beliefs and emotions. Dry facts and figures on child development do not always convey the cognitive complexity and emotional weight of children's views of death. More useful are specific anecdotes. The child psychologist Brent (1977) offers an excellent example in his account of a conversation he had with his two-year-old son concerning death. The child had begun to wake up terrified in the middle of the night, crying bitterly and demanding a long-discarded bottle of sugar water. Eventually, Brent decided to try a firm approach and told the boy that he was too old for a bottle and to go back to sleep. But when he noticed the little boy's despair, the father hugged him and asked: "What will happen if you don't get your bottle?" The boy answered through tears, "I can't make contact." "What does that mean, 'you can't make contact?' " "If I run out of gas, I can't make contact—my engine won't go, you know!"

At this point, the father remembered that during the summer they had traveled widely and had once or twice run out of gas. "What are you afraid will happen if you run out of gas?"

the father probed further. "My motor won't run and I'll die," the young boy replied. The boy's words reminded the father of a recent incident when the family had sold its used car. The buyer had tried unsuccessfully to start the car and said things like: "it's probably not making contact. I guess the battery is dead." Since the boy had been witness to this transaction, the father felt that he was beginning to grasp his son's confused understanding. He asked him: "Are you afraid that your bottle is like gasoline and—just like when the car runs out of gas, the car dies—if you run out of food, you will die?" The boy nodded. The father tried to explain: "Well, that's not the same thing at all. You see, when you eat food, your body stores up energy so that you have enough to last you all night. You eat three times a day; we only fill up the car with gas once a week. When the car runs out of gas, it doesn't have any saved up for an emergency. But with people it isn't anything like that at all. You can go maybe two or three days without eating. And even if you got hungry, you wouldn't die. People aren't anything like cars."

The father's attempt to differentiate between living and nonliving things brought only a small amount of relief to his son. He tried to explain again: "You're worried that you have a motor like a car's, right?" The boy nodded his agreement. "So," continued the father, "you're worried that if you run out of gas or run out of food you'll die, just like the motor of a car. Ah, but the car has a key, right? We can turn it on and off any time we want, right? Where is your key?" The father poked around the boy's belly button: "Is this your key?" The boy reacted with a laugh of relief. "Can I turn your motor off and on? See, you're really nothing like a car at all. Nobody can turn you on and off. Once your motor is on, you don't have to worry about it dying. You can sleep through the whole night and your motor will keep running without you ever having to fill up with gas. Do you know what I mean? Okay, now you can sleep without worrying. When you wake in the morning, your motor will still be running."

Brent's report succeeds in conveying what systematic scientific studies often fail to convey. It relates the experiential essence of death for a small boy. Brent's young son is very concrete in his conceptualization. For him, words have concrete meanings, almost as an object does. Gas is always gas regardless of the context and situation. It has the same meaning whether it is the gas of the car or the gas in a bottle of sugar water. The death of the motor is the same as the death of myself. The word *death* has an existence and a being all of its own. The father's abstract explanation of animate and inanimate objects is too symbolic and too far removed from the boy. In the end, the father succeeds in unraveling the muddle only when he begins to see things from the child's concrete point of view: The car's engine is ignited with a key, whereas ours is not. To an adult, the tangible example of the key seems trivial, but for the child it is filled with a very important meaning. This key stands between the child's feeling of great despair and his eventual relief.

Although the child is an active learner, the quality of his learning is influenced both by the style and the content of his thought. The story shows that young children attribute vitality to all things, living or not. They project their own internal experiences onto the world of objects. Thus, it is no wonder that the child struggles to discover the difference between a motor's dying and the death of a human being. Time, objects, causality, change, and identity all have different meanings for the young child than they do for the adult.

It would be inappropriate, however, to hold that the child's view is simply illogical. Indeed, as Brent's anecdote reveals, a child engages in inductive and deductive thought processes just as an adult does. Brent's son had learned that a car has a motor and that the motor can die if it runs out of gas. He had also learned that all animate things have a motor and that these motors can die. He concluded that both the living and the inanimate have motors, which give them life. It is a simple step to deduce that, if he does not take care, his motor will die. He also made a logical connection between gas and life. The motor dies without gas; gas is created by fuel and also by a bottle of sugar water. On this basis, the child can easily arrive at the conclusion that he has to drink the bottle of sugar water in order to keep on living.

Brent's experience with his son takes us back to the question "What do children know about death?" How do children begin to understand the adult concept of death? How do they cope with the notion of death? Does the accuracy of a child's perception of death influence the likelihood of suicide? Do children who try to kill themselves really understand the meaning of death?

Even after one puts aside all emotional overtones, the concept of death remains extremely complex. Death is defined as the total cessation of all life functions. It is an irreversible, unavoidable, and universal process. It may be the final stage of a natural gradual deterioration or the result of a massive injury. How much of this do children understand, and at what ages? Within the literature, one can identify at least eleven separate components, which come together to form a full realization of death. First, one must understand the word *death* itself, must be aware that death occurs, must distinguish between life and death, and must recognize the finality of life. Full realization of death also involves an awareness of death's irreversibility and universal necessity as well as its dominion over all forms of living creatures. Moreover, it requires an acquaintance with the causes of death, the relationship of death to aging, and the distinctive appearance of death. At the same time, a mature perception of death involves the recognition of death as a process, not only a state, and an awareness of the relationship between death and separation.

## Developmental Acquisition of the Death Concept

Speece and Brent (1984), in their survey of literature on cognitive development and children's grasp of death, note that young children have a good grasp of death and its meaning, even though this comprehension will continue to widen and deepen with age. In an early study on this subject, Gesell and Ilg (1946) compiled a description of the growth in children's understanding of death. Although their conclusions were based on casual observations, their precision exceeds that of research done much later. They present a dynamic approach that considers both cognitive change and the parallel emotional reactions, and their description relates to continued development through adolescence. Their central conclusion was that the main bulk of development in grappling with death occurs by age seven.

Gesell and Ilg broke down the stages of development year by year in the following manner:

Ages 1–3:  The very young child has a limited or no understanding of death.

Age 4:  At this age, there is a limited or unclear usage of the word *death*. Although the child is capable of expressing the idea that death is related to sorrow and sadness, the word does not arouse an emotional reaction.

Age 5:  The concept of death is more specific, factual, and precise. The child is aware of the physical aspects of death, such as the dead person's inability to move, along with the finality of death. Attitudes toward death are matter of fact rather than emotional.

Age 6:  Major awareness of and interest in death arises, as the child begins to respond to it emotionally. There is noticeable concern for the possible death of relatives, especially the child's mother. Curiosity appears about the causes of death, such as murder, illness, old age, and accidents. There is an interest in death rituals, funerals, and burials. The child still does not believe that he will ever die.

Age 7:  The concept of death is more realistic. The child continues to be interested in the causes of death and rituals related to it.

Age 8:  A budding interest appears in what happens after death. The child accepts the inevitability of death for all living things, including himself.

Age 9:  The child shows a deeper understanding of the biological processes of death and their finality. There is less fear of death, and the reaction to it is less emotional.

Age 10:     The child adopts a realistic, matter-of-fact attitude toward death, without any special interest
in its philosophical aspects.

Age 11:     The child begins to ask theoretical and philosophical questions regarding what happens after
death and becomes involved in discussions about
those who have died.

Age 12:     The preadolescent is occupied with questions
about life after death. However, he remains skep-
tical about its actual existence.

Adolescence:  Speculative and philosophical interest is focused
on life after death. There is a dominant and
magical fear about death, accompanied by strong
emotional reaction.

Researchers following Gesell and Ilg have demonstrated
that by age seven the child begins to acquire a more or less mature understanding of death. Until age seven, the growth in the
child's understanding is quite gradual. Then, at age seven, there
is sudden insight into all facets of death. The growth of this
complexity is well illustrated in the work of Barbara Kane
(1978, 1979). Kane examined the concept of death among
children between the ages of three and twelve. She reports the
following findings: At age three, there is only a slight awareness
of the existence of death. At age five, death is perceived as a
condition of immobility and separation. At age six, the concepts of irreversibility, causality, lack of bodily functions, and
universality are acquired. By the age of eight, death is perceived
as the nonfunctioning of the senses. Finally, by age twelve,
there is a clear understanding of the distinctive appearance of
the dead compared to the living. Kane's research appears to describe three stages of development. At the first stage, the child
is aware of death and perceives it as a separation and lack of
movement. In the second stage, children appear to understand
all aspects of death, but only in concrete terms. During the
third stage, these aspects begin to be understood on a more abstract level.

Research similar to Kane's has been conducted with chil-

dren between the ages of five and twelve (Orbach, Gross, Glaubman, and Berman, 1985; Orbach, Talmom, Kedem, and Har-
Even, 1987). Five subconcepts of death—old age, universality,
finality, causality, and irreversibility—were assessed with an objective questionnaire. These concepts were examined in relation
to the death of people and the death of animals. The children involved in the research were broken into three age groups: six to
seven, eight to nine, and ten to eleven. Furthermore, IQ scores
for each child were used to assign them to low-skill and high-
skill groups. In relation to death in people, the concept that was
most difficult for the younger children to understand was causality, although the youngest children also had difficulties with finality. The four concepts of finality, irreversibility, universality,
and old age were incorporated almost simultaneously by the
seven- and eight-year-old children. However, a grasp of causality
arose only among ten- and eleven-year-olds. Furthermore, intelligence influenced the children's ability to understand all the
subconcepts except causality.

   Although these studies employed somewhat different
conceptual measures from those used by Kane, one is impressed
by the commonalities. Both works indicate quite a realistic perception of death at a young age. Even young children believe
that death is final and irreversible. Some aspects, such as causality, are much more difficult to master. They appear to require
cognitive development, as well as knowledge and experiences
that are acquired with age. Thus, the development of a full concept of death appears to require both experience and cognitive
maturation.

   The studies by Orbach and his colleagues also offer interesting findings regarding the conceptualization of death in animals. Here the basic pattern of difficulty in understanding reappeared, except for one element—old age. Although old age
was easily grasped in death among people, it was one of the last
concepts to be acquired in relation to death among animals. Indeed, it was acquired at about the same time as causality.

   These findings appear to belie the common belief (Mitchell, 1967) that our grasp of death in animals precedes our grasp
of death in people. It suggests that our understanding of death
does not necessarily involve an initial encounter with the death

of an animal, which the child then generalizes to people. Rather, our concept of death seems to be nurtured by other experiential processes, such as cycles of sleep and wakefulness, separations, or various fears. This understanding then becomes generalized to animals (Anthony, 1972).

In the case of old age, the external bodily changes in animals are much more hidden than among people; therefore, the child finds it harder to generalize. Aging among people is a process that can be both observed and experienced in continuous personal interaction and is therefore the easiest subtopic to comprehend. Universality and irreversibility are things that cannot be ignored. Although adults try to force children to believe that there is life after death, the immediate experience that children have is that the dead do not return. Whereas certain elements of finality, such as the absence of movement, are visible and easily understood, other elements, such as the cessation of thoughts or emotions, are not. Most difficult of all is understanding causality, since it is dependent on knowledge and learning of processes that cannot be readily observed. This explanation suggests that the order in which different concepts are acquired depends on one's opportunity for direct observation of the biological processes involved. The more hidden or latent a process is, the harder it is to comprehend.

Recognition of the multiple concepts prerequisite for an understanding of death (the concepts used in the preceding studies, as well as even more basic concepts—such as time and the existence of objects apart from one's perception of them) highlights the importance of general cognitive growth. Piaget's (1954) structural theory of cognitive development offers a useful springboard for linking changes in concepts of death to a wider framework. Piaget articulates four general stages in the development of thought: sensorimotor, preoperational, concrete operational, and abstract operational stages. These stages have been employed by Lonetto (1980) and others to elucidate parallel changes in the quality of children's thoughts of death as reflected in their statements and their artwork. In the following sections, each of Piaget's stages is described along with changes arising in the comprehension of death.

*Sensorimotor Period (Birth to Age Two).* The emphasis

of the sensorimotor stage is on the development of motor and perceptual capacity in encounters with the world. At this point, the child has no general concept of object permanence (that is, the notion that the existence or nonexistence of objects does not depend on one's immediate perception of them), although during these two years the child is beginning to develop an awareness of permanent figures—mainly, the parents and the immediate environment. Followers of Piaget claim that at this age there is definitely no attention to death and certainly no comprehension of it. However, this declaration is contrary to clinical evidence, such as that shown in Brent's anecdote about his son.

*Preoperational Stage (Ages Two to Seven).* The preoperational stage starts with the initial acquisition of language and symbolic thought, allowing for a broader comprehension of self and the world. In the first part of this stage (ages two to four), thoughts are characterized by egocentric animism and magic. The child sees herself as the center of the universe. Everything is centered around the child's wants and wishes. Thoughts and words are powerful agencies with magical powers. During the second part of this stage (ages four to seven), there is an accelerated acquisition of language and enhanced use of symbolism and abstract thought. However, cognitive functioning is still based on what Piaget terms prelogical thinking. The child is still bound to the concrete world, to things that can be perceived by the senses. The pattern of learning and solving problems is basically by trial and error. In this second part, there is a drop in egocentrism. The child begins to deal with problem solving in a practical manner, going beyond immediate wants and desires. Moreover, a growing interest in causality is manifested in repeated questions of "why." Nonetheless, the child's perception of time remains a matter of subjective experience; time is not yet perceived in a continuous flow toward the future. Finally, the first real signs of self-definition and the first breaking away from family toward the child's own age group are seen at this stage.

What are preoperational children's thoughts of death? Anthony (1940) concluded that, as early as two years old, children can be troubled by and preoccupied with death. She based this conclusion on parents' reports of their children's games, her observations of children's drawings, and her talks with the children. Following the psychoanalytic approach, she believes that children's emotional reactions arise either from anxieties about losing control over aggressive impulses or from a fear of abandonment. Nagy (1948), a research pioneer, came to different conclusions regarding the beginning of children's interest in the subject. He placed it somewhat later than Anthony did—between three and five years old. During this particular period, in Nagy's view, the child perceives death as a separation, a temporary disturbance of life, not as something total or final.

Koocher (1974) has addressed quite directly the tenor of preoperational thoughts on death. The following questions, among others, were posed to children assessed as preoperational:

1. What makes things die?
2. How can one come back to life?
3. When will you die?
4. What will happen when you die?

The children's answers to these somber questions were refreshing and direct. A little boy of six answered the first question this way: "If they eat something bad, if you go with a stranger and he gives you some candy with poison in it, if you swallow a bug." Another child aged six answered the question "How does one comes back to life?" this way: "If you know a lot about science, and you give them [the dead] some pill, then you can do it." These sample responses bear out the limitations in preoperational thought regarding causality and reversibility of death. The impact of an immature grasp of time on perceptions of death can be seen in answers to the question "When will you die?" Although children on the average placed their death above a comfortable eighty-five, responses ranged from "In a year" to "After three hundred years."

Research examining children's drawings reveals that preoperational children between the ages of three and five focus mainly on the physical aspects of the dead (for example, lack of movement). They also show great interest in the immediate conditions of death (such as a dead person's position) and often associate death with abandonment and neglect. At this stage, there is difficulty in differentiating between death as a state and death as a natural process (Lonetto, 1980).

As research findings demonstrate, the preoperational stage is characterized by a partial understanding of death and its causes, accompanied by distortion as well. Children at this stage relate to death in a concrete situational manner, which is overlaid with magical thinking and generalizations. Death is often seen as a temporary and reversible condition, much like other phenomena in the child's world.

*Concrete Operational Stage (Ages Seven to Twelve).* Children in the concrete operational stage begin to apply logic to problem solving. These children are capable of categorizing objects on the basis of differences and similarities and are able to make deductions or inductions. They can now think sequentially, with one logical step following another. They can go back over a problem and break it down into its different elements. There is less dependence on the senses and greater reliance on logic and imagination. For example, a child can "imagine" taking a car apart and putting it back together again, and can plan the building of an airplane even if the materials are not in front of him. Despite these impressive advances, concrete operational children still lack the ability to create abstract hypotheses. They have difficulty in grasping relations of cause and effect. Although they are capable of representing the world in symbols, they still falter in their expression of possible relations between these symbols.

This period is one of explosive growth. There are initial steps toward comprehending concepts such as time, space, conservation (that is, the realization that an object remains the same even though the container that holds it is changed), and causality. These cognitive advances are paralleled by an extended sense of self and a growing feeling of autonomy. On the social plane, there is a greater awareness of the child's social image, and greater importance is given to relations with other children. Social norms and rules gain significance as children become capable of learning from others.

Nagy (1948) asserts that children who are at concrete operational ages begin to perceive death as the final cessation of all life functions. Nonetheless, death is still understood as something that can be prevented or avoided. Death is not yet seen as universal or likely to occur to one's self. Nagy found that children at this stage tend to personalize death. They see death as a human figure with desires, wishes, and demands, who can be influenced and controlled. As a result, one can have relationships and contacts with death, and it can be avoided. The causes of death are perceived as external and not as the internal biological process of wear and tear.

Koocher (1974) found that children at this stage gave concrete reasons as causes for death: cancer, heart attack, old age, poison, guns, disease, drugs, and drowning. Although all these answers are correct, they all remain linked to the concrete world. They do not reflect an ability to abstract the underlying biological or spiritual processes. However, in Koocher's work, there was no evidence that children personify death as a human figure, despite Nagy's claims. The difference between the findings may reflect no more than sociocultural influences or developmental stages.

Lonetto (1980) divides the development of concrete thought into two substages. In the first substage (ages seven and eight), the child begins to understand the use of social sanctions for inappropriate behavior. Children at this age believe that moral codes are absolute and cannot be questioned or altered. At this age, children also display an interest in, and fear of, the supernatural: ghosts, gods, witches, monsters, and the forces of nature. They begin to show an intense interest in death, are anxious about family members' well-being, fear possible abandonment, and begin to understand the process of aging and their own place in the universal scheme. Time is experienced now for the first time as a unilinear process. These changes bring about a clearer understanding of the essence of death.

During this early part of the concrete stage, Lonetto argues, there is a significant interest in burial rituals and in games about funerals and death. Children, particularly those from religious backgrounds, begin to wonder about life after death (Anthony, 1972). Lonetto believes that most children at this age tend to personify death and to perceive the causes of death as external, with no relationship to internal processes. Children's artwork reflects, in addition, emotional difficulties in dealing with the finality of death.

In the second half of the concrete operational period (ages nine to twelve), important changes, which alter perceptions of death, take place. Children begin to develop independent moral judgments instead of automatically accepting the moral codes of others. Although parents remain the main voice of authority, their opinions are questioned. There is an increasing tendency to relate to frameworks outside the home and family. With regard to death, this second stage is characterized by a continued interest in the supernatural. Children's drawings at this stage reflect their fears of the deaths of relatives, such as parents and grandparents. They attribute death to age and disease—in other words, to internal forces. Their drawings reveal their feelings about the different appearance of animate and inanimate objects. They also reflect the children's preoccupation with their own death.

*Abstract Operational Stage (Ages Twelve and Above).* At this stage, children reach completely mature thought. Thinking is objective, abstract, logical, and hypothetical. There is a good grasp of laws of nature and physical processes, as well as a mature perception of time. The formal and logical qualities at this period shine through in answers given to questions about death (Koocher, 1974): A boy of fifteen, when asked about causes of death, replied: "In the physical sense, [death is caused by] the destruction of an important organ or an internal life force." A twelve-year-old answered: "When the heart stops beating, the blood stops flowing, you stop breathing and that's it. Yes, it can happen in different ways, but that's actually what happens." Some children reach this developmental stage at a younger age. An eight-and-a-half-year-old gave this answer: "Sometimes they die when they don't have the things they need in order to live, like food, water, or clean air."

### Emotional and Experiential Perspectives
### in Understanding Death

At an intuitive level, it is appealing to view the developmentally expanding conceptualization of death as a function of increasing cognitive ability. Implicit in this perspective is the notion that children's knowledge of death is no more than a by-product of their broader attempts to understand the natural phenomena in their lives. Yet this cognitive perspective has been seriously challenged by psychologists who argue that the understanding of death is not a by-product of development but, rather, one of the central focuses and challenges of personal and emotional growth. Death both reflects and threatens the basic issues of existence and selfhood from the beginning of life. These psychologists argue that the central task for the child is not just understanding death but coping with and defending against its awesome implications for the integrity of personal well-being.

Our everyday experiences point out that death is integrally bound up with primitive fears and anxieties. As a result, we often relate to death with defense and distortion. The issue is not how much we know but how much we are willing to admit to ourselves. These notions of emotional attitudes to death have been taken up in different fashions. Some dynamic writers have emphasized that primordial fears are goads to an ever-widening quest for knowledge. Others insist that children's tacit knowledge of death is intact at a very early age—and that they cope with the fears that accompany this knowledge by adopting defensive camouflage and distorted views of death. Common to all these approaches is the view that the developmental transitions in the grasp of death are entwined with our existential understanding of self and processes for maintaining emotional integrity.

In the following sections, various emotional perspectives on the concept of death are addressed and amplified. This focus on emotional processes surrounding death puts a different slant on the question of how children's notions of death influence suicide. The question is no longer whether children know the meaning of their lethal actions but, rather, how they cope with these fears despite their knowledge. Answers to these newly framed questions offer a key to eventual treatment and prevention of suicide.

*Fears About Death as a Basis for Understanding Death.* A number of psychologists and psychoanalysts have emphasized the primordial nature of anxieties surrounding death, independent of specific comprehension. They focus on emotional and not cognitive development. For example, Klein (1948) believes that the fear of death is a primary and instinctive emotion, a murky but all-encompassing fear of annihilation and extinction. At a later age, this fear takes the form of fear of internal deterioration following separation.

More traditional psychoanalysts, such as Anthony (1940, 1972), concentrate primarily on children's fear of separation from their parents, a main source of security, as the foundation for fears of death. This fear is intertwined with the young child's anxiety over possibly hurting the parents in an uncontrolled expression of instinctually based aggression. Children are panic stricken by the possibility that unleashed aggression may cause parents to abandon them, even if it does not cause any real damage. In either case, the fear of parental loss is at the heart of the fear of death.

Other analysts, such as McCarthy (1980), also emphasize parental loss and separation; but in this view, death fears are related to the child's fear of leaving the parents, rather than the parents leaving the child. Here recognition is given to the symbolic separation that occurs when the child begins to differentiate himself as a being independent from his parents. In early life, according to this view, the child's experience of existence is bound up with the intimate unity with the mother; consequently, the growth of feelings of independence and differentiation from the parents strikes at the experiential source of being. Separation paradoxically arouses a sense of "not being." Fear of separation is generalized to a fear of death. This approach suggests that certain periods in the child's life amplify fears of death more than others. Periods of passage toward independence—such as starting school—become particularly problematic. In later stages, such as adolescence, the crystallization of a separate identity may subtly alter the view of death.

A more experientially bound approach (Maurer, 1960) links fears of death to the cycles of life: day and night, wakefulness and sleep. This cyclical experience receives cultural expression in such early games as "peekaboo." From the infant's perspective, we disappear and reappear as we cover and uncover our faces. The world itself seems to disappear and reappear and shift from darkness to light again. Covering the face causes a feeling of suffocation and loss, which is then followed by relaxation and joy when the cover is removed. One senses a strong but distant analogy with the experience of life, death, and the return of life. At a later stage, the child will eagerly initiate the game and repeat it again and again. The game becomes a source of great pleasure and only minimal discomfort. Later, the child learns to say "all gone" and to recognize that objects can disappear and not come back again.

Kastenbaum (1967) puts great emphasis on the link between the experiences of disappearance and loss and the concept of death. Very young children feel intuitively that death is something of great importance and that it is frightening. Kastenbaum cites the case of a one-and-a-half-year-old boy who found a dead bird in his yard. Usually curious and alert, the boy was shocked at the sight of the bird and did not attempt to touch it. A few weeks later, he found another dead bird and asked his father by hand motions to put the bird back on the tree branch. His father did as requested, but the dead bird fell off again. The young child insisted that the bird be put back again and again. Later, the boy became very interested in a leaf that had fallen off a branch. He tried many times to replace the leaf on the branch, but with no success. The boy's repetitive actions indicate that his first encounters with death left a deep impression on him.

Later, Kastenbaum argues, distinctions between temporary, long-term, and final separations form the foundations for the experiential understanding of death. A four- or five-year-old learns that her father goes away in the morning but returns home at evening time. In contrast, she finds that grandfather goes to the cemetery and will never return. It is at this point that children begin to show a great interest in death, especially that of close relatives. Only during "middle childhood" (ages six to seven) do children begin to succeed in emotionally distancing themselves from the subject.

Yalom (1980) takes an existential approach that also highlights the child's "all gone" as the core in grasping death. He has given a new meaning to the anal stage in children's development. Past psychologists have emphasized the aspects of sexual pleasure surrounding excretion. However, Yalom believes that toilet training may arouse fears of nonexistence and deterioration. He notes that the disappearance of the child's secretions is actually the disappearance of part of the child's self. As such, toilet training can unleash a fear of general self-deterioration. The child's passive resistance to excreting on command is an expression of the child's need to control the feeling of self-annihilation. This need for control leads the child at the same time to use the game of peekaboo as a means of manipulating the world. For similar reasons, the child begins to enjoy blowing out the candle, throwing away the garbage, and removing the bathtub plug to let the water out. At a later time, war games become a part of the child's tools of coping with the same problems and fears. Yalom maintains that the emotional experience of death is a major force behind the cognitive grasp of it.

Another view of the role of emotional forces is offered by Rochlin (1959, 1967), an adamant believer that children know about death from a very early age. Rochlin points out that the young child has numerous sources of information about death. Visits to the market reveal dead fish; walks in the field uncover dead insects. Talking with parents, watching television, or just going out into the street provides added information on death for the child. Faced with these realities, children begin to organize and assimilate them in a meaningful attempt to understand themselves and those around them.

Rochlin (1959) unhesitatingly puts forth the view that the "childish" viewpoints and distortions children express in their early years reveal no more than defensive coping with their fear of death. Their rejection of the concepts of irreversibility and finality is partly a defense mechanism aimed at lessening the blow. Children cushion their sorrow with magical animism. Since their cognitive functions are not yet fully formed, it is easy for them to deny death in this manner. Rochlin's (1967) conclusions regarding early death concepts were based on sensitive observations of children's play, where the subject of death arose irrespective of any immediate experience of the death of someone close. Rochlin's observations can be summarized as:

1.  Children react very emotionally to death and give vent to anxiety in particular.
2.  They persistently attempt to controvert information that might "correct" their misperceptions regarding death.
3.  Children can flexibly pass from a "proper" conception of death to a distorted one in the same breath and even in the same sentence.
4.  Children try to escape or disregard the subject of death when they feel cornered or attacked but will spontaneously initiate the topic at a later time.

Some of these elements are seen in Rochlin's (1967, p. 84) discussion with a four-year-old boy, David (D):

*D:* Last night I found a dead bee.

*Dr.:* Did it look dead?

*D:* He got killed. Someone stepped on him and it got dead.

*Dr.:* Dead like people are dead?

*D:* They're dead but they're not like dead people. Nothing like dead people.

*Dr.:* Is there a difference?

*D:* People are dead and bees are dead. But they're put in the ground and they're no good. People.

*Dr.:* Are no good?

*D:* After a long time he'll get alive [the bee]. But not a person. I don't want to talk about it.

*Dr.:* Why?

*D:* Because I have two grandfathers alive.

*Dr.:* Two?

*D:* One.

*Dr.:* What happened to one?

*D:* He died a long time ago, a hundred years ago.

*Dr.:* Will you live long too?

*D:* A hundred years.

*Dr.:* Then what?

*D:* I'll die perhaps.

*Dr.:* All people die.

*D:* Yes, I will have to.

*Dr.:* That is sad.

*D:* I have to anyway.

*Dr.:* You have to?

*D:* Sure. My father is going to die. That is sad.

*Dr.:* Why is he?

*D:* Never mind.

*Dr.:* You don't want to talk about it.

*D:* I want to see my mother now.

*Dr.:* I'll take you to her.

*D:* I know where dead people are. In cemeteries. My old grandfather is dead. He can't get out.

*Dr.:* You mean where he is buried.

*D:* He can't get out. Never.

Rochlin's (1967) central claim is that children first learn what death is and only then begin to distort and deny. These distortions may take the form of viewing death as a reversible selective process. Animism and magical thinking complete this defensive system. Finally, Rochlin inserts Freudian notions by claiming that childhood narcissism and perceptions of self as the center of the universe are nothing more than a generalized defensive reaction to vague but strong feelings of impending annihilation.

Rochlin argues that the existential feeling of nothingness gives rise to a defensive feeling of human omnipotence and centrality in the universe. For Rochlin, there is little doubt that children know death as the extinction of all life and are unwilling to accept it, either pragmatically or philosophically. Children reflect the duality of knowing and denying the existence of death.

Even adults appear to display a shifting understanding of death, often in response to circumstances. One study (Leviton, 1971) contrasted the perceptions of parents caring for difficult, disturbed children with those of parents facing the care of normal children. The findings revealed that parents of problematic children tended to idealize death as a situation of peace much more than parents facing a lesser burden. Moreover, the burdened parents defined life as disappointing, tiring, and without hope, while the second group perceived life as more satisfying. At the same time, the parents of problematic children showed less fear of death than the other group.

*Coping with Feelings About Death.* The fear of death is complex. Its variations are as great as the differences between individuals. A review of the literature on adults suggests that it is best seen as a multidimensional structure. As such, it is open to multiple forms of defensive coping. Multiple facets of death fears have been identified (Kastenbaum, 1967). They include fears of the hereafter, the unknown, annihilation, and loss of identity or control. Also included are fears of ghosts, loss and separation, and deterioration of the body.

Is the range of child fears equally great? Zeligs (1974) has documented the fears of death among young children. These fears focus on the loss of their parents, on seeing a dead body, on themselves dying, and on abandonment. Anthony (1972) feels that there are three main components to children's fear of death: the fear of abandonment and loss of dependence, the fear of aggressive impulses directed toward parents, and the fear of being vulnerable. The knowledge that death is lurking out there creates a sense of constant exposure to its danger.

Yalom (1980) offers a comprehensive summary of children's knowledge of death and the fears it incurs. He, like Rochlin (1967), argues that encounters with death arouse anxiety, which, in turn, evokes defense mechanisms. He highlights a number of these defenses and distortions as they appear among children of varying ages.

1.  *Denial of Death.* Death is belittled as a temporary condition, as life under improved conditions, or as sleep.
2.  *Belief in the Uniqueness of Self.* Death is seen as a selective force, not applicable to the self. "It won't happen to me." "It doesn't happen to the good people." This is a childish, egocentric viewpoint.
3.  *Belief in a Savior.* There are beings with power over death who can intervene in times of need. The savior can be the doctor, the parent, medicine, love, or any other means. Even if the person does die, these figures can reverse its effect.
4.  *Denial of Death in Children.* Death exists, but it does not affect children. It only occurs to adults or old people. Since killing is seen as a form of death that is controllable and avoidable, children hold to the belief that they will not die unless something kills them. Part of this system is a subsequent fear of growing older.
5.  *Personification of Death.* Death is seen as a human figure, a skeleton, or a ghost that can decide who will be killed. Personification offers the child the illusion of entreating or tricking or otherwise controlling death. Simultaneous with these beliefs is the notion that death as an external force is not as inevitable as an internal process such as aging.
6.  *Provoking Death.* One means of older children and adolescents for coping with death is to provoke it. Through rhymes ("If I should die before I wake/Know it's from a tummy

ache") and games, they mock death and are unafraid to draw it close. In this way, they seem to be proving their own vitality and actually distancing themselves from death.

How do children's death anxieties and defenses change with age? One of the best-known studies of the subject (Alexander and Adlerstein, 1958) assessed the galvanic skin response (GSR) of children aged five to sixteen as they listened to words associated with death over earphones. GSR responses are known to be a good measure of the strength of emotional reactions. Findings were quite surprising: Both the youngest (five to eight) and the oldest children (thirteen to sixteen) had the most emotional responses; the middle group (nine to twelve) showed practically no anxiety at all. Interpretations of this finding vary. Some argue that it reflects the relative emotional stability of various periods in the child's life, since the fear of death is a part of the more general emotional status. Thus, the great emotionality of the youngest and oldest groups would indicate a generally low stability of both age groups. For the five- to eight-year-olds, this instability results from transitions from the sphere of home to that of peers. Adolescence is also known as a period of strong conflict and crises, accompanied by internal upheaval and confusion. In comparison, it is argued, ages nine to twelve are fairly calm, since they do not demand new readjustments.

Yalom (1980) offers a slightly different interpretation. He believes that during ages five through eight the child is dealing with the concept of death. At nine to twelve, the child has succeeded in creating defense mechanisms, which preserve an internal balance between the knowledge and the fear of death. As a result, children at these ages are relatively at peace. In adolescence, the balance is disturbed as the early defenses of denial and personification lose their efficiency. Balance will be restored only when the adolescent creates more sophisticated means of coping, such as rationalization and emotional distancing.

No matter what the interpretation is, it is clear that the greater knowledge of older children does not make them more immune to anxiety. This conclusion is borne out in another study (Melear, 1972), where the researcher evoked death anxiety by

asking children a direct question concerning death. The data indicated a direct relationship between death anxiety and the
child's understanding of the concept. Although older children
understood the concept of death better, they were also more
frightened by the idea.

The complex interplay of anxiety, age, and intelligence
was examined in more detail in a study by Orbach, Gross, Glaubman, and Berman (1985). This study, cited earlier, focused on
children's comprehension of five aspects of death in animals and
people. Those who were brighter or older had a better understanding of death, while those who were more anxious had a
poorer understanding. Moreover, anxiety interacted with intelligence and age. The impact of anxiety was greater among the
more intelligent and among the younger age groups. As a result,
the bright first graders who were not anxious displayed an
understanding of the concept of death almost on the same level
as that of the bright fifth graders.

These findings indicate that a number of variables influence the child's perception of death, both singly and in unison.
One appears to be errors in understanding, resulting from low
intelligence or lack of information. Another seems to be anxiety. It is interesting to note that the three factors of age, intelligence, and anxiety had a different impact on the five aspects of
death surveyed. Age was associated with all five concepts: finality, irreversibility, old age, universality, and causality. Intelligence was associated with all but causality. However, anxiety
influenced only the concepts of universality and old age. Here it
is reasonable to assume that anxious children would believe that
death is selective and does not affect children.

This study suggests that the understanding of death is related to coping processes. This conclusion parallels Rochlin's
claim that emotions alter children's tacit understanding of death.
Thus, even children as young as four may have a mature grasp
of death, but it is often overlaid by additional emotional defenses and distortions.

*The Impact of Encounters with Death on the Concept of
Death.* Children's approach to mortality is revealed in a dramatic
fashion in the quality of their encounters with death—for exam-

ple, the loss of a pet or, more significantly, the tragic loss of a family member. An examination of these encounters lays bare the emotional processes by which children approach death and the manner in which society may either abet or defuse defensive distortions. Although one might suppose that direct contact with the death of a loved one should broaden the knowledge of death, clinical cases and research demonstrate the complexity of this issue.

In a study of children between the ages of one and three, Speece (1982) found that half of the children had had some experience related to death, including the loss of a person close to them. The children's reactions to their experiences were clear and distinct. Some searched for the missing person or animal; others asked questions regarding a dead animal's lack of movement. A number expressed a great anger over the loss of their cherished pet. Finally, others worried about what happens after death and expressed concern about relatives.

The enhanced understanding of death through direct encounter is seen clearly in a study by Reilly, Hasazi, and Bond (1983). These investigators compared three types of children: those who had lost someone close through death, those whose parents had divorced, and those who had never suffered these forms of loss. Among the five- to ten-year-olds surveyed, an experience of personal loss through death sharply affected the understanding and acceptance of personal death. Children in this group had a deeper, more mature view of death. Moreover, the experience of separation as such did not seem to be behind the impact, since the views of children whose parents were divorced did not differ materially from those of children who had not experienced loss through death or separation through divorce.

This research extends earlier findings (Nagy, 1948), which indicated that experiencing death provides the child with a better grasp of the concept, at least up to the age of six. These younger children who had experienced death displayed an understanding beyond that which cognitive theories might have predicted (Kastenbaum, 1977).

Contrasting social influences may alter the impact of death. Some adults feel a need to soften the blow for the child.

Others attempt to help the child face the true dimensions of reality. These contrasting approaches and the conflict they incur are evident in the case of Suzy, described by Furman (1974). Suzy was less than three years old when her mother died. When told of the mother's passing, she immediately asked, "Where's Mother?" Her father first reminded her of the dead bird they had found and buried only a short time before. He then explained that her mother was also dead and buried. He promised to show Suzy where her mother was buried any time she wanted. A month later, Suzy told her father that a neighbor's boy had told her that her mother would come back soon. "That's what his own mother told him. I told him that it's not true, that my mother is dead and when you die you can never come back again. Isn't that true, Daddy?" Despite her few years, Suzy speaks of death in a mature manner. She reflects on her father's explanation, given in simple words and taken from her frame of reference. This explanation did not in any way lessen the pain or shock of loss, but it did help the child adjust. In contrast, the neighbor's comments only confused matters.

Mystical explanations are often frightening and confusing. For example, a five-year-old girl, who had a good but rather concrete understanding of death, heard from someone that to die means that "God takes away the person." She was troubled by this information and tried to reconcile it with her old perception that to be dead means not to breathe, see, hear, or move, and to be buried. Her partial explanation was that God takes the dead person by a rope and brings him up to the sky, but only if the person was bad. In this manner, she incorporated the confusing disinformation into her realistic but concrete conceptualization.

Another example (Anthony, 1972) is of a five-year-old boy who talked about death with his mother, a professor. The child asked his mother if in the end animals die. The mother answered yes, that animals also die. All things come to an end. The child replied that he didn't want to come to an end. He wanted to live longer than anything else. The mother quickly calmed him by telling him that he would never have to die but would live forever. The mother's attempts to relieve her son's fears may easily have created a false concept. Even if her words offered temporary relief, she may have contributed to long-term confusion, whereby the boy will attempt to cope with his fear of death through distortions of reality and "self."

Clearly, a number of aspects must be considered when one discusses death with children. Most of their questions have an emotional connotation. That is, in addition to seeking practical information, children are also expressing emotional distress. As such, they do not necessarily demand assuagement. Rather, the listener is asked to hear the child out and accept his embarrassment and questions. Yet, even when an air of realism is invoked, drawn-out lectures and explanations about everything concerning death are ineffective and often produce results contrary to those expected. They are likely to confuse and embarrass the child even more, especially if he is unprepared to hear everything. The child must be allowed to determine the pace. Answers must be simple, concrete, and to the point, framed at the child's cognitive level.

Encounters with death, particularly in its violent and aggressive forms, are common during wartime. In some countries, such as Israel, Northern Ireland, Lebanon, and South Vietnam, war has served as a continual backdrop for generations of growing children. Logic and psychology suggest that such a reality will drastically influence children's perception of death. However, research about the impact of war is minimal. Few if any cross-cultural comparisons have been made between groups at war and at peace.

One single field study (McWhirter, Young, and Mazury, 1983) done in Northern Ireland indicates the diffuse effects of war. Children of different ages and religions and from different geographical locations were interviewed to elicit their awareness and perception of death. War seems to have increased children's awareness of death, but it did not notably alter their views of death. That is, children did not connect death primarily to war and aggression—possibly because, the researchers suggest, they more frequently had encountered instances of death from causes other than belligerence, despite the state of war and terrorism; or they may have made a gradual adjustment to the state of war, so that its influence was limited. Of course, such adjustments also reflect cultural influences (DeVos, 1980; Florian, and Kravetz, 1985).

The Holocaust in World War II provides an overwhelming pool of recollections to and experiences of death in its most brutal form. The horror and enormity of this period make it difficult even to formulate the appropriate questions to ask. The Holocaust raises questions about generalizations regarding normal development. Yet, with all these hesitations, one wonders how children of tender years dealt with death in its most monstrous form. What was its meaning? What did they feel about the death of a parent or sibling in that inferno? What did they experience when they were more than passive witnesses to the most awful forms of death? The profound limits of human experience in the face of death are exposed by one Holocaust survivor from Czechoslovakia. The older of two daughters, this woman had celebrated her ninth birthday at the end of World War II. Her family was the only one in the village to survive the oppression. Yet they too had been separated. The father had been sent to the concentration camp at Auschwitz. The mother had held on to her two daughters through a series of camps and escapes. They too were separated and then miraculously reunited.

The woman's recollections today are colored by the many years since the war. During this time, she has made an amazing comeback to a healthy and satisfying life. It is obviously difficult to sift out the words of the little girl from those of the woman of today. These memories are by no means an exact documentation, but their strength and depth are unmistakable. In the following account, the interviewer's questions appear in parentheses.

(When do you remember encountering death for the first time?) I was six years old. We and mother escaped from Theresienstadt but were caught by the Slovak police. They interrogated mother for a long time in order to find out if we were Jewish or not. But mother denied it and told them a pack of lies. She borrowed our maid's life story. We play-acted until they almost believed us. Suddenly another police officer came in. He looked at us and asked, "What are you doing here, Mrs. Cohen?" He was one of father's friends from school. When he realized what he had done, it was too late. The officers held long discussions between them and decided to send us to another camp. This was not Theresienstadt, but it was also used by the Germans as a cover-up. It was a front they put on for the Red Cross.

We fell into a routine. On the evening of Yom Kippur, Kol Nidre, two people came in and said to everyone in the synagogue: "We killed the guards, all the gates are open, everyone run." We were 324 Jews when we all ran into the forest to the Partisans. The Partisans led us to a safe place. But we first had to cross through an area that was swarming with Germans. We had to cross over the valley and then climb a mountain. This after three days without food or water.

The Partisans instructed us to cross over on our own. People began to run in the direction of water and jump into the puddles down below, but mother held us back and told us not to run. When the people ran to the water, the Germans started firing on them. They were shot down. Later, at night, we crossed through the valley and there we met those that had remained alive. They were now only about a hundred.

I saw a man with glassy eyes holding a package in his hands, holding it close to his body. I told mother I thought he had a baby there. Mother went to the man and asked him to let her take care of the baby. The man pulled back and grasped the package close to his chest. He said: "No, no, she needs warmth so that she won't get cold." I looked closely at the package; it was a baby without a

head. (As a child of six, what did you feel?) Nothing.

Later, that man was killed. He had a black
coat that was warm, and I wanted to take it. Mother pulled me to keep going, but I insisted. I took
the coat off the body. I saw his face and his bulging
dead eyes, but I only thought of the coat and how
to get it off the body. That coat saved me. In the
end only me, my sister, and my mother were saved
from all the Jews that escaped. All the rest were
killed on the way.

(What did you think of death then?) Death
was a simple matter. It was a German soldier.
(What were you afraid of?) That a branch at night
wasn't a branch, but the hand of a German, that's
what I was afraid of.

When we reached the village, there were a lot
of Partisans and they hid Jews. All in all, there
were five Jews in that village: us, another girl, and
a boy. We lived like Christians, we went to church.
The priest knew. I remember when I would go in
for confession, the priest would say, "I know. You
don't have to say anything. Just sit here for a while
and then leave." One day, the Germans came and
ordered all the men to go to the yard of the church.
They were told to strip off their clothes. We saw
the Germans when they found the Jewish boy.
Four soldiers went to one side of him, and four
went to the other. I don't want to tell you what
they did. (What did they do?) Everyone closed
their eyes. They covered their faces with handker-
chiefs and crossed themselves. I looked straight at
them. They ripped him in two. (What did you feel?)
I thought how much it must have hurt him. I didn't
feel anything. The whole time, I spoke with God. I
was afraid of God because many times I stole food
and I thought he would punish me. But I spoke to
him, and I told him that it wasn't right. I said that

I was hungry and didn't have a choice. Nothing else frightened me, not animals, nor rats, not the dead, nothing.

(Were there times when you wanted to die?) Of course not. Not even for a moment. The whole time, I thought how to live, how to survive, how to find a comfortable tree to sleep against at night and what to eat. (When you thought that you might die, what did you think about? What frightened you about dying?) To die meant to be torn in half. The pain.

Later, when I was eight, I was alone without my sister and mother. I walked through the forest at night. When I reached a village, I approached a house and knocked at the door. A farmer opened it, and I asked for some food. He gave me a stern look, then brought me into the house. He took me to the kitchen, and the family gave me food. I kept thinking what to do if they left the kitchen. That would be a sign that they were going to inform on me. I prepared how I would escape through the window. But they were all right and never left.

The farmer asked me, "You're a Jew, right?" I didn't say anything. I wanted to leave. He said to me, "You're not going right now. We'll take care of you." They let me sleep there. Towards morning they led me to a root cellar where they kept the potatoes from freezing. I stayed there during the day, and at night they would bring me to the house to sleep with warm blankets.

That's how it was for three days. Then someone informed on me. When they didn't come to get me in the evening, I started to leave the hiding place on my own. It was no easy thing to do. You had to know how to get out. First you peeked a little, then a bit more, and afterwards you lifted up the cover. I went out to the yard, and then I saw the family. The father, mother, and all four chil-

dren had been hanged in a row. And I was so happy
that it wasn't me hanging there, that it wasn't me
they caught.

I still don't get emotional about death even
today. Only when things have happened to my
family do I suddenly feel something. Yet even
though I don't get flustered, everyone else in the
family gets in a panic when someone suddenly dis-
appears for a moment. The fear of rats and cock-
roaches has only come back to me after many
years. And that happens only when my husband is
at home. When he isn't at home, nothing scares me.

Any attempt at psychological analysis can only detract
from the sober horror of this account.

*Coping with Death in Terminal Illness.* The Holocaust
tends to diminish the brunt of most other forms of human experience. Yet its terror at the personal level may be matched by
the fright of a little child who must face death from a malignant
disease. What does illness and the knowledge of imminent de-
mise do to a child? How does such a brush with death affect
one's understanding and emotional response?

Some striking conclusions can be drawn from research
(Shneidman, 1982; Kastenbaum and Aisenberg, 1972) with
adults who know that they are about to die. Most of these individuals are not flooded by anxiety. Many give an outward impression of calm and resolve, remaining logical and planning
their last moments with dignity. For these people, death is but
one final act in the human experience.

Studies conducted with children suffering chronic and
terminal illnesses point to the subtle manner in which these children's fears and coping abilities are altered in their encounter
with death. Bluebond-Langner (1978) conducted participant
observations as she walked the wards for children with cancer. In
her voyage into waiting rooms and treatment cubicles, she was a
silent witness to these children's inner worlds and emotional up-
heavals. Most important, she was able to evaluate the treatment
process and the children's relationship with their families and

the staff doctors. Since she saw the children when they were alone and when they wore their public masks, she learned to identify the maze of false communication between the parents and the children. These falsehoods were there to protect all concerned from the depths of the child's solitude and despair. Bluebond-Langner learned what dying children know about death and how they cope with it. Her work is an instructive human document about these children and the special culture in which they live and die. She describes with tender realism the course that children undergo, starting from their first encounter with the hospital. A multistaged process evolves, in which disease, death, and the "self" become forged into a new identity.

According to Bluebond-Langner, these children create new self-images in five stages. In the first stage of diagnosis, the children recognize that they are facing a serious disease. In the second stage, they learn the name of their medications and the various side effects. During the third stage, the goal of the treatment and the different processes related to it are learned. In the fourth stage, children learn about the gravity of their illness and the hopelessness of a remedy. In the fifth stage, there is recognition of the inevitability of death. Though theirs is a disease with ups and downs, progress and intermittent regressions, death always lies waiting at the end. Each of these stages is accompanied by gradual changes in the child's self-image. First is the image "I'm very sick." In the second stage, the image is one of "I'm very sick, but I'll get well"; in the third stage, "I'm sick and I'll never get well, but there will be good periods"; in the fourth stage, "I am sick and I'll never get well"; in the final stage, "I am dying."

The transition from stage to stage involves certain prerequisite encounters. These may be a certain number of visits to the clinic or the experience of remission and relapse. The final stage is broached when the child learns of the death of another child in similar straits. Throughout the passage from one stage to another, the children acquire a storehouse of knowledge about their disease, its medications, differential diagnoses, and the goal of each treatment. Everything is impregnated with meaning. Bluebond-Langner notes that some children fear therapy not so much because it involves pain but because it means regression.

The passage from stage to stage determines children's knowledge and understanding of death more than their cognitive development of intelligence. A four-year-old boy of average intelligence may know more about death than an intelligent nine-year-old. Moreover, in their travail, the children develop different modes of communication in order to acquire or transmit their knowledge. They learn whom to speak with, whom to hide information from, whom they can trust, whom they cannot burden too much. They learn who can deal with their pain and who cannot bear to stay around.

Most information is received from other children further down the line. Some is learned through cunning and shrewd means, mostly from the staff. Tom may say to a nurse, "Jennifer died last night. I have the same thing, don't I?" The nurse: "But they're going to give you different medication." Tom: "But what happens when they run out?" The nurse: "Well, maybe they will find more before then" (Bluebond-Langner, 1978, p. 156).

By continually comparing themselves to others, the children attempt to evaluate their conditions. Benjamin: "Dr. Richard told me to ask you what happened to Maria." Mira: "What do you think happened to Maria?" Benjamin: "Well, I know that she didn't go to another clinic or home." Mira: "She was very sick, much sicker than you are, and she died." Benjamin: "She had nosebleeds. I had nosebleeds too but mine stopped" (Bluebond-Langner, 1978, p. 187).

One little girl, Mary, took a round-about route to indicate that she knew she was dying. Her mother had tried hard to protect her daughter from the knowledge of her condition and was convinced that she had succeeded. The therapist turns to Mary: "What should I do with these dolls?" Mary: "Put them in their grave, in the Kleenex box. Let me do it. Bring it over here." Mary's mother: "That's the first thing you've offered to do since the doctor said we could go home." Mary: "I'm burying them carefully, each doll between two sheets of Kleenex" (Bluebond-Langner, 1978, p. 117).

The children's emotional reactions follow the stages of their death. Reactions include sadness, anxiety, anger, and attack. One child yelled at his brother, "I won't be here for your birthday," and crawled under his sheets. Denial and assumed ignorance, aided by masks of falsehood, are later means of coping. The end is marked by a gradual distancing from the environment, a preparatory separation involving either anger or introversion. When asked why he yelled at his mother, one lad answered: "This way, she won't miss me when I'm gone." The mother pointed out that her son knew she would leave since she couldn't take his yelling. His yelling was a sign that she should leave him alone.

Mutually protective falsehood is one of the keynotes of parent-child relations throughout the illness. When the parents are around, the children act as if they are not aware of the significance of their illness. Yet as soon as the parents leave, the subject is raised with other children or other adults. This duplicity explains some of the lack of clarity concerning the bounds of children's knowledge of death. In fact, these children's grasp of death is realistic and without illusion. Their description of death ends at the grave, without mention of their life after death. Death is seen as termination, the end of games, television, school, and acquaintances. Death means separation and leave taking. Although the children relate to death in a "scientific" manner, occasional expressions of magical thinking slip in, such as a fear of mentioning the name of a child who died.

Death is also a foreshortening of the future to the immediate present. These children request that birthdays be celebrated early and that presents be given long before holidays take place. There is panic to get everything done in time. These children are not willing to wait. They know that life is short.

Bluebond-Langner argues that children facing death have at their command multiple paradigms of death, which they display as a function of their immediate circumstances. Both realistic and animistic understandings, gross personification, and ultimate abstractions lie side by side in the child's awareness. What determines their expression is the child's immediate feeling and company. Bluebond-Langner concludes, as do others, that the verbalization of death and the knowledge of the meaning of death are not identical. A child does not communicate everything she knows about death, and not everything said by a child about death is evidence of the child's complete understanding of it. Bluebond-Langer argues that these multiple perceptions are available to healthy children as well, irrespective of their age or intelligence.

*Perceptions of Death Among Suicidal Children.* Does the suicidal child really know what it means to die? That is one of the first questions asked by adults and even professionals when confronted with a child who is threatening to commit suicide. The findings presented in this chapter make amply clear that children seven years old or younger know what death is. Yet it is still not certain that children with self-destructive tendencies have an accurate perception of death. Their acts may be fueled by a perception based on imagination, misinformation, or wishful thinking. Moreover, emotional defenses and distortions may be involved in acts of self-destruction. The basic psychoanalytic approach (Van Hellmuth, 1965) formulated at the beginning of this century is that the death wish is intended to achieve no more than temporary separation. The suicidal child may perceive death as a friendly figure with no harmful intentions. This friendly image is nurtured by the child's unconscious and by culturally acquired images of death as no more than sleep.

This psychoanalytic view that those with suicidal tendencies regard death as a temporary or positive experience has gained general popularity. Kosky (1983) quotes an eight-year-old boy who wished he were dead because he already knew what it is like to be alive and he wanted "to see how it is in the sky." An eleven-year-old boy wanted to die in order to join a beloved grandmother. Another lad explained that he wished for death so that he could "have peace and sleep for a long time." Orbach (1981) reports that a six-year-old boy who tried to stab himself with a knife expected to go to heaven and be greeted by God, a good-hearted old man with a beard, candies, and toys. When they finished having fun together, God would return him to his parents on a special ray of light. These scattered anecdotes and systematic observations suggest that suicidal children see death as less final and more positive than do other children their age. Moreover, this tendency of suicidal children seems to reappear in adults. There are a number of examples (Leviton, 1971) of suicidal adults speaking about death in terms of a better life, peace, quiet, and love.

Is it possible that the perception of death as life under better conditions pushes suicidal people toward their desperate acts? Only two research studies so far have tried to answer this question directly (Orbach and Glaubman, 1978, 1979a). Both compare the death perceptions of children with self-destructive tendencies to those of aggressive children and normal ones. Questions included: How do things die? What happens when they die? Can something dead come back to life? The children's responses were then categorized and compared.

All three groups gave distinctive types of answers. However, the suicidal children's responses were particularly unique, since their portrayal of their own deaths was strikingly different from their portrayal of death in general. Neither of the other groups offered this split portrayal. Moreover, the suicidal children's descriptions of death in general were surprisingly like those of the other groups. The suicidal children portrayed their own death as the continued functioning of life. Sentences frequently started with such words as "I'll feel bad," "I'll want to . . . ," "I'll be glad to . . ."—all indicating a continued form of existence. Furthermore, the suicidal children believed in personal resurrection or life in heaven and hell more than the children in the other groups. Yet when they talked about death in general, the suicidal portrayed death as final and irreversible, with no option of an afterlife. This contradiction in perceptions of personal death and death in general did not appear in either of the other two groups.

The death perceptions of aggressive children were replete with violent phenomena. Death was seen as the result of murder or fatal accidents. No aggressive child related to the possibility of peaceful old age or disease. Descriptions were cruelly realistic. Portrayals emphasized rotting, stench, disintegration, and bare bones. For these children, death is final and irreversible.

The normal children described death mainly as the result

of disease and old age. They related to death as a total cessation of life. They were the only ones who took into consideration the reactions of the bereaved family and described sorrow and sadness as responses to death. They, too, believed death to be irreversible and did not believe in life after death.

It might be theorized that the suicidal children's concept of personal death is a defense mechanism against the terror of death. Similar defense mechanisms of distortion were pointed out by Rochlin (1967) in his work with normal children. The distortion of children with suicidal tendencies may be no more than an exaggeration of this process. Children considering suicide stand before the terror of death in all its strength. They are faced with two options: to accept death and its horrible finality or to continue living with intolerable pain and suffering. Yet these children choose a third option. They distort death in a way that makes the execution of it or the consideration of it easier. These notions were first raised by Schilder and Wechsler (1934).

Defensive distortions were examined in a second study (Orbach and Glaubman, 1979a), similar to the one just described. As before, three groups of children participated: children with suicidal tendencies, aggressive children, and normal children. The children were also given a short intelligence test, as well as a questionnaire related to their concept of life. Comparisons of intellectual capabilities revealed no gross differences among groups, indicating that the source of the suicidal children's unique beliefs was not intellectual in nature. Furthermore, no group differences appeared between the suicidal children and the other two groups in regard to their concepts of life. The only difference was in their concepts of death.

These findings are consistent with the notion that suicidal children's view of death is a defensive distortion. Clinical observations indicate that this view is far from stable; rather, it changes in accordance with changes in the child's life—as is demonstrated by the case of a ten-year-old boy initially seen for abusing another child. Almost from birth, the child had lived with his grandmother. Since two previous children in his family were stillborn, a spiritual healer had advised his parents to remove him from an "accursed" home. Yet in the child's mind, it was not the house that was cursed but he himself. He believed that he was cursed with the magical power to kill. An intimate relationship that developed with his grandmother was cut short when the grandmother became ill and was hospitalized. The young boy, sure that she would die, threatened to kill himself. He described what death meant to him: "We'll live together in the sky just like we did here. We'll continue eating together and sleeping together, either in heaven or in hell." Later, when the grandmother had recovered and returned home, the child began speaking of death in a different light: "It's frightening. I don't want to die. It's frightening to be in hell."

This young boy's words clearly illustrate how the temporary distortion of death played a crucial role for him. It helped make suicide feasible. When the idea of suicide could be abandoned, the defensive concept of death was dropped. Any attempts to upset these distorted views of death often engender fear and hostility. When pressed to detail their concepts of death in therapeutic sessions, suicidal children display a great deal of anxiety. Some ask to stop the discussion, some react with anger, and others deliberately change the topic. In many cases, the children tenaciously cling to their distorted views, as if they were about to be made to give up a cherished possession.

Signs of similar changing views of death have been found among suicidal adults. Neuringer (1970) examined the positive and negative values attributed to death by adults hospitalized for serious suicide attempts. The first evaluation was made about two days after the suicide attempt; the second was made two weeks later, following therapy. The patients attributed more positive values to death immediately after the attempt. Yet at both times, high positive values were given to life.

All in all, professionals agree that a preoccupation with death is a sign of suicidal intention. Yet this research suggests that a distorted concept of death and a split concept of personal death and death in general are added signs of high suicidal risk. A perception of personal death as life under improved conditions may be telling evidence of suicidal intent. Further research support for this idea is presented in later chapters.

Whatever its causal role, it is clear that the death concept is essential for comprehending the motives behind suicide and for evaluating the life conditions that bring one to the act. The contents of death fantasies reveal the context of pain and suffering, as well as the underlying motives involved. The fantasy of a little boy that death means sitting on the lap of a kindly old man who dispenses candies suggests a life lacking in satisfaction and love. It makes us aware of his need and expectation to receive warmth and kindness and to be treated as a little tot. These fantasies are keys to understanding the emotional complexities that bring these children to the brink.

One should not overlook the therapeutic implications of the concept of death. If distorted concepts of death offer us a mental defense for suicide, then therapeutic confrontation can raise death anxieties and defuse this defense. Death anxiety can definitely be used as a temporary blockade to delay the execution of the planned or impulsive suicide.

## Summary

Despite popular beliefs, children's suicide does not seem to be the result of misunderstanding. Both cognitively and emotinally, the suicidal appear to have ample grasp of the true meaning of their actions. The suicidal understand the finality of death, just as others do. Therefore, it would be wrong to view their acts as games with tragic consequences or accidents with no agent. If self-destructive children differ from others, it is not so much in knowing the face of death as in their judgment of its instrumental value. The suicidal appear to view death as a possible alternative to the here and now. This view is sometimes bolstered by defensive distortions, which allay anxieties over the ineffable and bolster hope for a positive hereafter. Yet most central to this view is the perception of death as a viable option to present despair.

# 7

# How Family Life
# Contributes to Child Suicide

Previous chapters have touched on specific factors in family life
—such as the death of a family member, divorce and separation,
neglect and abuse, and family aggression—that might lead to
child suicide. However, a number of more general attempts have
been made to offer integrated pictures of facets of family life
that contribute to the growth of suicidal tendencies. Three of
these general approaches are presented in this chapter.

The first approach is concerned with the "multiple-
problem family," where a series of grave problems and crises
disrupt the child's normal growth and deny the fulfillment of
even basic needs. With no ability to cope, the child becomes
weary and disillusioned and, ultimately, suicidal.

The second approach focuses on a "deadly message" that
family members broadcast to the potential victim. This message
is part of an unconscious plan to rid the family of an unwanted
or scapegoated child. The goal of this plan is to resolve internal
conflict or unbearable family conditions. The suicidal child is
seen as a partner in his or her own destruction.

The third approach, which emphasizes "destructive family processes," deals with undramatic but often devastating patterns of family interaction. One such pattern of enmeshed symbiosis is characterized by schemes to prevent family separation
at all costs, including the use of sadomasochistic coercion. This

139

pattern destroys individuality, instills fear and anxiety, and denies any possibility of independent life outside the family circle. The bind between children's desires for freedom and their inability to be separate is seen as the root of self-destructive behavior.

## The Disintegrating, Multiple-Problem Family

Reading through cases of child suicide, one is impressed by the recurrent picture of family disintegration and crisis. This picture appears, for example, in Farberow's (1981) profile of a prospective suicide. His family has programmed him to feel bad about himself and filled him with feelings of guilt, shame, and a desire for self-punishment. He has been encouraged to deny and suppress difficulties and to be inflexible in solving problems. The family has scapegoated him and deprived him of his identity. He has been blamed for recurrent family tragedy and at times abandoned. Family chaos has made him feel lost, rejected, and the source of family woes. In a foster home, he feels inferior to other members of the foster family. His chances for survival are further reduced if his father has committed suicide and his mother blames him for it.

Farberow's hypothetical portrait of the suicidal youth is similar to empirical findings with adults. Maris (1981), for example, has concluded that suicidal children and adults come from families suffering multiple problems and crises. He emphasizes that suicide is an outcome of the continual pressures engendered by a variety of longstanding difficulties covering a range of areas. These pressures, rather than any single event or factor, lead to family disintegration and the growth of destructive family patterns. It is interesting to note that suicidal individuals themselves, and not just the researchers, tend to perceive their families as beset by multiple problems in multiple areas.

This hypothesis of "multiple problems" or "family disintegration" has been invoked to explain suicide in children by a number of authors (Tishler, 1980; Shafii and others, 1984). The general picture is of an unstable family lacking any positive means to cope with the debilitating changes that beset it. Hussain and Vandiver (1984) use a variety of clinical and research evidence to demonstrate that suicidal children are more likely than other children to have experienced such events as the death of a family member, separation, divorce, or longstanding family problems. Their parents' lives are often littered with job loss and change, prior marriages and divorces, and hospitalizations for illness. Family function is often absent, as in the case of children placed in foster homes, or filled with tension and sadomasochistic tendencies. Many of the family members display health problems, alcohol abuse, depression, and anxiety; and often one family member has attempted suicide.

The pattern of crisis suggests that the parents are trapped by their own problems and have little time for nurturing their children. This neglect can take on disturbing forms, such as covert or overt rejection of children; some children have even been physically attacked and abused by their parents. These expressions are usually directed toward one child, the one who eventually turns to suicide.

The role of these family conditions in children's self-destruction is highlighted in a number of documented clinical cases. Tishler (1980) relates one such case of attempted suicide. J is a five-year-old boy who was brought to an emergency room after swallowing forty-seven aspirin pills. He wanted to die because his brothers would not play with him. He wanted to meet Jesus and his grandmother, who had died a half year before. His grandfather was about to be remarried. J had a history of problem behavior—such as lighting fires, running away from home, and abusing animals. His mother described him as "hopelessly spoiled." J's mother had been married three times. Her first spouse died of a drug overdose. Her second husband, J's biological father, was an addict. Her current husband, as well as her previous husbands, frequently beat her, and J usually witnessed the beatings. His mother had been hospitalized in mental institutions at least twice.

Similar patterns of crisis and disintegration appear in the family of Jerry, an eleven-year-old suicide described by Shafii and his colleagues (1984). Jerry was found dead in a closet, strangled by a rope connected to the clothes bar. He had five brothers and sisters, all from his mother's previous marriages.

When he was four, his mother had left his natural father, after the man had raped one of Jerry's stepsisters. Jerry's mother, when she was eleven, had seen her own mother kill her alcoholic father in self-defense. A year before Jerry's death, he had been a witness to the deaths of two friends, one by drowning and the other in crossing the street. A few months before his death, Jerry had been expelled from school because of his "disgraceful behavior." Just days before his suicide, he had been harshly punished by his mother and stepfather.

The basic premise of the "multiple-problem" hypothesis is that the ongoing family chaos continually wears down the child's ego functioning and ability to cope. It may also disrupt and hinder normal emotional development and damage self-esteem. Suicide provides an escape from painful experiences in the face of mounting problems in life.

## The Deadly Message

Clinical observers of suicidal children (Sabbath, 1969; Glaser, 1965; Gould, 1965; Toolan, 1962) report that they have frequently experienced strong parental rejection. This rejection begins early in life and can even arise before the child is born. Among parents trapped into parenthood, the tragic feeling that "maybe it would have been better if he weren't born at all" echoes for years. Of course, such feelings can surface from time to time even among the most loving parents; but here we are dealing with a strong, pervasive attitude of rejection. The accident of pregnancy is only one of a number of accidents and disasters, all of which snowball into rejection of the child. Actual flaws or birth defects only intensify the rejection by childish or egocentric parents.

Paradoxically, this parental rejection may actually increase the child's dependence on the parents (Toolan, 1962). It is sometimes painful to see how these children desperately reach out to the same parents who reject and neglect them. This behavior, of course, is driven by the overwhelming terror of abandonment that these helpless children feel. Panic stricken, they have no choice but to turn for hope and security to the parents who brought about their state of fear and panic.

Parental rejection is often hard to identify because it can take many forms. One common pattern is that of bipolarity: love/hate, closeness/distance, involvement/aloofness, concern/neglect. Parents' sudden flips from one extreme to the other leave the child bewildered, uncertain, and emotionally drawn. A second pattern of rejection is that of emotional unavailability. The harried parents, caught up in their own concerns, are unable to recognize the child's needs. They ignore the child and react angrily when the child attempts to remind them of her presence or asks them for help.

Children do not take always accept such rejection in a passive manner. They often express their rebellion through behavior problems, phobias, provocations, and school failures. These sources of parental discomfort are both a protest against and an outcome of their emotional burnout. However, they often only serve to refuel parental rejection.

With time, a pattern of mutual hostility develops. The parents' stance is one of continual violent anger directed at the child—over his behavior, his demands, his very existence. This attitude is well reflected in a remark made to me by a mother of a child who had attempted suicide soon after his father's death: "That boy gets me so angry that I would like to throw him out of the window." This mother and her child played out many of the elements of rejection. The mother had felt anger toward her son since the day he was born. She felt that he had never really been hers to begin with, and she had pushed him out of her life as if he were a stranger. Her rejection of her son was made all the more clear by the contrasting love and affection she showered on a younger daughter.

Her son struck back in his mother's weakest spots. He dirtied up the places she had recently cleaned, he ate hungrily but with disgusting manners, he forgot her requests, and he chronically disobeyed rules. Yet he never gave up on his mother's love. At times, he would fawn over her like a small child and try to win her heart. At other times, he would try to win her over with tears or the heartrending plaint "Why do you hate me so?" His attempts were to no avail: his mother never once touched him or kissed him or tried to soothe his anguish.

One final destructive element of rejection is that of isolation and scapegoating. The parents and sometimes even the other family members begin to feel that the rejected child really is not a member of the family and might somehow infect the others. For example, the parents of one suicidal child refused to bring the other children to therapy because, they insisted, they wanted to protect them from the "curse." They complained that this child was ruining the others and constantly bothering them. Although these complaints were groundless, they did have the power to protect the parents from looking closely at the roots of their own problems.

Familial rejection provides the spawning ground for a deadly message: "I don't want you, get out of here." This message may first arise in hidden thoughts and wishes but later takes on more explicit forms in word and deed. The case of two career-oriented parents with a six-year-old son makes the point. The boy's birth had been unplanned, unwanted, and untimely. For the first year, he had been given to his grandmother for care. The guilt-ridden mother continually tried to make up for this early abandonment, but her acts always seemed to lead to contrary results and made the child feel all the more isolated and unwanted. For example, when the parents would buy gifts for the children, they somehow would forget to buy something for the boy. No words were passed, but the message was clear.

Sabbath (1969) gives examples of the commonplace phrases that convey the deadly message. One mother would tell her fifteen-year-old daughter to "drop dead." A father would tell his daughter, "If you've got one rotten apple in the barrel, you have to get rid of it." More indirect is Glaser's (1965) example of the mother who told her daughter not to follow in the footsteps of a suicidal father. The message of death was clearly understood, as evidenced in the daughter's subsequent attempt to end her own life.

For one uninitiated in the ways of pathological families, the notion of a deadly message seems unbelievable. Yet newspaper clippings bear witness to the phenomenon. Stories of abuse abound, and cases where parents have actually tried to kill their children are not unknown. The deadly message is earmarked by dramatic and repugnant elements: rejection, hostility, isolation, and scapegoating. Against this background, the child gets the message that he must leave. Hints of death point him in the desired direction. In this light, the child's suicide becomes an ultimate submission to parental will.

## Destructive Processes of Symbiosis

Richman (1971, 1978, 1979a, 1979b, 1984) has written widely about the devastating effects of hidden family processes that often appear at first sight to be harmless. He highlights a number of such processes, including symbiosis without empathy, closed family systems, secret communication, denial of independence, inability to separate from family of origin, and the passing down of problems from generation to generation.

Symbiosis is a state where a strong mutual bond exists between a mother and child, so that each is abnormally dependent on the other. The distinction between the two becomes lost, and mother and child begin to regard themselves as one undivided unit. The continued dependence of the child as he grows older may result in a total lack of independence and identity throughout life.

Similarly, a symbiotic family has a massive generalized identity, with little distinction among the different members. All are seen as parts of one larger whole. Each member feels complete only through the emotional mix with the others. In this extreme drive for unity, members of symbiotic families are often left with the paradoxical feeling of isolation and loss of self. At the same time, symbiotic parents perceive their strong emotional demands as expressions of loyalty and love.

Symbiosis often continues across three family generations. It may start in one generation and then continue in the next, since the children in adulthood then seek out partners to fulfill their needs for parenting and dependency. The symbiotic bond between these parents is then extended to include their children. In this manner, a new set of dual loyalties, complications, and conflicts emerges. Examples of these conflicts can be seen in the demands expressed by one symbiotic father to his wife: "I want you to understand me like our daughter does, without words. How come my mother can understand me without words and you can't?"

In essence, symbiosis involves an effacement of the self, a destruction of all that is individual and unique. Symbiotic partners are frightened by true emotional contact and blending with others because, they believe, such contacts may do away with any remaining threads of selfhood. They cannot believe that emotional relations do not necessarily require a loss of self.

Richman's clinical experience has led him to conclude that symbiosis is a frequent element of the dynamics of suicide, especially when it is accompanied by an absence of empathy or sensitivity to the feelings of others. Symbiotic parents frequently do not even allow their children to express their feelings. Richman (1978) describes a treatment session with a suicidal girl and her mother. When the girl broke out into tears, her mother scolded her: "You don't care about me, you only think about yourself." Indeed, research has shown that mothers of adolescents attempting suicide display less empathy than mothers of those hospitalized for other reasons (Topol and Reznik, 1982).

Another aspect of empathy also appears to be absent in families of the suicidal: the ability to give warmth and sympathy. The parents often appear distant and estranged. The children of such parents therefore are placed in an unbearable position: a forced, strangling bond without any expression of love or warmth. This combination of symbiotic bonding and emotional distance creates a tendency for the trapped family members to abuse one another.

Richman (1979b) points out that suicidal families are also closed systems. Symbiotic families tend to cut off their members from the outside world by walls of suspicion and antipathy. The only permissible social contacts are shallow, controlled, and functional. The only permissible display of loyalty is inward toward the family; only there may one seek emotional fulfillment. Any overture toward the outside world is met with hostility, discouragement, and fear tactics. A symbiotic husband may, for example, attack his wife if she expresses a desire to work outside the home: "Anyway, you can't really do anything or succeed at anything. How many pennies could someone like you earn?"

One outcome of this style of life is a complete taboo on intimate relations outside the home. Richman (1979b) quotes one mother of a suicidal daughter as saying that she would hate anyone who loved her daughter or her parents. This mother was beset by fears that someone would kidnap her family and leave her alone. In similar fashion, Richman describes a father who ripped the phone from the wall because his daughter was talking with a boyfriend. These expressions of hostility and violence arise from fear rather than inherent ill will.

Among the children, intimacy with others is accompanied by feelings of shame and betrayal of trust. The youngster must choose between complete separation from the outside world or a complete break with the family. Moreover, it is inevitable that the feelings of confinement and isolation will be carried into relations within the family as well. The children begin to feel alone and estranged from their most intimate relations. Almost all the cases of attempted suicide in children that I have encountered have been marked by these feelings of isolation.

One of the most destructive results of symbiotic demands is the installment of a deep fear of separation. The children come to believe that any sign of individuation, even in the simplest words, is likely to bring about the disintegration of the family and overturn their internal world. These children feel that they have no ability to exist independently from their family.

Communication in the symbiotic family is whispered, indirect, wrapped in secrecy. One mother of a boy who attempted suicide notes: "I never get angry at him, but when he does something bad I get depressed." Her nonverbal message thus comes across as infinitely more threatening than any direct verbal one. Even the use of silence can be terrifying. I remember one boy in treatment who was driven wild by his mother's ominous silences in response to his misbehavior. The boy would beg, "Do whatever you want with me, punish me, hit me, yell at me, just say something." The mother here used her lack of words to underline her punitive rejection.

The absence of communication can erupt in violent outbursts of anger, accompanied by shouting and slamming of doors. The closed, secretive atmosphere serves to heighten feelings of anger, which is sometimes expressed in abuse of others and sometimes in abuse of self. The life pattern is, at its roots, one of slow self-destruction at a symbolic and an actual level. The symbiotic family as a whole becomes fatigued and unstable over time, and its members become weakened and vulnerable as their resources for coping are leaked away.

The members of a symbiotic family are trapped from every direction. They are cut off from the outside world, yet they lack the resources to break free. The family is demanding and stifling, but each member feels isolated and alone. Each searches for selfhood but can find it only within the all-encompassing bonds of mutual dependency. The family members seek warm emotional contact, yet they fear that it may threaten their remaining threads of identity. They invest their all in family loyalty, yet they are filled with pervasive feelings of betrayal. It is easy to see what devastating results can occur when they are finally forced or drawn to the outside world.

Richman's concepts of the closed family and of symbiosis without empathy seem to have particular relevance to understanding suicide among children. Although they are by no means the only explanatory tools available, they do point out why children may view suicide as a preferable way of dealing with their problems. In this regard, it would be useful to contrast these processes in families marked by suicidal threats as opposed to those without such tendencies. The following comparison of two families with suicidal children and one family without this background outlines factors that can make these processes lethal.

The first case of suicidal symbiosis is that of Ron, a handsome man of twenty-eight who was saved from the brink of death. One of three children, popular and a high academic achiever, he had always been the family success story. Life with his parents and siblings had always been marked by harmony. His parents had expected excellence from him, and he had conscientiously followed the trail they marked. Their plans had included army service in a select unit, a central command post for a few years, and then a position in the family firm. As Ron faithfully plodded his course outside the family, he maintained close relationships with his parents. He made them full partners in his plans and took their counsel. The family was a sacred value to him and to the other family members.

Ron's father was an assertive, authoritarian man who ran his business and family affairs with a firm hand. Unable to delegate authority to others, he involved himself in even the smallest details of his business. At work and at home, he constantly interjected himself, even to the point of instructing others in table etiquette during meals. Ron's mother was also a dominating person who constantly involved herself in her husband's and children's lives. A stormy woman, she was nevertheless emotionally cold. Empathy or sympathy seemed to her to reflect childlike needs for mollycoddling. As long as family members toed the line, she swelled with pride, but the slightest deviation was met with stifled anger and rejection: "How can you be so weak, that's just not manly." It was surprising how effective her cutting remarks could be.

Family harmony was broken when Ron married at age twenty-six. His parents objected that he was too young, that she was not the right choice, that the in-laws were less than distinguished, and that the timing would upset his military career. Yet Ron held firm until they succumbed. With the marriage, Ron's mother decided to take his wife under her wing by dictating everything in her life, from the style of her clothes to the timing of childbirth. A hidden struggle developed between the two women over Ron himself.

In this struggle, Ron took a place on the sidelines. He did not want to stand against parents or spouse. After initial attempts to mediate failed, Ron found himself slowly surrendering his independence and resolve. He felt fatigued and worn. For the first time in his life, he felt that he was not effective at his job and therefore concluded that he should resign from the army. His resignation brought on a massive depressive reaction that lasted for months. He lay curled up in his bed until finally he required drug therapy to get hold of himself. He then broke up with his wife and returned to his parents' home and his mother's watchful supervision. Yet once home, he suddenly fell silent within himself, as if by refusing to talk he could broadcast his anger more safely. During these trials and tribulations, he tried to kill himself.

From the moment that Ron's parents called about treatment for him, they attempted to dictate to me the nature of his problems and the way they should be handled. After he entered treatment, they constantly were calling to check up and get reports. My initial attempts to exclude them in order to develop a working relationship with Ron were met with anger and shock. Ron himself seemed completely indifferent about their all-enveloping presence. Even so, I invited them in only months later, after Ron had had a chance to get over his crippling depression.

The joint sessions with the parents revealed a family portrait of fury. First, the mother abused Ron's wife, blaming her for all his woes. Then she blamed Ron for dividing his loyalties. Finally, she castigated him for what he had become: "You're not the one you used to be, you're not my child, you're not my man anymore." The father also berated Ron for the error of his ways: "You really need a hearing aid. If you would just listen to us, everything would work out."

Ron's statements of selfhood were met with anger. His expressions of independence were castigated as hopeless, foolish, fatal errors. His mention of feelings only incited his mother. Even therapeutic overtures were met with total rejection. These stormy family sessions would end with the parents showering abuse on me and with Ron closing up in a shell of silence for self-protection. Ron remained dependent on his parents and was a recluse in their home, refusing to work, meet friends, or even talk. Our meetings were his only social contact.

Ron's therapy involved a series of delicate maneuvers. On the one hand, I encouraged his expressions of selfhood, his speaking out freely, his individuality. On the other hand, I had to help release the smothering grasp of the demanding parents. The parents had to learn to accept Ron's self-expression, even if it seemed to them capricious; Ron had to learn to attain selfhood by establishing boundaries without cutting lines of communication.

The roots of suicide in Ron's family can be seen in their

symbiotic rule, their nudges to toe the line, their demands for family loyalty, and their anger at any signs of individuality. In spite of the genuine concern for Ron, there was a complete lack of warmth, closeness, understanding, or acceptance. Ron's suicidal behavior is an example of symbiosis without empathy, where suicide becomes an option in times of crisis.

The deadly consequences of symbiosis without empathy reappear in the case of Jimmy, an eight-year-old who tried to end his life by jumping out of a window. The immediate details of his attempted suicide are somewhat banal. During a class break, one of his classmates pulled Jimmy's pants down to his ankles, to the amusement of the others. Humiliated and shocked, Jimmy ran to the second-floor classroom window and yelled, "I'm going to jump." The speedy efforts of two classmates prevented him from carrying out his threat. Only later did Jimmy tell his teacher that he had decided to kill himself long before the incident.

Jimmy's family life illustrates Richman's description of the symbiotic family. His father appeared soft and gentle mannered, a man who was tirelessly dedicated to his family. In fact, he had often changed jobs and turned down advances in order to maintain a constant, close family presence. Jimmy's mother seemed worn and tired, beset by an outside job that she did not want but family economics required. Both parents felt that their strong commitment to their children was an outcome of their own less successful upbringing as latchkey children. Their own parents had had to leave them for long hours of the day under others' care while they worked. Both of Jimmy's parents had felt the lack of a loving touch and tried to ensure that their own children would never suffer this want. To compensate, they would spend all their spare time with Jimmy and his younger sister and call frequently throughout the day to oversee their activities.

Yet behind this idyllic state of affairs lurked a darker presence. The mother's actions clearly manifested overprotectiveness, rather than mere concern. She demanded that the children get home as soon as school ended, and even the slightest tardiness would throw her into a panic. Once, she abruptly left work and ran home to make sure that all was well with the children. Her calls home were filled with orders and threats of punishment. She would give Jimmy long lists of tasks and threatened him with punishment if he should fail to carry them out. If he was doing his homework, she would ring up frequently to check his progress. And when she got home, the threats of punishment were carried out.

Outside social contacts were strongly discouraged. If Jimmy asked to go out and play with friends, his father would accuse him of lacking filial affection in preferring his friends to his parents. He would be directed to find alternate activities at home. Social occasions for the family meant going to visit the grandparents. Infrequent outings with other families generally ended in Jimmy's getting punished for one thing or another.

Warmth and affection were absent. Once, when Jimmy rested his head on his mother's shoulder during therapy, she brusquely pushed him off: "Move away, you're already past the age when you need to be spoiled like your sister." Jimmy's responded by silently, restlessly tapping his foot in the air.

Jimmy's parents frequently expressed their dismay over his lack of gratitude: Jimmy just didn't know how to appreciate their dedication and sacrifice. If it weren't for him, they knew that their life would be much more enjoyable, just like other parents. Their own relationship was posed as one of ideal harmony, lacking any tension or conflict.

A small role-playing task during therapy dramatically pointed up some of the deadly processes that had led to Jimmy's suicide attempt and the violence behind the family ideal. By accident, Jimmy let slip that his father had broken a table with a single blow. The father explained apologetically that Jimmy had angered him so much that he had vented his feelings on the table rather than his son. "I explained to him," the father related, "that I had done to the table what I wanted to do to him." When asked why he was so angry, the father recollected that they had once gone to see a movie with a group of other children. After the show, Jimmy had asked for ice cream in spite of the fact that he had gotten candy earlier. This type of request drove him mad.

Jimmy responded enthusiastically to the suggestion that father and son change roles and play out what had occurred. The father hunched over and whined, "Dad, I want ice cream." Jimmy replied gruffly, "Not now." "But I want ice cream." "Shut up you idiot, you fool. Aren't you ashamed, you spoiled brat, all you do is want and want." With that, Jimmy leaned over and slapped his father. The father's grudging affirmation of this reconstruction put an end to the myth of the ideal, protected family.

Jimmy's family shares certain characteristic qualities with other symbiotic families: the stifling repression, the overwhelming hold on the children, the reclusiveness, the distancing of the outside world, and the lack of warm emotional bonds. At the same time, one senses certain unique qualities, such as the extreme violence, the punitive humiliation of the children, and the placement of private woes on the children's shoulders as scapegoats. It is no wonder that Jimmy turned to suicide when beset by humiliation within the classroom as well.

Yet symbiosis can arise without such deadly qualities, as can be seen in the case of fourteen-year-old Dina. The second of four children, Dina had suffered from chronic bedwetting since early childhood. Clinically speaking, Dina's role in life was to maintain the close bond between her family members, a task she accomplished by keeping everyone's attention riveted on her problems. This unconscious tactic had twin goals: it prevented conflict between her parents, and it gave her a special role in the family.

Discussion with the family returned over and over to themes common in symbiosis: loyalty, trust, separation, boundaries, relations with others. Dina was constantly worried over such questions as what she could keep to herself, what she should tell her family, and how much time she should spend with friends. Dina, her mother, and—to a lesser degree—the other family members professed beliefs in complete loyalty and absolute sharing among those who loved each other. Any separation among family members was a cause for crisis, and many a trip was cut short for this reason.

Yet this symbiosis in Dina's family was qualified by a

large measure of empathy and love. In spite of the hidden conflicts, there were frequent attempts to communicate. One often
saw expressions of intimacy, participation, and sharing of
thoughts and feelings. Moreover, Dina's family displayed none
of the hidden hostility and sadomasochistic tendencies common
to other symbiotic families.

In comparing Dina's family with those of Ron and Jimmy,
one is struck by the differences in family closure and the open
expression of affection. These differences gave a completely different meaning to the symbiotic features they held in common.
They seem to confirm Richman's conclusion that self-destructiveness arises primarily when symbiosis appears without the
cushion of empathy and affection.

## Summary

This chapter has presented three approaches to familial
processes in children's self-destruction: the multiple-problem
family, the deadly message, and the problem of symbiosis without empathy. A common theme in these approaches is the deadly damage wreaked by families that deny love, joy, fulfillment,
and selfhood. One sees a portrait marred by internal animosity
and the sadomasochism of hatred, rejection, and overwhelming
demands. Yet clinical experience suggests that this air of animosity is not always a necessary feature of suicidal families.
The following chapter demonstrates that self-destruction can
grow even in an atmosphere of loving concern.

# 8

# An Adolescent's Suicide: Family Dynamics and Childhood Origins

The case of Sonia, a seventeen-year-old suicide, illustrates many of the family processes discussed in Chapter Seven. Yet, as we shall see, it shows that suicide can occur even in the context of a family filled with mutual love and concern. This family seems to match Richman's description of symbiosis, yet it lacks the bluntness or hostility that he describes. Rather, Sonia's family was caught in a complex web of unique codes and idealistic values that placed its members at odds with outside reality. Because of these rules and expectations, family members found it difficult to get along in the outside world and were vulnerable to failure, even when they succeeded.

Sonia's family offers a penetrating view of processes common to many suicidal children of younger years. Although Sonia's death occurred when she was seventeen, the seeds of suicide were sown and nurtured long before her life was cut short. The roots of self-destruction can be seen in unique patterns of family communication, in limitations placed on expression of emotion, in the creation of self-entrapments, and in the continual references to death.

## The Bereaved Family

It was night when Sonia rose and took the gun that her father had recently taught her to use. Wrapped in a warm coat, she left the house quietly without waking her family. She walked through the cold night, making her way to an orchard a quarter mile away. She entered along a well-worn path between the trees; walked for a while; and then sat down, her back against a tree. Placing the gun barrel against her forehead, she put an end to her life. Her body was found a few days later, still resting on the tree trunk. The note in her pocket was laconic: "Mother, Father, Mike, John. I have come to a point of no return. I am worse than nothing. All that remains for me is my dependence on you till the end of my life. I am sorry for your pain, but this is the best way for me. Sonia."

She had been a brilliant student. By skipping a grade, she had finished high school early and had received high marks and honors. Friends found her agile, sharp, direct, and firm in her convictions. She was quick to express appreciation to those she felt deserving, and she was piercing in her criticism of those who fell below her high standards of fairness or performance. Moreover, she had a tendency to rebel against the arbitrary or patronizing use of authority and position. With no little daring, she would demand explanations for instructions or requests that she considered unreasonable. Yet she demanded as much from herself as she required from others.

In spite of an active social life, Sonia was often distant, and her acquaintances had learned to approach her with caution. Although she was held in high esteem by teachers and peers, they were also frightened by her criticisms and rejection. It was as if Sonia lived on a lofty peak of excellence and morality, which left her remote from those around her.

About two months before her death, a quick succession of blows had driven her to the edge. In characteristic fashion, Sonia had decided to dedicate the "vacation" year before her army induction to volunteer work in a poor neighborhood far from home. Yet there she began to feel—perhaps for the first time in her life—the bitter sting of failure. She had started out bursting with energy and full of dreams, glad for the opportunity to turn her values into realities. Yet translating hopes into action and motivating her new group to follow her in the effort proved too much for her.

She had been so sure of her ability, so firm in her course, so certain that she was right. Yet, suddenly and without warning, reality refused to acquiesce to her will. Nothing fell in place. All at once, Sonia found herself face to face with the failure and mediocrity she had despised in others.

Sonia had volunteered for community work with a group of peers who were also waiting to be drafted. Since none of them had known her before, she had no history of past glory to bank on. In trying to surge ahead, she only fell behind. Her duties, she felt, were inconsequential and far below her aspirations or capacity. Yet, even so, she was stunned to find that she was simply not succeeding.

Sonia did not give in easily. She tried with all her resources to break through the barriers, to convince, explain, and push forward—but to no avail. One can only wonder at her astonishment at failure, at the depths that suddenly opened before her, at the fear that awoke within her. A girl who had tasted only the sweet fruits of success was suddenly brought to write in her death note, "I am worse than nothing." As Sonia now confronted what she regarded as abject failure, her joy in life disappeared. She lost her appetite, could not sleep at night, and even ceased to have her menstrual periods. She withdrew into herself; when others spoke, she answered as if from a deep sleep. Often, her answers made it appear that she was simply responding to voices within.

At home, the first danger signs came in the form of frequent telephone calls, expressing a homesickness and longing she had previously disdained. She suddenly began to "pop" home for short visits, even though her home was many miles away and the trip took several hours. Such visits gave her renewed vitality, but she never stayed long. Her mother recalled:

> Once she called ahead to say she was on her way and I could sense the urgency in her voice. She had a pressing need to talk, yet when she got home she barely said hi. Just put down her pack, hit the phone, and started to talk to a friend. Talked and talked and talked, with no logic to her words. It

seemed like she held on to her friend as if gripped by a sudden fright. I waited and waited but it just went on and on. I got so tired that in the end I left her a note that I was going to sleep and she should wake me when she was done. When I woke early in the morning, she wasn't in bed and there was no message. She was just gone.

[At another meeting during the winter holidays:] We spent long hours talking into the night. She talked about her disappointment, her difficulties, her depression. I tried to calm and ease her, but it didn't help very much. Sometimes she held her ears as if to close them. My words didn't seem to get to her, and she answered as if from a distance. I couldn't make contact. She answered me as if from her own world.

She was completely confused. She asked for advice and instructions. She couldn't do even the smallest thing for herself, as if she had lost her internal sense of direction. Even so, from time to time she could pull herself together and calm down, but then she just went through it all again.

In one of her brief periods of clarity, she began making holiday gifts for all of us. She seemed driven by a fury. Yet by the time the holiday rolled around, she hadn't gotten one yet for her youngest brother, John. It put her into a panic. . . . She had to get it done. Now I know that this was the first time she was disclosing her secret plan for suicide.

Later, three weeks before the suicide, there was a sudden calm. Sonia seemed to return to herself. The signs of confusion disappeared. She decided to go back to her new group of friends. The whole family was relieved, and her parents decided to go ahead with the vacation trip they had planned, in spite of their initial doubts. But ten days into their vacation trip, a sudden call from the oldest son, Mike, cut everything short.

Mike had gone to visit his sister and found her in a terrible state. He had forced her to return home, almost dragging her. Her confusion and depression had returned with all their fury. Mike's call brought the parents home immediately. Sonia fell on them, begging them to beat her and punish her for not being good. She exclaimed that she had disappointed everyone and fallen below their expectations. With equal fervor, she begged them to take her back to her friends and her volunteer duties. Her parents tried to dissuade her, but in terms that denied her basic strengths: "Not now, rest up a little. You're not on your feet. Now you're the weak link in the family, and it's up to us to help you get back together. Don't think about us. You cannot cope, you aren't functioning right now."

Sonia agreed and went one step further: she asked to be hospitalized in a mental institution. Her parents countered with the suggestion that she see the family doctor. Although Sonia refused at first, she finally made one appointment but refused to go back again because, she said, she did not believe in drugs. The topic of mental treatment was not brought up again.

The endless talks through the night returned. It seemed that what particularly troubled Sonia was the thought that she was now a burden, that she was not giving enough, that she was a disappointment. Comforting protestations that everything was all right, that she was the one who needed help right now, were of little use. Sonia stuck to her self-flagellation.

She now brought up the topic of suicide in a direct but offhand fashion: "Maybe I should be done with myself and not make it hard on everyone." Her mother, feeling trapped, tried to fashion her response with care: "Sonia, you have to think about yourself now, not about others. Don't think about us, think about what's best for you."

The mother's intent was that Sonia should stop considering herself a burden, since her parents and brothers were only giving back to her what she had given them in the past. Yet the message was complicated, and Sonia interpreted it differently. In the end, she would do what she felt best without concern for others. Later, aggrieved and guilt ridden, her mother felt that everything would have come out differently if only she had made herself clearer to Sonia. If only she had said, "No, not suicide; it would drive me mad with sadness," maybe then she could have saved her daughter.

The mother's words were echoed by the father in one therapy session: "I'm sure if she had known what sorrow it would cause, she would never have done it. We just gave her too wide a margin of freedom. We shouldn't have let her be so independent. What a terrible feeling to be so close to a loved one but unable to help her from drowning before you."

Indeed, the whole family was trapped. The father, watching with fear and distress, tried to divert Sonia from her pain by taking her out to dinner and to shows. Her parents spent hours with her so that she would not feel alone, and her father often called from work to check on her. In a similar fashion, her elder brother tried everything, dragging her to movies or on trips. He lectured her to snap out of it. He humored her without realizing that he was pressing her all the more. The younger brother watched it all at a troubled distance, uncertain, a silent participant.

And the emotional roller coaster continued. One day, it seemed as if Sonia had come to her senses; but the next day, she would drop back into depression and confusion. Three days before her suicide, Sonia blurted out to her mother, "What will be left behind me? You have to take good care of John." Yet even this blunt message was not really understood. It seems that a mother must have a deep well of internal strength to accept the fact that her child is talking about imminent death. All the same, worry crept into the mother's heart. She asked where the gun was kept. She wanted to be rid of it.

And then one day, Sonia arose quiet and refreshed. She had come to the surprising decision to finish painting her room, a long-delayed piece of unfinished business. She painted until early afternoon and then went out for the evening with her older brother. When she returned, she calmly went off to bed. Everyone breathed a sigh of relief: the storm had ended. That night, Sonia shot herself.

Two months after the tragic event, the family came for therapy, seeking a return to normal functioning. "Return to functioning" was the key phrase throughout the therapy. The family members believed that they knew what had led Sonia to her end, and they were not looking for any explanations or guilty partners. Rather, they sought advice for a range of problems: Should John go to boarding school now? Should Mike return home? Should the mother go back to work? How do you go back to living? Each was in a world of his own, carrying his own hurt in his own way. Yet beyond this uniqueness were characteristics so alike that they united the family into a whole—a pattern of relationships that had probably surrounded and molded Sonia as well.

*Sonia's Father.* The father was a heavy-bodied, thick-featured man of fifty-five. A figure of power, he protected his loved ones with unquestioned resolve. His forcefulness was threatening, carrying an air of sudden explosiveness. It was expressed in his tense, high-pitched voice and in the aggressive lean of his body while he was talking. Yet he could also be vulnerable. His face could suddenly flush with pain, his eyes tear at Sonia's name. A tremble would shudder his body as he quieted the pain.

He was the central figure of authority, always guarding the family in its contact with the outside world. He was the gatekeeper, ever watchful of those coming and going, planning discourse with the wider world. The keys to permission, denial, judgment were kept in his hands. To me, he often seemed like a fierce lion guarding his cubs, wary and willing to attack any threat.

Areas of trespass were many: talk of anger, love, emotion, communication. In treatment, he would often push me away in brusque fashion if I ventured on intimate grounds: "I'm warning you, that's not your business, you're making a big mistake you'll regret." Even in the confines of therapy, he was still threatened by implied criticism of the family.

Sonia's father always emphasized an intellectual approach. He would discourse on philosophy, offer historical references, make literary allusions, even delve into physics to prove a point. At times, he would carry on at such length that the others would fidget in their chairs, helpless to cut off the flow. But, although they found his soliloquies a bother, they would be horrified at any interruption on my part.

The father could not bear to deal with his spouse or children on an emotional level. If strong feelings arose, he would deny them, overlook them, or change the topic. At best, he would sit on the sidelines while his wife dealt with their children's expressions of emotion. It was as if he feared that opening even the smallest crack to feelings would leave him hopelessly overwhelmed.

He held firmly to the view that the family should do everything together. Trips, decisions, even pain and suffering were joint endeavors. Long family sessions preceded any group decision, and if something could not be done together, it would not be done. As a result individual needs often had to be forgone. The slightest deviation from the family was regarded as betrayal. During therapy, if anyone expressed a wish for greater freedom, he was hurt and angry.

Family roles were equally clear-cut. Emotional and educational concerns were secondary and within his wife's purview. "In that sort of thing, I depend on my wife." She arranged all the outings, food, education, and heart-to-heart talks. Only when he sensed that she was faltering would he cut in to provide needed resolve and direction.

His relations with his wife involved a heady mix of adoration and dependency, ranging from protective concern to childish, overbearing demands. He regarded his wife as fragile and delicate but felt helpless without her. He was fiercely protective of her time and activities. His expectations of his sons were precise. They were to be movers and shakers, decisive, innovative, and—above all—coolheaded. Any emotional waver constituted weakness.

His relations with Sonia were not completely clear to me. He loved her deeply but preferred never to draw close to her. He was unable to talk with her and felt at odds when he tried. As in most areas of intimacy, he kept his feelings walled within and held her at a wary arm's distance. He had viewed Sonia as the family's intellectual, who would achieve great things because of her brilliance. In the weeks prior to her suicide, he had taken little part in the emotional maelstrom. Not knowing what else to do, he had passed the initiative to his wife. Yet he was willing to do anything that was required, including pushing Sonia to accept needed remedies when she was reluctant. His wife revealed that he had been left a single child when his older brother had died in early childhood. He had been a dedicated and loyal son, taking care of his parents faithfully. Yet ever since she had known him, he had suffered from periodic highs and lows resembling a manic-depressive disorder. In manic periods, he would become elated and talk endlessly, dragging the family into all sorts of strange projects. He would slowly become unbearable, passing from argumentative and overbearing stages to ones of threat, aggression, and abuse.

Although these attacks never passed the border of sanity, they created a family atmosphere of escapism. Everyone hid in a corner and avoided crossing his path. The mother became the father's interlocutor with the family and the outside world. She absorbed the abuse and straightened out the rough edges, accepting any demand if only to keep the peace. As his attacks would stretch into weeks, she would become drained.

Relief would arrive only with the father's passage into a depressed state. These were periods of quiet, reclusiveness, melancholy. Then he would slowly return to himself. He had suffered these bouts of highs and lows numerous times, yet there had never been any serious attempt at treatment.

*Sonia's Mother.* The mother was thin and attractive and radiated a quiet internal force that belied her fragile, sensitive features. At close to fifty, she still had some of the striking features of a young girl. During the first meeting, she wore clothes that had once fit Sonia.

The mother was the emotional spokesman for the family. The spiritual burden that this role placed on her cried for release. Yet, from the very start, she would always forgo her own needs to permit another family member to discuss his problems or distress. When that person faltered, she would aid, encourage, and help break through the difficulties. In the end, she would retreat and silently withdraw.

She had invested endless hours in care for her children and husband. Every act was carefully worked out; every step was part of a wider educational plan with long-range goals. She left no room for randomness or uncertainty in regard to her family; everything had a purpose. She spent much thought on what books to bring home, which types of diversion had educational value, what food was healthiest. Her days were carefully orchestrated to leave room for her job, the home, cooking, attention to her husband, and play with her children.

Even the relationships in the family were not left to chance or spontaneity. She planned out who would meet whom, who would be best for whom, and when the chosen individuals should meet. She tried to figure out how to ensure that her children would learn the consequences of their acts. She even tried to plan how to help her children search for independence and how to give them just the right challenges to reinforce their ability to cope. She could see nothing paradoxical in her attempts to instill independence through rigid controls.

All these numerous responsibilities fit under the simple term *functioning*. One of her greatest worries was that she might be unable to continue functioning; she could think of no greater misfortune. She was equally concerned about her children's ability to function and kept close watch over their weaknesses while encouraging their strengths. The weaknesses she attempted to soften by "instilling means of coping," a common term that often recurred in this family. All this she did in complete selflessness, dedication, and the certainty of attaining her goal.

It was clear that she had little knowledge of the possible damage that might arise from her continuous probing under the surface. It was also clear that her efforts were motivated by deep concern and respect for the other family members. Yet often, in spite of her strong belief in honesty, she was far from open. The hidden corners of her heart held more secrets than she revealed, and she always "knew" more than she spoke. These hidden truths guided her in her endeavor to help, but left a certain wariness.

Not only her husband and children but also her parents, her in-laws, and every other intimate figure were the recipients of her loving care. She kept equally close relations with her husband's extended family as with her own. And on them, as on her own family, she lavished careful attention and planning.

Most striking is the fact that, with all her giving, she still found time for herself, her career, and her personal growth. Yet her multiple concerns demanded constant activity and caused pervasive fatigue. "I'm always running to keep up with myself," she remarked. But then, during her most difficult periods, she seemed to reach her highest levels of efficiency. She would take charge and run things until the crisis had passed. Her fears would often arise days after danger had waned, at which time she would give way to her anxiety.

In therapy, she could cry endless tears, yet she more typically made no emotional display. Her expressions of feelings almost always missed their mark. Statements of anger, love, or intimacy were set in such precise language and complex allusions that they became stiff, intellectual exercises. Even when she made caustic or ironic remarks in a humorous way, to blunt their edge, they still left a bitter aftertaste. (This Machiavellian humor appeared to form part of the private language used by the family as a whole.) I never saw her offer physical closeness, and only rarely did she display maternal softness. She would express support and understanding, but always at a distance.

The mother was one of two children; her parents were idealistic intellectuals who were public figures. The death of her younger brother in a horrible accident had dropped a cloak of depression over the entire family. Her father had never truly recovered. Throughout the therapy with me, she found it difficult to relate to her bereavement over Sonia without allusion to her brother's death.

The death of her brother had marked the beginning of her own burdens of responsibility. At that time, it translated into concern for her parents and effacing her own needs to ease their burden. She had to compensate for her lost brother. The air of melancholy within her parents' home thickened with time. The mood was so unbearable that during her adolescence she had to leave home for a period in boarding school. Yet the mother's bonds to her family did not weaken.

Sonia's mother was clinically depressed when I saw her. She felt that depression had always been close beside her. "A spinning whirlwind dragging you down into a pit with smooth walls, all alone. Trying to get out, you only slide back in." She always started her descriptions of her depressed feelings with the word "you" rather than "I," as if trying to remove herself and return to functioning.

She used all her energies to ward off depression until her husband would come out of one of his "attacks." She would gather all her forces to escape her dark mood long enough to aid, calm, reassure, or bolster. When she was alone, she would return to her depression. Perhaps that is why she kept herself busy with others' needs. I often feared for her, especially at one point when she and her family had begun to recover from the trauma. She was stunned by the fact that one can get over even the most terrible events, a realization that flooded her with anxiety.

She had thought of suicide herself a number of times, long before Sonia's death. Many times, she had caught herself at the last moment and made a desperate attempt to fight for her life. She saw death as a deep restfulness, a solution that reflected personal bravery, and the only permissible form of selfishness. Late in therapy, she admitted that she was jealous of her daughter's courage. Fighting back guilt and shame, she related that at one time after Sonia's death she had felt relieved: Sonia had chosen the best path in her condition.

The mother's revelations made more clear to me what the family had said, at the outset of therapy, about understanding Sonia's motives. It also explained in part why they were not angry. The mother at least believed in full conscience that Sonia had had no choice and that death was better than the life of pain she had known. One can only wonder whether this belief had limited the mother's ability to help Sonia and to respond to her death cries.

*The Brothers.* The elder brother, Mike (aged twenty-four), was at first glance the most emotionally open of the family members. In the initial meetings, he was the first to speak of the family's anguish. He was filled with anger, pain, and puzzlement and did not hesitate to share these feelings with others. Mike clearly was coping best with the tragedy, yet his emotional openness was only a temporary measure.

Mike believed that one could get over things quickly, and in one step, by explosively ventilating one's feelings. One should give in to pain, talk about it until one was rid of it, and then hermetically close the cauterized wound. He pushed all the other family members to embrace his approach: Talk! Speak out! Feel the pain! Get it out! He was driven by a desire to "get back to how life had been, all of us together" as quickly as possible. Impatient, he was unable to deal with the others' slower pace.

He demonstrated much the same resistance as his father when the therapy turned beyond the immediate distress to touch on longstanding problems of parental relations, habits, and communication patterns. He did not feel that the family had to change at all, and he wanted to chart out a therapeutic plan within certain boundaries of time and focus. His approach to Sonia's distress had taken much the same form. He had completely dropped his regular affairs and dedicated whole days to being with her. He had spent all their time together trying to convince her to give up her pain. He urged her to go out, forget about things, take action, and start functioning—anything to rid herself of her depression. He felt personally responsible for his failure to help her, as did all of the other family members at some level or another, but he could not think of any other course than the one he had taken.

Mike felt that it was now his duty to get the family going again. Throughout therapy, he demanded that the others return to "normal function" and was frustrated by their lack of response. He wanted the whole family to recover at the same time. He once asked to meet separately with me in order to receive legitimization for feeling different from the others. He needed permission to return to his life and separate from his family; he was afraid of the betrayal.

Although Mike eventually went on with his own life, he continued to be involved and followed his parents' renewed crisis with rising anxiety. He expressed his fears and love in the honored family tradition. He called on his mother with the words: "Mom, you aren't functioning like a mother. You have to get back on your own two feet. You can't give in. Your not functioning isn't good for the family." In point of fact, he had really only wanted to say that he loved her and was worried about her.

Mike's response to crisis displayed another family characteristic: he began to organize everyone's lives. He pushed John to look out for Dad, Dad to look out for Mom, and Mom to look out for John. He planned out what everybody had to do for everybody else. The only difference between Mike's planning others' lives and his mother's was that his was done openly rather than covertly. This pattern of control, of course, often caused conflict, since it clashed with the father's own efforts in this regard. For Mike, confronting life and problems and trapping them in plans of action were ways of coping with issues similar to those that Sonia had faced.

Mike's brother, John, was the youngest at fourteen. He was caught up within himself, struggling hard and unsuccessfully to cry over the family tragedy. When he first entered therapy, he was filled with distortions. Every emotion was twisted, and whenever he tried to express himself, he found himself blocked. In the end, he would come up with some sterile, intellectualized comment: "Certainly it doesn't make me happy" or "Let's say that it's not the best thing that could happen."

John was so shocked by Sonia's emotional disintegration that he was afraid to deal with any of his own feelings. He feared for his own sanity. As a result, he tended to overwork his normal tendency to frame emotion in intellectual terms. In this, John displayed in exaggerated form some of the most characteristic family speech patterns. One was to use formalistic sentences containing interchangeable words whose meanings were indeterminate: "In this condition, you do not know whether it's one or it's two." "Here it's important to determine who, when, and where." "Then you're not certain if it's up or it's down." Another pattern was a type of equation linking factors and an outcome: "If A does this to B, then he'll get C or D" or "If one doesn't take care of himself, then the outcome will certainly not be good." As a whole, the style was quite functional in rejecting emotional contents, giving a generalized intellectual veneer, and being so vague as to avoid any possibility of conflict or disagreement.

John came across as a mixture of child and adult. One frequently had to remind oneself either that he was already fourteen or only fourteen. He was highly intelligent, capable, and filled with sadness. As the youngest, he was the object of all maternal instincts in the family. He filled a large portion of his mother's thoughts, his father was endlessly concerned with easing his way and removing all dangers, Mike directed and guided him, and Sonia had cared for him with faithful responsibility.

His bond with his mother was strongest. His mother, he felt, was the only one he could talk to heart to heart, and they filled the night with their conversations. His father was more distant and wary and as uncomfortable with him as with the others. John's father could not bring himself to hold his son's hand, stroke him, soothe him, or even look him in the eye. Yet they could spend long hours talking about everything under the sun except themselves.

John, too, had had thoughts of suicide. A few years before, he had suffered from migraine headaches. The pain was incapacitating and depressing. Although he had never made specific plans, he thought about suicide frequently. A homeopathic cure in the end did away with the headaches and, with them, his thoughts of suicide.

John, like Sonia, was also held in high esteem by his friends and also felt to be distant. He did not find a common language with them and was unable to meet them at their level. "Running wild" with the gang had never attracted him; it seemed too childish. In fact, he was embarrassed by expressions of friendship and felt comfortable only in arguments about events and values. Only after the suicide did he conclude that he had to become friendlier and not retreat from expressions of love in others. Happily, his efforts were successful.

## Sonia: Vignettes from Childhood

From the descriptions of family members, Sonia appears as an intelligent, idealistic, energetic, uncompromising young person. She was committed to the welfare of society but had social difficulties because she was very demanding and full of contempt for those whom she did not respect. She was respected by many but was liked or loved by very few. She did not have a boyfriend or a close girlfriend. Her parents related that "she always preferred books to friends and games." Her apparent aloofness may have served the defensive function of self-protection against fears, the exact nature of which is not clear.

Sonia's father refused to talk about any problematic characteristics of Sonia, insisting that she was a healthy and well-adjusted child. The suicide, he believed, could only be attributed to the events in the last few months of her life. Sonia's mother was less defensive. At some of her individual sessions, she disclosed that, as a little girl, Sonia displayed many extreme and contradictory behaviors. She was very adventurous in her games and was not frightened by any danger. "I always worried about this. Once she flew out of the window as if she was jumping into a swimming pool. She made me worry about such things many times." Outside the home, Sonia was far less flamboyant. At the age of six, she actually suffered from a school phobia. During the first few weeks of the first grade, her fears seemed to grow from day to day until she was sent to see a therapist. After four months in therapy, the fears disappeared completely. At that period, Sonia also suffered from sleep disturbances and was excessively attached to her mother. She rejected all of her father's attempts to reach out to her in times of crisis. At a later age, there were a few periods of extreme fears of death. Sonia was preoccupied with death and was especially concerned about her mother's death. She would be terrified by the sight of a dead insect. One can only speculate that Sonia's difficulties in those days were related to her parents' difficulties—the mother's depressions and the father's outbursts—and the special familial processes that dominated their lives at that time. One wonders whether Sonia's phobias represented an attempt to protect her mother from her father's stormy outbursts and from the mother's own depression. The few details we have about Sonia do not allow us to give affirmative answers.

In one of her individual sessions, the mother brought in a file with Sonia's drawings from kindergarten through the third grade. Some of the drawings reflected sadness and depressive qualities: dark colors, black skies and earth, black flowers and trees. Most of the drawings, however, were rather colorful and cheerful. Nevertheless, there was a conspicuous absence of figure drawings, self-portraits, or portraits of the family.

Sonia's suicide note is most revealing in what it does *not* contain. In the entire letter, there is no single word of love for her parents or brothers—no comforting words, no real concern for their welfare or pain, no attempt to alleviate their guilt feelings. Rather, there is a flavor of accusation and anger. Indirectly, Sonia clearly indicates that she blames her parents for making her so needy of them and so insecure: "All that remains for me is my dependence on you till the end of my life."

It is very difficult to trace Sonia's suicidal tendencies in an exact way to these early life vignettes, but there is enough to make us speculate that, along with the real love the family had for Sonia, there were undoubtedly some harmful processes very early in Sonia's life that led her to her angry suicide. Some of the impressions related by the mother hint that Sonia had to carry out a role of protecting her mother from her own depressions, fears of abandonment, and suicidal wishes, and probably from the father's emotional instability.

### A Family Analysis

Sonia's family members demonstrate many of the characteristics common to symbiotic families with undifferentiated identities. These are families that value togetherness and shared activities more than anything else. Each member of Sonia's family tried to think, feel, and act for the others. In the end, they required no communication, since each believed that he or she knew what was best for the others, as if some symbolic mental link bound them together. Part of the pattern was the belief that each had to fall in line with the others. Deviation from the family front was regarded as almost criminal. Because of this heady mixture of togetherness, they did not realize that they were losing their lines of communication or shedding their individuality. It was shocking for the family members to realize that their beliefs about the others might be wrong. Therefore, they either denied the possibility of error or tried to force the others to act in accordance with these beliefs.

The family members were in a state of symbiosis, but they lacked empathy. As one body, they felt complete responsibility for what the others did or felt. This mutual responsibility allowed one member to push a second to act on behalf of a third, as if they were simple extensions of one another. Without knowing it, they had reached a point where one family member was no longer permitted to cope alone.

Signal within this wider enmeshment was the interdependency of mother and father. The father's dependency on the mother often took the form of childish jealousy as he demanded that they spend every spare moment together. The mother, in turn, was dependent on the father's instrumental ability to bring about change and discourse with the outside world. Whenever problems loomed in her work or with the authorities, she turned to him to solve them. This interdependence had within it the seeds of their children's overdependence on the family circle. Side by side with the enmeshment was a clear differentiation of family roles. The mother dealt with emotions and interpersonal growth. The father took care of providing and protecting. Sonia was to care for John and to achieve academic success. Mike was to mediate the parents' relationship. John was to be the baby. And, above all, each had to *function* to fill his task.

These processes created deep conflicts within each member—conflicts between individuality and familial responsibility. For an extended period, individual expression was pushed aside. Even recognition that individual needs existed was considered a betrayal of the common cause. Moreover, each family member was afraid to let the others down by failing to live up to the group's expectations. Although these expectations were never expressed openly or directly, everyone recognized their powerful presence. To fail in the family plan invoked overwhelming internal anxiety and external disapproval.

The normal angers and conflicts in all families were not allowed to surface in this enmeshed group. They simply could not be discussed, ventilated, or released. Differences over artificial, inconsequential matters were tolerated, but discord or negative feelings regarding family life were taboo and caused shock tremors. The family lacked any tools for dealing with such cracks in family accord.

In general, the family lacked the ability to tolerate emotion of any magnitude, even if it was positive. When I tempted family members to express such feelings, they were almost incapable of doing so fully. They could never reach a point of full emotional release. As soon as they started, internal emotional pressures would rise to such a state that they would balk and retreat behind a dense thicket of words, definitions, or learned pronouncements. Escape from full emotional expression could also take more concrete forms, ranging from a quick walk for a breath of air to an extended vacation. More simple still was to suddenly get involved in other pressing affairs until the storm had passed.

Intellectual problem solving was their central tool for day-to-day coping and adjustment. All problems were phrased in concrete, practical terms. At that point, everyone could then join in finding a practical solution. Even emotional problems that required simple ventilation received this practically oriented treatment. If someone would bring up emotional distress, the immediate response would be: "What would make you feel better? Shall we go to a restaurant?"

Their defensive reliance on intellectualization was so massive that any slip in cognitive skills was felt to be a major threat. Simply forgetting a fact or misplacing an object became a cause for panic. Moreover, there was no place for relativity, contradictions, or lack of clarity. Everything had to be precise.

Another form of defense was to blame the outside world, which was held at a convenient arm's length. I myself was the target of this longstanding family tactic, in which anger was directed in vehement disproportion at those outside the inner circle. Those within the family were not scapegoated in this fashion. Excluding and blaming outsiders served as complementary processes in idealizing intrafamily relations. Their effect was heightened by the complete taboo on sharing family information with others.

Paradoxically, although the family held itself separate from the world, it was by no means apart. All the members were involved in a variety of social groups and social causes. They played host to a series of social and cultural gatherings, many focused on social reforms. Yet this social investment was often flawed by a patronizing attitude, as if the family members had the patent on how things should be done.

All in all, Sonia's family had created unique rules and codes that led them to be estranged from the outside world and vulnerable to its ways. For example, each family member was expected to give to family and friends but never to accept aid from others; receiving was considered a sign of weakness. Another code related to the place of outside authority. The children were not expected to obey school figures or their regulations, even in such matters as homework. If requests did not seem reasonable, they did not have to be obeyed.

Another rule that set Sonia and her brothers apart concerned enjoyable activities. No fun was acceptable to the family unless it had some ulterior educational or social motive. In a similar fashion, Sonia's family believed that material things, such as money and possessions, were actually to be despised. Sonia's family also insisted that one should always have complete control over events; anything less was simply a sign of poor planning. Spontaneity could only lead to tears and disappointment.

In retrospect, these family rules created a basic mismatch between Sonia and the outside world. They led to a general misunderstanding of life and the means for coping with it. Sonia had learned about life within the singular close-knit family circle. Yet the rules there did not necessarily work on the outside and required massive adaptation.

Sonia was also hampered by the pattern of family com-

munication. Although clear and precise, it was void of direct
emotional expression. Indirect, formal, full of allusions, it permitted little intimacy and served only to isolate. Families that
speak in the second person ("you") leave little room for the
first person ("I"). The family speech was cluttered with special
codes and catch phrases, which often short-circuited the free
expression of views. For example, a phrase like "It's time for
Sue's special soup" implied that someone in the family needed a
special treat in order to get over a period of family stress. All
the listeners understood the implied message that the recipient
was having problems, an implicit understanding that was often
inaccurate and generally left untested.

In family conversations, pessimistic utterances popped up
with alarming frequency: "You're finished." "You're wiped
out." "You're through, a real goner." Allusions to death and
suicide were common: "If you did that, you'd be better off
jumping from the roof." "It would be better to plummet into a
pit." Even if one takes into account their recent brush with
death, it still seems that their use of such metaphors was part of
a more longstanding style.

Suicide and death appeared to be seen as realistic options.
The family history was replete with more than its share of tragedy and suffering, and each of the parents carried private burdens. Suffering loomed strongest in the mother's life story but
was also a central feature for both the father and John. Sonia
herself—who displayed normal behavior for most of her short
life, was full of ambition, and had had many successes—suffered
from severe anxiety whenever she had to meet reality on her
own. She needed treatment to overcome her school phobia, was
apparently very attached to her depressed mother, had a complicated relationship with her father, and exhibited some depressive features early in life. Having felt anguish often, the family members were prepared for incipient tragedy as well. And it
seemed to me that they all carried within them the idea that
death was a possible solution to the trials of life.

Yet it would be unfair to conclude that Sonia had in any
sense been the focus of these thoughts of death or had been

chosen to carry them out. It is certain that numerous misunderstandings may have plagued the other family members' discussions with Sonia following her suicidal talk. Yet these fell far short of any attempt at scapegoating her or ejecting her from the family as a solution to their woes. Quite the opposite seems likely, for there is no doubt of the deep love that bound them all, in spite of the cloud of anger in her suicide letter. Unfortunately, the shared suffering and pessimism had contributed to a silent understanding that suicide was a possible and preferable alternative to the exigencies of life.

One can see within Sonia's family life an endless supply of paradoxical action and self-ensnarement. The strong feelings of love and affection were defused by faulty communication. The desire for mutual support ended in mutual injury. The attempt to reach utmost clarity ended in clouded misinterpretation. The parents' excessive structuring of their children's independent existence led to feelings of total dependency.

The description of Sonia's family life can be reduced to a schematic of the reasons behind her suicide. As a whole, the family had a history of pain and suffering, in which suicide was a potential option. The mother was chronically depressed, and the father suffered from periodic emotional disturbances. Sonia herself was an anxious child with depressive features and difficulties in adjusting to new surroundings. The family dynamics sowed a dense minefield of emotional traps and double binds: high demands for success, complemented by a view of failure as betrayal; expectations for social involvement in which one could give but not receive; and a complex weave of dependence and independence, involving total group loyalty and responsibility side by side with completely independent action.

The thicket of rules governing Sonia's family left her ill prepared for coping with life outside. Moreover, when emotional storms raged fiercest within her, family tradition made it inconceivable that she should express her feelings or seek relief from them in the outside world. But to turn to the family to accept aid in the face of defeat was a cause for feeling even greater failure. Their demands that she return to immediate functioning only increased the pace of disintegration and despair and accentuated guilt and self-disappointment. As she began to feel a total failure, her most cherished hopes fled, her self-esteem plummeted, and the ever present option of death beckoned. In Sonia's terse final words, she was "at the point of no return," "worse than nothing," looking at the despairing failure bound up in "dependence on you till the end of my life."

# 9

# Explaining Child Suicide: Several Theoretical Perspectives

The previous chapters have reviewed a broad array of theoretical and empirical works on the psychological and social processes involved in suicide. The present chapter focuses on a number of models that attempt to explain the essence of suicide in childhood. One of the most basic models, the psychoanalytic one, employs much the same principles to describe child suicide as adult suicide. A second type of model mixes family processes and personality characteristics fostering suicidal tendencies. A third type emphasizes the step-by-step development of self-destruction. A more eclectic view is seen in the multidimensional approach, which tries to categorize the complex overlapping dynamics involved in suicide. A fifth approach spotlights biochemical concerns.

   Each of these theoretical models can be placed in a separate category, depending on its emphasis on the specific conditions that bring about child suicide. Yet none of these models allows us to determine when suicide is likely to arise or why it, rather than other types of pathology, is likely to occur. As a result, I conclude this chapter with a theoetical perspective that emphasizes the uniqueness of the self-destructive behavior of children and its distinction from other pathologies. A central element in this approach I call the dynamics of confrontation with an unresolvable problem.

## The Psychoanalytic Model

*Internalization of Aggression—Schechter.* Schechter (1957) attempts to apply classic psychoanalytic explanations of adult suicide to suicide among children. In his view, suicide among children represents an introjection of aggression originally directed toward a loved one. In this view, a child who tries to hurt herself is actually expressing murderous aggression toward those she loves and depends on. This tremendous unbounded anger is a reaction to frustrations, unfulfilled desires, punishment, or even the pain of separation. The loving yet frustrating parent becomes an internalized figure. Anger is directed at this internalized representation rather than at the actual person. This process occurs at an unconscious level, since the child would feel great anxiety and guilt if she knew that she nurtured such feelings toward a loved one.

The child is likely to commit suicide when her anger mounts to uncontrollable levels and she becomes aware of her unbounded animosity toward her parents. There are twin motives in this type of suicide. One is to vent angry feelings that can no longer be contained; the other is to avoid any recognition of such anger against the parents.

It is Schechter's thesis that, because the child lacks the ability to execute a complex plan of suicide, most self-destructive drives are given indirect and unconscious expression in the form of accidents, frequent injuries, or aggressive antisocial behavior. The child may perform these clumsy acts in order to get attention or, in more psychoanalytic language, to restore the bond with the attachment figure.

Psychoanalysts link subtle changes in the nature of attempted suicide to the evolving stages of psychosexual development and the particular traumatic events they invoke. For example, separation from a parent can engender the same sort of depressive process found among adults. In such instances, a child's suicide may reflect an attempt to renew bonds with the lost object through a confrontation with death. This type of suicide attempt often is accompanied by hysterical responses similar to those in psychosomatic illnesses that have no physical basis.

When the child is older, suicidal responses occur as a self-punishment for hidden sexual impulses toward the parents. Both hysterical responses and suicidal thoughts manifest an escape from these incestuous impulses. With the onset of adolescence, the suicidal impulse is motivated by a need to suppress forbidden thoughts and drives surrounding the renewed arousal of the Oedipus conflict. Obsessive behavior allows the adolescent to be so preoccupied that he no longer has to confront frightening drives and impulses. When obsession loses its efficacy as a defense, suicidal thoughts and actions may begin to appear.

Psychoanalysts have also pointed to the role of character disturbances in some suicides. These disturbances are usually reflected in stealing, aggression, running away, or disciplinary problems of similar ilk. At the root of these behaviors, one usually finds a mixture of latent depression, low self-esteem, and anger toward the self and others. The child gets into trouble as a defensive measure to alleviate the pain brought about by these disturbances. However, these dangerous tactics can easily lead the child to the brink of death.

In spite of its appeal and simplicity, this theory basically disregards the fact that we are dealing with children rather than miniature adults. Since its formulation in 1957, subsequent research data and experience have suggested that introjection of aggression is not really a central factor in suicide even among adults. Thus, the notion of internalized aggression seems relevant only to a small number of suicide incidents among children.

*Fear of Losing Control over Instincts—Ackerly.* The clinical researcher Ackerly (1967) has modified Schechter's psychoanalytic thesis of suicide as an introjection of aggression. In Ackerly's view, children's suicide is fueled by anxiety over losing control of aggressive sexual impulses toward the parents and not merely by a reversal of aggression. Losing control over anger or sexual desires toward one's parents reflects regression to a primary infantile stage. It demonstrates a psychopathological weakness in the ego structure's ability to repress drives and desires. The child fears that he will be unable to restrain himself and that he will kill or sexually attack his parents, particularly his mother. Certain situations, such as sadistic parenting or loss of a father, may heighten the danger of losing control. Suicide may offer a release from the tyranny of the child's internal drives.

Ackerly points out other potential factors in child suicide, such as identification with a parent's depression or internalization of a parent's anger toward the child. Identification, in and of itself, is an essential part of the growth process; the child has no choice but to identify with parental figures. Yet if the parents are depressed, or display anger or rejection, the child will internalize these feelings and.display them toward himself. Such feelings of worthlessness and self-hate help pave the way to suicide.

Ackerly believes that suicide is an end result of severe pathology. One sign of its severity can be seen in suicidal children's gross distortions of death. He notes that some see death as a continuation of life, while others see it as a means to rejoin the mother through rebirth. Such conceptions of death, in Ackerly's view, indicate an underlying psychopathology.

Ackerly mixes a rich weave of additional theoretical threads in the pattern of suicide: aggression, egoistic-narcissistic aspirations involved in primitive sexuality, a punitive superego, and retreat from emotional or libidinal involvement with the world. These theories overlay the more basic ones of identification with parental depression, loss of self-esteem through introjection, a distorted view of death, and rebellion against the tyrannical rule of one's own drives. All in all, these far-ranging dynamics can be grouped into the three categories that Menninger (1938) highlights in adult suicide: the wish to kill, the wish to be killed, and the wish to die.

In spite of its richness, Ackerly's work suffers from certain basic flaws, not the least of which is that it is laden with superfluous explanations. In emphasizing the intrapsychic processes, he has downplayed the role of children's environment. Thus, it is difficult to predict which situations will be likely to lead to suicide. Furthermore, he glosses over the destructive potential in certain types of interpersonal relations. Finally, current research suggests that Ackerly's view of how children see death gives them less credit than they deserve.

*The Sadistic-Masochistic Nucleus—Furman.* Furman (1984)

has attempted to amend the classic psychoanalytic explanation of child suicide as a response to guilt over forbidden impulses or fears of losing control. This search for alternate explanations has been rooted in the belief that children under twelve have not yet developed the mental structures responsible for guilt as seen in adults. Furman offers a fascinating thesis—namely, that suicide results from the early formation of sadomasochistic tendencies. In this view, the nucleus for self-destruction arises from otherwise normal developments in the instinctual sexual drive and its expression in physical self-love. Sadomasochism refers to an unusual fusion of sex and aggression in such a way that the aggression toward self or others arouses sexual feelings and results in sexual satisfaction. In other words, the act of physical injury creates ecstasy and pleasure.

The sadomasochistic mix exists in children of all ages, especially in the earliest developmental stages. Certain conditions can crystallize this fusion of pleasure and pain. For example, parents with highly ambivalent feelings toward the child may combine rejection with love toward the child. For the child, displays of love may be accompanied by humiliation or even physical pain. Another condition leading to the crystallization of the sadomasochistic tendency is the exposure to frequent love-hate relations between the parents. In other words, suicidal children face not only the ambivalence of love-hate toward themselves but also a melding of pain and pleasure. When confronted by similar patterns in later life, they are likely to burst out with self-aggressive responses that are accompanied by sexual excitement.

A second character trait that Furman highlights is a lack of love for one's physical self. Primitive physical love is seen as the basis for later emotional or mental love of self, and it is this love that protects us from causing ourselves bodily injury. In most cases, relations to self are modeled on a motherly love that is gentle and protective. Absence of this maternal love not only exposes the child to immediate physical danger of neglect but also encourages a later indifference toward one's body.

Identification with parental apathy may take the passive form of inadequate self-protection in the face of danger; a more

active expression may appear in attempts at self-inflicted injury. For example, some infants bang their heads against their
cribs, as if the painful rhythm has a calming effect. Needless to
say, this nucleus of bodily indifference eventually has emotional sequelae in a lack of self-esteem, general apathy, active
self-abasement, or failure to avoid emotionally dangerous situations such as humiliation.

In Furman's view, developmental distortions—in the form
of sadomasochism and lack of bodily love of self—become
nuclei of an infantile personality with suicidal tendencies. Thus,
Furman's theory is one of the first theories to posit that suicidal
tendencies arise at a very young age. Furman defines in clear
and simple terms the relations that are likely to foster deviant
developmental tendencies.

Unfortunately, Furman's explanations seem far removed
from the subjective feelings expressed by children with suicidal
inclinations. Only in a few cases can one find signs of sexual excitement or even pleasure arising in children as a result of their
suicidal acts. Thus, while Furman's model has undoubtedly revealed an important mechanism in child suicide, it is likely to
be pertinent only in a minority of instances.

## Models of Family Processes

*The Expendable Child—Sabbath.* Sabbath's (1969) theory
regarding the rejecting family atmosphere and the destructive
messages passed on to the children was discussed in Chapter
Seven. His basic premise is that suicide arises when the child
feels that he or she is an expendable part of the family. This
feeling of superfluity, Sabbath believes, appears in families
where relations between parents are unstable and filled with extreme conflicts. Frequently, the relation toward the child is
ambivalent from birth, especially if the child was unwanted to
begin with. The child rebels against this status by displaying
various behavioral disturbances or disorders. The parents, because of their own conflictual relationship, are unable to handle
this threat to familial harmony and therefore may view the
child as an even greater burden. Their reactions to the child

then may become even more negative, with even greater ensuing deterioration in the child's behavior.

Even when the parents try to deny their rejection, it often bursts out in their words. For example, a mother yells at an unruly nine-year-old son, "Go break your head in two." When the child bangs his head against the wall in a subsequent therapy session, he explains that that is what his mother wants him to do. Such messages sink into the boy's consciousness: he is unwanted, abandoned. Sabbath argues that these destructive dynamics threaten the family's existence. At this stage, a suicide attempt can save the family by drawing the parents together and by enabling the child to avoid coping with the painful thought that he is superfluous.

Sabbath (1969) has formulated a second version of the dynamics of the superfluous child. In this version, the child acts as a scapegoat for the parents' anger at their own weaknesses and conflicts. By blaming the child for the faults they find in themselves, parents rid themselves of tension brewing between them. Although scapegoating holds the family structure together, it means that the child is valuable only as long as a scapegoat is needed. When problems between the parents subside, the child, since he is no longer necessary, begins to get the message that he is expendable.

All in all, Sabbath's approach links child suicide exclusively to life and family situations rather than personality dimensions. He portrays the suicidal child as someone who is completely dependent on his parents and feels the heavy weight of rejection, abandonment, and worthlessness. The suicidal child takes his drastic action in order to fulfill his parents' expectations. His subconscious hope is that in his death he will finally win the affections denied him in life.

*Object Relations and Negative Self-Image—Pfeffer.* Pfeffer (1981a) has borrowed concepts from the developmental theory of object relations in order to explain child suicide. Her model falls within the broader psychoanalytic approach, yet she emphasizes the parent-child relationship over general issues of psychosexual development.

Pfeffer interprets child suicide as a product of a complex

family system in which both parents are still dependent on their own parents. Because of these earlier dependencies, family boundaries are broken, and conflicts from the original family are interjected into the daily life of the new one. Serious conflicts between the couple ensue. Pfeffer, like Sabbath (1969), argues that the child becomes the bearer of negative feelings in order to prevent family deterioration.

The child becomes trapped between her dependence on and love for her parents and the angry hate that she feels toward them. One result is that the child begins to view the world in dichotomous terms as good or bad and is unable to forge these concepts into a whole. The child also comes to view her own good and bad features separately. In the words of object relations theory, an internal split arises that cannot be bridged. Since the relational system with the parents is mostly negative, the child's negative self-concept becomes dominant.

Pfeffer, following Richman (1971, 1979a), believes that strong symbiotic bonds between mother and child heighten the child's dependence and ensure exposure to continuous negation and punishment. As in all symbiotic relations, the child tries to internalize and deny the anger that inevitably accumulates. In trying to idealize her parents, she turns her anger toward herself and thereby strengthens the negative self-image and feelings of self-hate. When anger mounts beyond control, the child turns with full vengeance on herself and commits suicide. At the price of her death, the suicidal child preserves a positive image of her parents and their love for her.

Criticism of Pfeffer's approach reflects a more general criticism of object relations theory. In spite of the theory's explanatory strength, it describes processes whose existence is not easily amenable to assessment. In adapting the theory to suicide, Pfeffer does not explain why a given family situation or circumstance evokes suicide rather than a different reaction. This criticism is particularly telling since the developmental conditions associated with suicide are often limited by object relations theorists to a variety of developmental disturbances, including the borderline personality. From a developmental standpoint, the concept of object relations seems more appropriate to the interpretation of adolescent suicide. At younger ages, personality probably has not sufficiently matured. Nevertheless, Pfeffer has definitely advanced the understanding of childhood suicide by her attempt to provide a comprehensive theoretical approach to the field.

*Running Away from and Running Toward Symbiosis— Richman.* Richman's (1979a) explanation of child suicide focuses on symbiotic relations between parents and children. Even though Richman emphasizes issues relevant to adults and adolescents, his work seems well suited also to suicide at earlier ages. Because he attributes suicide to family processes rather than intrapersonal-structural processes, developmental levels of the children are less central. In Chapter Seven, we reviewed Richman's notion of nonempathetic symbiotic relations with all their negative ramifications. Essential features of this pattern include the clannishness and extreme interdependence of family members, the taboos, the restrictions on expressions of individuality, the arousal of anger, and the persistent feeling of confinement. One destructive result is a continuous conflict between the desire for total dependence and that for total independence.

Although many processes can take place in a symbiotic family, the connection between suicide and symbiotic relations rests on the simultaneous fears of either total fusion or total abandonment. Symbiotic families demand that the child give up any hope of independence. Any sign of a natural desire to express one's individuality is met with punishment and the threat of total abandonment. Since no other avenues for individuality are left open, the only remaining expression of individuality available is suicide.

A second dynamic in this context is the inability to cope with independence and repeated failures in one's endeavors. Symbiosis offers little preparation for the demands of outside realities. Therefore, when a child experiences failure in the outside world, suicide becomes a symbolic route for reunification and total fusion with the family.

When concepts of symbiosis and suicide are applied to children, a question arises. How can one say that young children, who are deeply dependent on their parents, seek individuality and independence to such an extent that they may, if thwarted, become suicidal? In order to answer this question, we have to distinguish between symbiosis and dependency. Indeed, the small child is dependent on his parents. However, symbiosis is not a nourishing relationship but an irrational denial of the child's individuality. Even small children seek to express their individuality by determining which game to play, which friends to choose, or when to do homework. Thus, part of healthy development is being able to say "no" to parents. Not every "no" indicates resistance. Some simply signify the need to be special or different. Yet symbiotic parents experience a child's "no" as a threat, since they cannot accept any form of self-expression. Their response is to threaten, "If you do such and such, then you're no longer my child." The child can sense the stranglehold on him despite his own dependency needs. In this light, suicide may be the only answer to the parents' symbiotic grasp or the child's failure to gain independence.

The family setting also can be linked to suicide when the family uses similar threats to prevent another family member from leaving the family framework. In other instances, the parent may indirectly encourage a child to take his life in an effort to bring back others in the family who are threatening to leave. This process often appears in suicide attempts of young children in the course of the parents' divorce. For the sake of the suicidal child, the parent returns home.

Symbiotic processes may also lead to suicidal tendencies across generations. A suicidal parent may pass these tendencies on to his children because of their symbiotic closeness. Children identify with what they see before them. In the same manner, the death of an immediate relative in a symbiotic family is likely to heighten a suicidal risk. Some symbiosis magnifies identification, the child attempting suicide in mimicry of the deceased or in an attempt to renew the broken symbiotic relations.

*Inheritance of a Pessimistic Attitude Toward Life.* Over and over again, research and clinical descriptions show us families that suffer from various difficulties and pressures. These families are distinctive in their pessimistic outlook on life, their view of death, their fatalistic style of speech, and their complaisance in the face of difficulty. This pessimistic and submissive attitude is then learned by the children—either through identification, or imitation, or the formation of negative expectations from life. Since these children miss out on opportunities to observe active coping with life, they are capable only of surrender, relinquishment, and the internalization of anger. The message passed on in varied ways is that life is hard and that sometimes it is better to die than suffer. Because of the child's limited experience, there is a greater chance that he will adopt this self-destructive viewpoint and arrive at its simple behavioral conclusion.

The following case illustrates the pessimistic inheritance at work. A ten-year-old boy started cutting himself with shards of glass in front of a group of children after having been hurt in a fight with his friend. A teacher was called for and stopped the self-mutilation. Later, psychologists were asked to intervene. The boy's mother, a tired and depressed woman, looked as though she was barely holding on to life. She was unable to take any responsibility because her complete self-absorption had totally clouded her judgment. "I don't know how to take care of my children, and I don't even know what's dangerous and what is not. I don't even know how to tell them to be careful crossing the street or what could be harmful to them. Sometimes I see them doing something dangerous, and I don't know how to stop them. Nothing helps anymore."

Some, following Sabbath, might interpret her words as an indirect message to her children that they were unwanted. Yet this mother did not seem to be urging her children to do themselves in because they were a burden to her. Rather, she seemed to be saying that life itself was an unbearable burden and that death was preferable. One of her children could easily acquire her pessimistic viewpoint and decide to act upon it when life's hardships increased beyond a bearable level.

### Gradual Development of Self-Destruction

*Accumulation of Problems and Ever-Growing Isolation—Jacobs.* Jacobs (1971) has developed a model of adolescent suicide that involves a gradual decline into total social isolation, which eventually leads to suicide. This model can also be applied to suicide in younger children. According to Jacobs, the route to suicide begins with the pain of dealing with long-term life problems that are perceived as being insoluble. Yet, unlike other children in similar situations, the suicidal child cannot share this heavy burden with anyone. A vicious circle of isolation and loneliness is set into motion. The adolescent attributes his failure to solve his problems not to any fault in coping efforts but, rather, to the fact that the problems simply have no possible solution.

At this stage, death becomes a possible relief for life's difficulties. Initial beliefs that suicide is immoral, pathological, or asocial are abandoned and cease to have any deterrent power. Moreover, the adolescent slowly comes to feel that he is no longer a part of society. At that point, suicide is no longer perceived as a potential solution but as the only solution. During the course of this destructive decline, new frustrations may serve as the breaking point.

With younger children, this gradual process is placed against a background of loneliness and alienation in the family context, not just the broader social one. The child, like the adolescent, is faced with problems whose nature he cannot even define. In initial stages, the child tries to rebel against his isolation. Since these efforts are generally provocative, they only aggravate the familial rejection. The child may begin to speak of death and suicide at some point as a means of testing the parents' love. He hopes to force a frightened reaction from the parents. The frequent lack of response is likely to push him toward carrying out his threat.

*Failure to Disconnect from the Mother—Novic.* Novic (1984), like Jacobs, has developed a model involving the gradual movement toward adolescent suicide, but he uses a slightly different theoretical facet. His model can be applied to younger children as well. Novic's theoretical approach also involves the accumulation of problems. Yet, unlike Jacobs, he believes that the problems are caused by conflicts with one's self rather than with one's surroundings. The adolescent is tormented by feelings of being mentally disturbed, particularly because of his sexual, at times incestuous, drives. After the adolescent leaves his home and family, he is unable to cope with this separation and re-gresses to primitive modes of behavior, such as sadomasochistic relations involving mutual pain.

Following the regression comes a sharpened awareness of one's dependence on home and mother. There is an increase of sexual and aggressive fantasies toward the mother. The adoles-cent tries to form new relationships to escape these frightening fantasies, but his efforts end in failure. As anger and guilt be-come stronger, they are accompanied by frightening murderous thoughts and drives toward loved ones. Once again, the adoles-cent reaches outside the family for social contact, but this time his efforts are only a thinly veiled search for rejection. When the sought-for rejection is attained, suicidal thoughts break out and eventually lead to a suicide attempt.

Novic's theoretical approach employs many of Ackerly's (1967) concepts regarding outbursts of sexual attraction and aggression aimed at the mother. The model can be applied to child suicide in response to parental rejection. Rejection arouses in children a whirlwind of impulses, varying from desperate at-traction to uncontrollable anger. These may slowly serve as the basis for suicide when no solution is found for the child's emo-tional dilemma.

Some of the dynamic elements that Novic discusses can be seen in the case of the nine-year-old girl who was rejected by her parents and sent to a boarding school against her will. At first, she tried to accept the fact but was unable to do so. After-ward, she embarked on a long series of provocations, which led to her rejection by the teachers and the other children. She then decided to starve herself and actually stopped eating. This type of suicide may be seen as a symbolic expression of the girl's outrage toward her unnurturant mother. Only when the young girl was sent home did she begin eating again.

### A Model of Multiple Dynamics and Types of Suicide

Most of the theoretical models of suicide addressed in this chapter have tended to spotlight one specific variable or dy-namic. However, many researchers and clinicians regard the phenomenon as a highly complex and interwoven pattern. As a result, these professionals have attempted to categorize and specify these multiple alternate paths and methods (Mattson, Seese, and Hawkins, 1969; Gould, 1965; Peck, 1982). In some instances, their categories overlap. One group of dynamics highlighted in suicide includes depression, desires to fuse with a loved one after death, and themes of guilt or revenge fueled by aggression. Another group of suicides includes those who attempt to manipulate and alter the environment and its relationship with them. At times, this attempt can also be seen as a cry for help in order to call attention to the person's mental anguish.

Another type of dynamic relates to isolation and closed communications. Some children are shut up within themselves. Emotional difficulties, bitterness, and feelings of unfair treatment pile up inside them. Parents of these children shield their self-images as good parents by ignoring their children's hidden problems and belittling those that are hesitantly whispered. An ever-widening gap yawns between parents and children, with the children starting to doubt the validity of their feelings. The children are pushed further away into their closed shells. In these cases, suicide does not proceed from a stormy confrontation but from an almost whispered plaint.

The accumulation of failures forms a separate route to suicide. Even young children can confront failure so repeatedly that it becomes destructive. Suicide arises among those children so worn down by feelings of failure that they cannot deal with the pressures of new demands made on them. Peck (1982) offers dramatic evidence of the role of failure. Among the suicidal children and adolescents he studied, half suffered from such severe learning difficulties as hyperactivity, distorted perception, and dyslexia. The frustration and misunderstanding flowing from such sources of failure led these children to the perilous brink.

Psychosis, loss of contact with external reality and loss of control over the inner one, provides another route to suicide. The psychotic child suffers from fantasies and wildly false apprehensions; her thought processes are distorted and her judgment impaired. In such cases, the emotional dynamics at work are not different from those in other types of suicide; however, the behavioral expression differs markedly. For example, the psychotic child is likely to take her destructive step as a reaction to "voices" that command her to kill herself. Similarly, a psychotic might starve himself out of a fear that his food has been poisoned. Another might try to fly from the fifth floor, confident that she has wings. In all these examples, a common motivating force seems to be the escape from suffering.

Suicide games give the form a completely different category. Some children get pleasure and excitement just from taking a deadly risk. It is as if coming close to death and surviving is a type of victory over the uncontrollable. At its core, this behavior reflects an extraordinary fear of death, with suicide forming a counterphobic response. Other researchers may include here such variables as masochistic behavior or latent depression.

This categorical, multidynamic approach to child suicide is promising, but it currently suffers from overgenerality. It lacks the dimension of in-depth description, which would permit differential identification of the processes involved. For example, it is still unclear whether these categories are different external expressions of a common process or whether they relate to different processes involving distinctive life circumstances or personality types.

### The Biochemical Model

A new tack in the analysis of suicide concerns the role of genetic and biochemical variables. Much of the research here deals with biological components in depression, under the assumption that depression is central to suicide. Another group of biological studies deals with the direct genetic influences on suicide. Although all the work in this area to date pertains to adults, it seems logical to assume its relevance to children as well.

Reiner (1984) offers an excellent summary of genetic factors in depression and suicide. One methodological approach in this area is to demonstrate the heightened frequency of depression among the relatives of a family member who is depressed. Unfortunately, this method does not permit one to discern genetic causes from obvious psychological explanations. A somewhat more convincing approach is to compare depression rates of identical twins with those of nonidentical twins. Similar comparisons have been made between the biological members and the adopted members of a family. These comparisons indicate that genetic components do seem to be associated with manic-depressive disorder, since this disorder has been found among those with closer genetic backgrounds. Yet the findings concerning other types of depression are not so clear-cut.

Regarding the role of biological factors in suicide, evidence is even less clear. Research with twins and adopted children does show trends toward genetic factors in suicide and depression. Yet counterfindings are not infrequent. For example, Roy (1983) found a higher suicide rate among family members of suicidal patients in mental hospitals than among family members of nonsuicidal patients. However, there was no difference in suicide rates as the blood relation was weakened; that is, the rates were similar for first-degree relatives and for second- or third-degree relatives.

Recent research on biological components has moved from simple epidemiological studies to more complex morphological and biochemical ones. For example, some morphological studies (Van Praag, 1986) have examined the relevance of different brain substances and neurotransmitters to major depression and suicide, mostly among adults. A relation has been established between disorders in the levels of these brain substances and depression and suicide. Since these disorders remain even after depression subsides, we may assume that they precipitate depression but do not arise from it.

Research has also focused on potential biochemical disorders in serotonin levels in depressed adolescents. Serotonin is known to be responsible for the regulation of moods and aggression. Thus, the presence of abnormal serotonin concentrations is highly suggestive (Ambrosini, Rabinovich, and Puig-Antich, 1984).

Current attention is now being directed to the potential role of endorphin, a pain reliever released by the brain in times of pain or distress. Past studies (Canon, Liebeskind, and Frenk,

1978) have shown that people who suffer from chronic pain have low levels of endorphin. Therefore, suicide and depression may be related to low levels of endorphin and serotonin because low pain tolerance and faulty regulation of aggression would cause the individual to be less satisfied, more sensitive, more frustrated, and therefore more vulnerable to suicide. No doubt, this hypothesis will be investigated in the near future.

### Three Basic Research Models

One can identify three different causal paradigms underlying almost all the clinical and theoretical material on suicide. The first attributes suicide to specific life conditions, such as a broken home or divorce. The second links suicide to developmentally accumulating pressures. The third, and most comprehensive, treatment attempts to address potential interactions between given circumstances and personality dimensions. Each of these paradigmatic approaches has its unique strengths and weaknesses.

The first model assumes that specific life conditions lead directly and uniquely to child suicide. For example, a broken home or a deteriorating family unit causes feelings of insecurity, abandonment, and rejection in the child. These feelings, in turn, give rise to a lack of self-esteem, low self-assurance, and a lack of direction—all of which bring about depression. Another example of the "specific factors" hypothesis is the child's internalization of the depression and suicidal inclinations of parents. When children internalize their parents' pessimistic outlook on life through identification, suicide becomes a preferred solution. Other specific factors are negligence and abuse on the part of parents in deteriorating families. The negligence and abuse generate uncontrolled aggressive drives in the children, who then internalize the aggression and eventually redirect it toward themselves. Similar hypotheses have been formulated with regard to loss, rejection, symbiotic processes, and so on.

The main weakness of such hypotheses is that there is no way of proving that these factors necessarily lead to suicide rather than to other pathologies. At the very least, a greater specification of the conditions whereby each factor leads to suicide is needed.

The second research hypothesis assumes that gradually mounting pressures wear down coping mechanisms, resulting in strong inner feelings of hopelessness. Breaking points arise when the child feels that she can no longer deal with the accumulated burden and that there is no chance for relief. Self-destructive reactions are differentiated from other pathological responses by the amount of pressure. A classic example of this research hypothesis is the work done by Cohen-Sandler, Berman, and King (1982). They discovered that children who attempted suicide were under much greater pressure than children exhibiting other pathologies, and that their burden had aggregated since late childhood. Pressures came to a head about a year before the self-destructive act. This model, however, does not consider personality variables that can moderate the pressures one is faced with. It is reasonable to assume that children react to pressure in different ways and that their breaking points vary significantly.

The third model hypothesizes that accumulated stress interacts with certain personality inclinations and that the different combinations of pressure and personality variables—especially coping styles—can produce various patterns of self-destruction. Coping refers to the particular manner in which an individual responds to failure, frustration, or conflicts. Individual differences in coping can explain why some people break under pressure and others do not. For example, it is clear that different children react in different ways to the loss of a loved one and to physical abuse or neglect by parents. Even if the loss of a close person, for example, turns out to be a common denominator in child suicides, it is obvious that not all children who experience such a loss take the drastic step of committing suicide.

Several coping styles are particularly relevant in this context. One is the ability to deal with frustration. People incapable of dealing with frustration in a relatively calm manner react in emotional outbursts, which only create new frustrations. Others are able to face frustration with relative tranquility. The way in which people react to attacks is another important facet of coping. Some react by counterattacking, others by running

away, and still others by refraining from response altogether
and- in effect—denying that any unpleasant event took place.
Coping styles may prove to differentiate between children and
adults who are vulnerable to suicide and those who are not.
Moreover, these styles may be responsible for the varying motives behind suicide. For example, a child with low tolerance for
frustration may commit suicide out of vindictive revenge for
wrongs done him. Here we can see the potential interaction of
personality with life circumstances highlighted by the interac-
tive model.

Strikingly few studies to date have attempted to mix
models or to undertake a multidimensional view treating specific life conditions, accumulative stress, and confrontation style.
Future studies in this direction could possibly shed light on the
nature of both child and adult suicide.

## The Unresolvable Problem

Another theoretical approach to child suicide—an approach that I call "the thesis of the unresolvable problem"—
seems to me useful in illuminating a unique dimension of suicide in children. The unresolvable problem refers to a phenomenological state of mind that reflects the child's experience of
being trapped and incapacitated. In viewing the distressful conditions in his life, a child comes to believe that his woes have no
end or resolution in sight and that no action can change this
state of affairs. This perception is likely to evoke depression,
despair, and feelings of rejection and, ultimately, to lead to
suicide.

Clearly, many of the issues involved in the unresolvable
problem are not unique and involve the reordering or reclassifi-
cation of earlier themes and concepts. Yet the reconceptualiza-
tion of child suicide in terms of the unresolvable problem offers
theoretical and practical benefits. From a theoretical standpoint,
this approach allows one to determine whether or not a situation will probably lead to suicide. For example, divorce may be
a harmful and destructive event at times. In other cases, it may
result in a situation that is, in fact, easier for the child to adjust

to than the situation before the divorce. Part of the difference for the child revolves around whether or not the divorce process poses an unresolvable problem. From a practical and therapeutic perspective, identification of an unresolvable problem may permit one to outline a therapeutic program for the entire family. Therapy of this nature, perforce, focuses on problems of the family as a whole and not just the distress of the child.

The notion of the unresolvable problem has appeared in the work of previous researchers. However, the term has never been adequately developed in the past, nor have its implications for suicide been elucidated. Moreover, past references (Teicher and Jacobs, 1966) to the phenomenology of the unresolvable problem among adolescents have tended to overlook the very real roots of these perceptions in intolerable life circumstances.

The unresolvable problem has a number of basic characteristics. First, the problem is beyond the child's capacity for resolution. Second, the situation involves a restriction of the child's choices and possible courses of action. Third, every attempt at problem resolution engenders new problems in its wake. Fourth, the child's problem camouflages a deep familial conflict. Each of these characteristics is addressed here in greater detail.

*A Problem Beyond the Child's Scope.* Unresolvable problems arise from highly complex family situations that are beyond the child's ability to resolve. The problematic circumstances are reinforced by overlapping and contradicting needs and interests of each family member. For example, when parents are consumed with hostility toward each other but deny these feelings, their aggression is often directed to the child as scapegoat. The child's guilt is then the glue that binds the family together. In this perspective, any attempt by the child to escape from his intolerable predicament (for instance, by improving his behavior or his school grades) will, in fact, lead his parents to find new reasons to attack him.

This type of dynamic arose in one case that was otherwise difficult to decipher. A ten-year-old boy had tried on numerous occasions to commit suicide, but it was impossible to find a discernible reason for his behavior. Family life was seem-

ingly normal, the boy's relationship with his sister was acceptable, and the family had experienced neither the loss of a close
relation nor any disruptive illnesses or maladies. The most not-
able fact was that the child was distant and removed from his
friends and excessively attached to his home. Astonishingly,
some background work revealed that the boy's older sister had
displayed suicidal behavior the year before. Only when she had
stopped her suicide threats did they appear in the younger sibling. It seemed that this family needed suicide threats.

Continued therapy revealed a concealed crisis in the family. The father had been threatening to divorce his wife over a
long time period. The mother was in a panic, but she hid her
panic through restraint and self-control. The father had postponed his divorce intentions after the daughter's suicide threats
and later after the son's. Surprisingly, despite the uncomfortable family atmosphere, the children appeared unaware of the
father's plans. Yet when the parents began dealing with divorce
in therapy, the suicide threats stopped almost immediately. This
chain of events supported the assumption that the children's
destructive behavior was directly connected to the parents' conflict. Unknowingly and unintentionally, the mother had trans-
mitted a message to her husband through her children: "If you
leave, someone here is going to die." She encouraged a feeling
of dissatisfaction and depression in her children and was passive
toward their suffering. Thus, when her son spoke of suicide, she
cautiously sent him to his father for help. Yet she did not bolster the father's efforts to help his son.

In this case, the mother used her children as a means of
preventing a catastrophe in the family. The parental conflict
posed an unresolvable problem for the children. Nothing could
help them short of solving the parental conflict, but this was
beyond the children's purview.

A subsequent tragedy in this family points out the unique
power of unresolvable problem situations. Two years after therapy was terminated, the mother died of cancer after a short
period of confinement. The family experienced intense mourning and bereavement, aided at times by therapy. Yet despite this
upheaval and distress, neither threats of suicide nor death wishes

reappeared. It seems that the destructive impact of the unresolvable problem was much greater than that posed by irrevocable loss and orphanhood.

The case of a seven-year-old girl whose parents were separated presents similar dynamics. The father lived abroad but would occasionally "pop in" to visit. These visits caused an emotional upheaval in both mother and daughter. Each time, the father promised that he would soon return because he loved them both very much. However, the final reunion was repeatedly postponed. After each visit, the mother and daughter experienced fresh emotional disappointment. Since the mother fostered secret hopes of reestablishing her family, she refrained from making new relationships or proceeding with divorce.

Just before one of the father's visits, the girl spoke of her wish to die. First she claimed that she would kill herself if her father came to visit. Then she said that she would kill herself if her father did not visit. A call by her mother brought her husband to therapy with their daughter to determine the reason behind the threats.

The sessions revealed that, despite her longings for her father and despite the imbalance in her life, the girl was not suffering from despair to the point of suicide. Rather, she was acting as an unknowing tool for her mother. Once the mother separated completely from the father and began to rehabilitate her social life, the young girl's suicide threats disappeared.

In a number of cases, irrational pressure is placed on the child to solve the unresolvable problem or at least to bear responsibility for it. This attribution of blame can be seen in a family with an eleven-year-old son and two older daughters. The parents were divorced, and there was a great deal of hostility between them. Throughout the therapy, the mother displayed ambivalence toward her son. Although she claimed that she loved him, she continually raised old and unclear complaints about him. New complaints cropped up all the time. The boy was in great distress and several times had threatened to kill himself. With time, the picture was clarified. The mother could not bear to look at her son because he resembled the husband she hated. Through symbolic distortion of other angers, the child became responsible for his father's sins. Even the sight of the boy aroused tremendous anger.

As this case reflects, parents may reject children for numerous causes beyond the child's control. As an extreme example, parents who had early conflicts over their own sexual identity may reject children because of their gender. Or parents may punish children for uncontrollable behaviors such as displays of fear or anxiety.

At times, the problems faced by children do have potential solutions, but their implementation is too much of a burden for the child. For example, one couple expected their ten-year-old boy to perform all the housework because they were too busy dealing with other matters. Clearly, this was too heavy a responsibility for such young shoulders. Death wishes in these situations are a drastic solution to a drastic problem.

*Limitations in Choice and Possible Courses of Action.* At times, the unresolvable problem arises because the child's courses of action or choice are systematically cut off. For example, the parents may force a child to take a specific course through threats, physical punishment, withholding of love, or constant preaching. Thus, the child must relinquish her own needs and free will; at the same time, she learns to direct all her energy toward one target, since to compromise or change goals is to fail. These compulsive patterns have an immediate effect on the child's quality of life.

The following sequence of events exemplifies this process and its ramifications in its most extreme form. A twelve-year-old boy took his father's rifle and shot himself in the chest. The bullet missed his heart by a fraction of an inch, miraculously saving his life. How did he reach this state of affairs?

The boy had always been an outstanding student. When he had skipped a grade a few months earlier, he had been put into his older sister's class. The boy now had to compete with his sister and to fulfill his parents' overwhelming expectations; he also had to try to adjust to an older social group. He asked to return to his previous class or at least to switch to another school. His parents refused these options, encouraged him to try harder, and would not permit him to bring up the subject again.

A few days before the suicide attempt, the boy dared to discuss the matter with his parents. The father recalls: "As soon as he started to speak, I slapped him for bringing up the subject. When he began, 'But father,' I slapped him again. He started to cry and I yelled at him to stop being a crybaby. He still tried to continue talking and to explain, so I slapped him again. At that moment he stopped crying and went to his room in silence."

These few lines recalled by a guilt-stricken man in tears illustrate how an unresolvable problem is created when courses of action are limited. The boy had no choice now, not even the right to express his opinions. He was chained to the high expectations of his parents. Coercion and limitation of actions led to a dreadful feeling of hopelessness, which preceded a final act of desperation.

The feeling of being "boxed in" was underlined in the boy's own recollection of the suicide attempt: "I took the rifle, put the magazine in, and loaded a bullet in the chamber. I pressed the trigger, but nothing happened. I understood that the rifle's safety lock was on. I felt this was a sign from Heaven that I must not kill myself. I tried to remove the magazine but was unable to do so. All I could think of then was what would happen to me if father discovered the magazine in the gun and that I had played with it. He would not believe me that I had tried to kill myself, so I decided to go on and kill myself." The boy's recollections bear witness to the deep feeling of being trapped, of being pushed into a blind alley.

We have already touched on cases where parents made their children's studies the most important project of their lives. Although their great enthusiasm is simply a cover for other life difficulties, it forces the child into the pursuit of only one goal in life: academic success. Parents can be very exacting and oppressive in this area. They speak only of the child's studies; they sit themselves and their children down for hours at a table to work on homework; they call from their places of work to see how the homework is progressing.

In a number of cases, parents restrict children's actions at the same time that they encourage their initiative. The child is called on to act or to take a stand, and then is punished for doing so. The covert goal of this maneuver is to perpetuate a family situation that the parents lack the daring to alter. This pattern, when repeated, leads to hesitation and final paralysis of independent action. For example, children may be pushed to widen their social activities and then punished for wasting time at these endeavors. Other children may be urged to take a stand in a family squabble and then be punished for interfering. Still others may be asked to help out more around the house, only to have their efforts sharply criticized. In each case, the final outcome of this push and pull is a feeling of utter hopelessness.

*Solutions Engendering New Problems.* One paradoxical facet of the unresolvable problem is that any attempt at resolution generates new problems in its wake. One source of distress follows another in an endless chain. Sometimes, the very act of doing away with a problem becomes a source of difficulty in itself. If a child is made responsible for the handling of this problem, he may become so distraught that he will slowly draw into himself and cut off contacts with the world around him. Other people's voices seem to come to him from a distance, from behind a thick wall. He begins to forget what people said to him or what they asked him to do.

This problem appeared in the case of an eleven-year-old boy who came for treatment with his family after expressing suicidal thoughts. The family included his mother, his stepfather, and a five-year-old brother. A baby sister had been left at home. The boy's natural father had passed away when the boy was two years old, and the mother had married one of the father's close friends.

The family's main problem was an inability to coalesce into a true family framework. Each member seemed to have an internal barrier against drawing close to the others. The mother still carried within her deep feelings of mourning for her previous husband and felt guilty at having remarried so soon after her husband's death. She felt that her oldest son still belonged to his natural father and denied her new husband any role in his upbringing. The stepfather felt guilty at having married his best friend's wife and did not permit himself to feel that she was now truly a part of him. The eleven-year-old boy yearned for warm relations with his stepfather but felt that such a relationship would sully his father's memory. The younger boy, brought into the world as a symbol of the new family union, envied his older brother. He preferred to believe that he too was a son of the dead man.

This complicated family picture serves as the backdrop for continual pressures that were put on the eleven-year-old boy. He had to be the best at school, always well behaved and obedient. Since he was never able to meet these expectations, he became a constant focus of complaints. His attempts to draw close to his stepfather were cut off by the mother. His attempts to draw affection from the mother were rebuffed as childishness. And the few times when he could find a moment's closeness and understanding with both parents were always disrupted by the jealous outbursts of his younger brother. The whole family was a pressure cooker with no safety valve. One way for the parents to cope was to dump all problems on the older son. He, in turn, found refuge within himself, shutting himself away. Finally, he sought haven in his suicidal thoughts and threats.

*The Camouflaged Family Problem.* The examples demonstrate that unresolvable problems are usually, in fact, camouflaged family problems. Although many forms of childhood psychopathology involve this subconscious pattern of family camouflage, it takes on special significance in childhood suicide. Examples given earlier demonstrate a range of camouflaged problems that express themselves in suicide. In one instance, a mother's own hidden drives for self-injury were expressed in her child's harmful acts. In a second, parents' mutual dissatisfactions were transferred to the child. In a third case, the mother's fears of abandonment by her spouse lay at the root of her daughter's suicide threats. In a fourth case, a child who was born in order to solidify his parents' shaky marriage attempted suicide when their relationship did not improve. In each case, camouflage efforts by the family members put the child in a painful bind. He is asked to wage war with a powerful but invisible enemy.

Unfortunately, the dramatic aspects of self-destruction often draw concern away from the family's problems. Suicide often is seen as an attempt to attract attention—a motive viewed as childish, unjustifiable blackmail. One common response is to deny the sought-after attention; another is to lavish excessive love and affection on the child. By latching on to this idea of attention getting, family members and therapists often avoid dealing with the more basic family problem and begin searching for solutions in the wrong direction.

*Threats to Selfhood and Alienation.* Two rival aspects of unresolvable problems are the nature of the threat they entail and the isolation that they engender. Almost any major problem that resists solution is likely to bring on feelings of hopelessness. Yet certain binds are especially destructive because they tap themes central to one's self-image and feeling of self-assurance—themes such as sexuality, rejection, or degradation. A child who is rejected entirely because of his sex, for example, may have such intense feelings of threat and turmoil that he will seek to escape by desperate means.

The threatening power of sexuality and rejection can be seen in the heartrending case of a seven-year-old who attempted suicide. The boy had been sexually abused by his handicapped older brother with his parents' silent permission. The attack itself, and the panic that followed, completely unbalanced the young boy. Moreover, when he turned to his parents for support, they accused him of lying. Suicide appeared to be the only option available to escape the threats on selfhood.

Side by side with the issue of threat is that of isolation. The fact that the unresolvable problem is camouflaged and that the child is the only one called upon to handle it creates tremendous feelings of isolation from other family members and the outside world. The child himself often does not recognize his isolated state. However, he does feel its effects. This state may engender self-estrangement and self-alienation. Moreover, since the child cannot easily identify or express what he is facing, he is unable to reach out for help from the outside world. Mistreated and alienated from his family, the child rarely has anyone else to turn to.

## The Link Between Suicide and Unresolvable Problems

A series of emotional states form the links in the chain between an unresolvable problem and eventual self-destruction. Many of these facets of turmoil and distress have already appeared in these chapters: depression, hopelessness, guilt, failure, frustration, and desperation. Confrontation with an unresolvable problem can evoke these states. Continual pressure to solve the unsolvable puts one between a rock and a hard place. Depression creeps in behind the sorrows of failure and guilt, as if the child were somehow to blame. These feelings are heightened by undefined responsibility that the child takes on himself to assure the well-being of the family members. Because the child does not know how to discharge this duty, continual failure inevitably causes diffuse clouds of guilt. The cornerstones of depression have been laid.

In rare cases, the child does succeed in drawing support from his surroundings. Unfortunately, the security and support that they offer can be no more than temporary, since they cannot resolve the problems that the family faces. Yet even this limited support can reduce by a substantial measure the chances of suicide. Repeated failure also brings with it the slow razing of one's self-worth. The child begins to see himself as worthless, useless, an empty vessel. The accumulation of these feelings sets the stage for passivity toward self and others: "Nothing can do any good anymore." As self-initiative drops, expectations for the future become dark and plummet. Another of the foundations for depression is cast.

Alienation and isolation take their toll. At the start, the child feels alienated from his parents. With time, he begins to lose touch with himself and others. He feels misunderstood and disappointed and begins to seek solace in even further isolation. In his lonely, silent abode, the voices of negation and destruction become louder.

The child's options slowly disappear. Initially, the family throttles his efforts at independence; yet with time, he himself begins to see the world in a narrow tunnel vision and quells his own creativity. Everything takes on a dichotomous hue, black

or white. The internal maelstrom forms the emotional background for the violent ultimatum "Either I get what I want or
there's no reason to live anymore." One patient put it best:
"I'm giving one last chance to life. Either something gets me
out of this fix or there's no reason for me to get up in the morning. I won't be long for this world."

The unresolvable problem is not the only factor in suicide. Yet it is clearly a central element in the totality of the dynamics that lead to self-destruction. It gives a unique destructive
slant to problems that in other circumstances might have been
manageable. Adults may be able to deal with the issue of unresolvable problems by realizing their ephemeral nature. But for
the child, they are a matter of life and death.

# 10

# Attraction and Repulsion of Life and Death: A New Way of Understanding Suicidal Behavior

This chapter presents a general framework that synthesizes research findings, clinical observations, and theories about child suicide. Despite its generality, this framework contributes to an understanding of suicide from a phenomenological point of view and aids in the evaluation of self-destructive behavior. Furthermore, it suggests a guideline for the treatment and prevention of child suicide.

Phenomenology describes experiences from the individual's point of view. Applied to suicide, the phenomenological approach provides an understanding of the act and its motives based on the subjective experiences of the sufferer and his pain. Shneidman (1985), for example, offers a phenomenological perspective in his book on the definition of suicide. The present chapter, using a similar approach, offers a systematic descriptive model of child suicide that should be equally applicable to adolescent and adult suicide.

## Ambivalence Toward Life and Death

One of the most striking aspects of suicidal children is their ambivalence toward life and death. In these children, suffering is mixed with pleasure, helplessness with initiative, and feelings of worthlessness with manifestations of talent and achievement. Their ambivalence is most pronounced in reference to death. At one moment, a child may distort the meaning of death so grossly that she does not seem to understand what death is. She may relate to death as a longed-for goal, somehow better than life. Yet sometimes, only moments later or when life circumstances change, the same child may reveal even greater insight and anxiety about death than normal children.

This ambivalence toward life and death appears also in the child's actions. As we saw in an early discussion, destructive actions and suicide involve a great deal of waffling and wavering. Even though the child's descent to suicide is overall a gradual one-way decline, it is filled with wide fluctuations of thought, feeling, and behavior. At one point, a child may want to dash herself against the rocks and yet only a few days later will cling to life at all costs. However, these fluctuations arise around the destructive nucleus, which remains intact unless decisive action is taken or a drastic change occurs in the child's life. Children's ambivalence toward life and death is reflected in the course of day-to-day behaviors, as was revealed in observations of suicidal children at play in their natural surroundings at school (Orbach, Gross, and Glaubman, 1981). The same children who are seen struggling with pain and distress in a therapy session may show the greatest joy on the playground. During recess, they can be seen actively engaged in social and emotional affairs. Unfortunately, these quick changes in behavior create the illusion that such children are not capable of experiencing profound pain; therefore, their suicide attempts are often misconstrued as merely attention-seeking maneuvers.

The quixotic changes in behavior reflect children's internal organization of experiences. Children can forget their distress for periods of time more easily than adults can, since they are influenced to a larger extent by environmental stimuli. This difference does not imply or prove that their distress is any less than that of adults. Many, misled by the sudden alternations in children's behavior, believe that child suicide is the result of a momentary urge. Such a view fails to recognize the underlying distress and the phenomenology of pain in children.

## Four Basic Attitudes

At its root, child suicide revolves around a basic conflict of attitudes toward life and death. It is more than a conflict between the wish to live and the wish to die. Rather, conflicts appear in each context separately. One can speak of four types of conflicting attitudes of repulsion and attraction toward life and repulsion and attraction toward death.

"Attitude" in this context refers to a web of ideas, perceptions, beliefs, and motives that combine to create an experiential quality or a unique state of mind. Attraction to life arises from feelings of gratification and happiness brought about by one's positive experiences with others. Repulsion by life involves the experiences of pain and suffering that arise from sources of anxiety, frustration, and stress. (See Figure 3.) Similarly, some of the feelings, beliefs, and fantasies cluster into an experience of attraction to death; others, into a repulsion by it.

These four attitudes of attraction and repulsion vis-à-vis life and death are active in everyone. However, the relative balance of these driving forces differs between a normal person and one who is in great distress. Moreover, throughout life, the balance between these attitudes is in constant flux. It is the specific balance between them that is a determining factor in the move to suicide.

The basic assumptions underlying this model—which holds that suicide is the result of a certain equilibrium between opposing attitudes and that this equilibrium fluctuates with life circumstances—are partially supported by a number of studies. One study (Kovacs and Beck, 1977b) found that adults hospitalized after attempting suicide expressed both a wish to live and a wish to die. Moreover, changes in these motives correlated with the severity of the suicide attempt. Other studies (Leviton, 1971; Neuringer, 1970) found that variations in degrees of attraction to life and death corresponded to variations in an individual's life circumstances. Thus, if attitudes toward life and death can be determined, acts of suicide might become more understandable. Intervention or prevention, in this light, would in-

Figure 3. This drawing by a seven-year-old girl (see also Figure 2
on page 40) combines positive and negative attitudes toward life.
The branches are reminiscent of swords, but the drawing also suggests
feelings of happiness.

volve the creation of a new, more positive balance. What are the factors determining these attitudes? Let us examine each in turn.

Attraction to life is influenced by the individual's feeling of security in interpersonal relations, the love he derives from others, the fulfillment of his basic needs, the availability of support and encouragement, feelings of self-love and self-esteem, and positive feedback from the environment. Attraction to life is also determined by the way in which the individual copes with difficulties, his assets, his ego strength, and the various defense mechanisms he employs. Thus, for example, a child can minimize frustration by compromising or by lowering expectations and by accepting criticism. These and other coping mechanisms can minimize feelings of failure and friction with the environment. In general, attraction to life rests on personality strengths and the support one receives from the environment. It is this attraction to life that prevents self-destruction.

Feelings of repulsion toward life reflect the pain and suffering that the individual experiences. We can list here the entire range of experiences alluded to in suicide: confrontations with unresolvable problems, the death of a loved one, divorce of parents, physical and emotional abuse, rejection, destructive messages, isolation, and alienation. We can add to these the destructive processes of the symbiotic, demanding, or suffocating family. Included also are negative, unsatisfying relationships with peers and adults. Internalization of self-destruction or identification with a depressed suicidal parent also figures in this category.

Personality tendencies also contribute to a repulsion toward life. Among other traits, we can find here sadomasochistic tendencies, inability to compromise, rigid demands on self, excessively high expectations, emotional inhibition, negative self-esteem, self-degradation, and deficient problem-solving skills. Pathology and ineffective defense mechanisms further strengthen an attitude of repulsion toward life. In general, this attitude reflects the intensity of a person's conflict with her surroundings and within herself. It can be seen as a motivating force toward self-destruction.

Attitudes toward death are not simply the antithesis of

attitudes toward life but are independent mental forces derived from the inevitable confrontation with death. Interest in death, among both adults and children, is not only a product of suffering but an integral part of existence.

Attraction to death embodies the belief that death is a mode of physical or emotional existence that is superior to, and therefore preferable to, life. Among children, attraction to death often comprises beliefs that God is a loving, fatherly being, that in death all one's desires are fulfilled, and that death is reversible. Adolescents, grappling with such existential issues as the meaning of life, often romanticize death, seeing it as a state of mystical union with a universal, supernatural force or with nature. Some adolescents believe that, in dying, one forms a unity with a powerful entity that provides protection and strength (see Figure 4). When adolescents approach suicide, they often inquire about death through discussions, readings, and introspection, and they reach the seemingly cold and logical conclusion that they have availed themselves of what life has to offer and now can move on to more promising worlds. Those around the adolescents fall into the trap of responding to their philosophical queries at an equally intellectual level, completely ignoring the emotional significance of the interrogation.

We have already seen that a view of death as a serene and peaceful rest is basically defensive. This duality in both children's and adults' perceptions of death is quite normal and not exclusively a product of pain and suffering. It is an integral part of existence, which is nurtured by personal experiences, religion, and culture. Yet among the suicidal, attraction to death takes on a greater weight and becomes a motivating force behind self-destruction.

Repulsion by death is salient even among people with strong tendencies toward self-destruction. This attitude stems from the realistic, frightening perception of death as an irreversible cessation and annihilation, but it is also colored by the individual's inner world. Thus extreme feelings of guilt may be expressed in an expectation of harsh punishment after death. The fear of loneliness finds symbolic expression through a concept of death as a state of terrible, eternal solitude. People be-

Figure 4. In this drawing, a suicidal adolescent girl depicts a powerful union between self and nature.

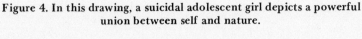

lieve that they will actually *experience* this loneliness, the heaviness and dampness of the grave, even when these idiosyncrasies disappear in the light of cold, rational analysis.

Repulsion toward death is a force that deters one from self-destruction. It is present even in people who are considering suicide and even in those who have taken preliminary steps in that direction: "If I had the courage, I would do it." However, its strength is often diminished.

Approaching the phenomenon of suicide from the perspective of opposing attitudes enables one to formulate a relatively simple hypothesis regarding the different strengths of these attitudes in people with and without suicidal tendencies. It may be assumed that most people are strongly attracted to life and strongly repulsed by death while evincing little attraction to death and little repulsion by life; in contrast, suicidal individuals might be expected to evince strong repulsion toward life, little repulsion toward death, a strong attraction to death, and little attraction to life.

The case of a ten-year-old boy who made numerous suicide attempts offers some clinical support for this analysis.
When speaking of life and death, the boy seemed to be following the theoretical model word for word. In an early therapeutic
session, he was asked about his thoughts of death and what
would happen if he were to die. He answered: "I see it as two
long, dark halls. One hall is death and the other is life. I'm walking down the hall of life and there are two rooms. One room is
dark and frightening, and the other is full of light and looks interesting. The room with light has lots of fun things like games
and toys in it and it's nice to be there. When I leave that room
and go to the other one, it's dark and frightening and there are
all sorts of voices and noises and I'm afraid to be there. In the
hall of death there are also two rooms. One is nice and quiet
and is pleasant to be in, and the other is the most frightening of
all. It's absolutely terrible there, and I quickly run out to the
hall and walk along until I reach a wall and I can't go any further. So I turn around and see that all of a sudden there's another wall in front of me and I can't go either forward or back-
ward."

### Evaluative Studies of the Model

This model was evaluated by studies that compared the
relative strengths of the four key attitudes among children
showing suicidal tendencies with those among children who
showed no such tendencies (Orbach and others, 1983; Orbach,
Feshbach, Carlson, and Ellenberg, 1984). A test involving several stories, each representing a different attitude toward life or
death, was devised to measure the strength of the four attitudes.
Each story involves a dilemma that the child must resolve. The
child's answer reflects the degree to which he identifies with the
attitude represented in the story.

The first story, which assesses attraction to life, resembles
the tale of Pinocchio. An artistic carpenter creates a doll so
amazingly lifelike that he wishes it to turn into a real boy. The
tester asks the child whether it is worthwhile for the doll to turn
into a real child. The child marks on a ruler how worthwhile it

is to make the doll real. Finally, the child is requested to explain his or her conclusion.

The story assessing repulsion toward life deals with the theme of rejection: A zebra is rebuffed by the other members of his herd, who do not like him, refuse to include him in their games, and abandon him to dangers. The zebra is presented with the opportunity of turning into an inanimate object and thus ending his suffering. Here the examiner asks the child whether it is worthwhile for the zebra to become an object.

The story concerning attraction to death is a description of a wretched horse who sees a gleaming marble statue of a stallion in the middle of town. Later, when the horse is carrying a very heavy load through mud and rain, he wonders whether he would be willing to change places with the statue. At this point the child is asked for an opinion. This story attributes a certain appeal to an inanimate object, which is taken to represent death.

The final story captures the attitude of repulsion by death. An ugly duckling yearns to become a swan. The opportunity arises for him to become a beautiful swan on the condition that he give up life. On impulse, the duckling chooses to be a swan. When his duckling friends see him floating lifeless on the water as a wooden swan, they consider making the same choice. At this point in the tale, the child is asked to take a stance and express an opinion.

The stories share a number of characteristics. All are based on familiar tales whose heroes are animals. Life and death are represented by the transformation from living beings into inanimate objects, an accepted technique for dealing with death in child literature. The children are able to identify with animals in stories, while maintaining a certain distance. Thus, the child can respond without too much anxiety. Two parallel sets of four stories were used to test the reliability of the children's responses over time.

In the first study (Orbach and others, 1983) where these stories were used, suicidal and nonsuicidal children (aged six to twelve) were compared. The two sets of stories were administered a few weeks apart. Changes in mental status of the suicidal children were assessed during the interval. Striking differences appeared in attitude profiles of the two groups. The suicidal children showed more repulsion by life, less attraction to life, more attraction to death, and less repulsion by it than the normal children. Strikingly, the smallest difference between the groups was in regard to attraction to life.

The internal organization of the attitudes in the two groups also differed notably. The suicidal children gave approximately equal weight to the four attitudes. At the same time, it was clear that the attitudes were distinguishable from one another. Among normal children, the weights of the attitudes differed greatly but were highly intercorrelated. In other words, suicidal children are both attracted to and repulsed by life and death to the same extent. Yet they have a deeper appreciation of the various aspects of life and death. In comparison, normal children have fewer conflicts in this sphere, and their attitudes are organized according to opposite dimensions. A child with a high attraction to life will have a low repulsion to life or vice versa. The same holds true for attraction to and repulsion by death. The normal child lacks an awareness of and sensitivity to various aspects of life and death. These findings support the idea that suicide is the result of a conflict between different forces and not the end point of a single unidirectional process.

Another finding of the study was that only one attitude—namely, attraction to death—varied with changes in the emotional state of the suicidal children. As the tendency to commit suicide grew stronger, so did the attraction to death—and vice versa. This finding supports the assumption that attraction to death is a defensive strategy, which becomes active when the child begins to seriously contemplate suicide. Therefore, this measure is sensitive to changes in the child's moods and can be used to evaluate the immediate risk present in a child's suicidal impulse.

As mentioned, suicidal children do not appreciably differ from normal ones in their attraction to life. This finding indicates that suicidal children by no means have totally rejected life. Their desire to live remains very strong even in times of crisis and perhaps even at the time of the suicidal act. It would be a mistake to believe that suicidal children are totally disgusted with life or are in complete despair. Even though they are in anguish and seek relief in death, the basic will to live remains. This conflict between inner forces is what gives the suicidal state its conflictive appearance.

By and large, the research findings are consistent with the theoretical assumptions of the phenomenological model. They indicate that the act of suicide is a dynamic process involving a unique balance between forces. Children with suicidal tendencies maintain their thirst for life; their attraction to death is a defense serving their self-destructive tendencies.

A second study (Orbach, Feshbach, Carlson, and Ellenberg, 1984) replicates many of the findings of the first and broadens the experimental population to include a group of children with chronic and fatal illnesses, such as cancer. These children must deal with the question of life and death as a consequence of the very real threat posed to their lives by their illness. It is reasonable to assume that, as a result of their struggle with death, they should exhibit a stronger attraction to life than either healthy or suicidal children. On the other hand, their defensive attraction to death should be greater than that of healthy children, although less than that of the suicidal ones, because their special situation necessitates a confrontation with death that leads them to employ such defenses as a distorted perception of death. In addition, it was hypothesized that the anxiety about death felt by the sick children would fall between that of the healthy and suicidal children.

Overall, the findings of this study replicated the earlier findings and confirmed the hypotheses regarding the terminally ill children. The three groups of children all displayed equally high degrees of attraction to life. The chronically ill children displayed the greatest rejection of death, but their attraction to death was almost as high as that displayed by the suicidal children. In some ways, the sick children showed much the same internal conflict between life and death as did the suicidal children—a conflict probably related in part to the anguish of their illness and the painful treatments. In other respects, they resembled the healthy children in the degree of anxiety they experienced about death.

One further finding appears to bear out the clinical implications of phenomenological models. Among the sick children, changes in attitudes regarding life and death were evident and paralleled advances or recessions in their maladies. Previous research (Kellerman, Zeltzer, Ellenberg, and Rigler, 1980) with chronically ill children has revealed similar vacillations in behavior and mood, including anxiety and feelings of control over the environment, as a function of disease status. The main contribution of this study is its identification of the unique constellation of attitudes toward life and death among chronically and terminally ill children. These findings validate the phenomenological model and the possibility of characterizing children and their behavior according to the four attitudes regarding life and death.

The phenomenological model can be extended beyond issues of suicide and death. Orbach and Florian (1986) studied the applicability of the phenomenological model to children of varying social and cultural backgrounds. The study compared the attitudes of religious and nonreligious boys and girls. The research method was similar to that of the two previous studies with one addition: the children were requested to rationalize or justify their responses to each story. The children's reactions were classified according to their content—for example, "escape from emotional or physical pain," "seek out new experiences," "self-fulfillment."

In general, the attitudes expressed by the religious and nonreligious children were similar to those given by the "normal" samples in the previous studies. The only difference was that religious boys and girls revealed a somewhat stronger attraction to death. Greater variation appeared in the rationales provided for these attitudes. Here the responses of religious girls diverged from those of religious boys, nonreligious boys, and nonreligious girls. The religious girls rationalized most of their responses on the basis of self-actualization needs, whereas the other groups singled out the need for interpersonal relationships as the most important reason for their responses.

The essential similarity of responses across the various groups speaks well for the robustness of the phenomenological model. The few dissimilarities also match intuitive notions of religious individuals' perceptions of death. The stronger attraction to death on the part of the religious children reflects their belief in the hereafter and, as such, is an expression of a cultural and religious norm, rather than of a distortion in perceptions of death.

The relatively high importance assigned to self-realization by the religious girls can also be explained by religious and cultural factors. The girls in the experimental sample were religious but not ultra-Orthodox; as such, they are exposed to such secular beliefs as self-actualization and yet are consigned by their own culture to a traditional role in the home. This situation appears to cause conflicts for such girls; thus, the notion of self-actualization colors many of their attitudes toward life and death.

## Clinical Applications of the Model

Taken together, the three research studies support the validity of the phenomenological model. The model makes an important contribution to an understanding of the dynamics of suicide. Furthermore, it aids in diagnosing and predicting the risk of suicide in children. It can be employed clinically to assess the danger involved in certain self-destructive behaviors, even in the absence of exact information about the strength of the four critical attitudes. The principles presented in this section can be used in the clinical setting to assess and treat self-destructive behavior.

*Assessment.* The application of the theoretical model begins with a general assessment of the situation, acquaintance with family members, and an understanding of the dynamics of the relations between them. When possible, use may be made of such external sources of information as teachers and family doctors. The impressions gathered can be systematically categorized in terms of the four attitudes toward life and death. Phenomena such as excessive punishment, parents' divorce, academic failure, overt rejection, and excessive demands can all be seen as contributing to the phenomenology of suffering, and thus to those forces in the personality that reject life. Similarly, attraction to life is indicated by factors in a child's life that contribute to his well-being: support systems, abilities and talents, achievements, social standing, and other sources of pleasure.

Attitudes toward death can be discerned from a conversation or an exploration of a fantasy of death. By studying these fantasies, one can see, for example, that a child looks on death as something that "corrects" life's flaws. For example, a young girl's claim that when she dies "God will turn me into a boy" or "let me meet my dead dog" reveals deep despair. It seems reasonable to assume that her words reflect rejection on the part of those who are close to her or her confrontation with an unresolvable problem.

Care must be taken with direct questions to children about their motives for committing suicide. Internal experience is not always translated adequately in words or in rational reasoning. Moreover, the child does not always consciously understand her reasons for wanting to die. Because of their stumbling and symbolic quality, the child's answers frequently seem irrelevant. A child might declare that she wishes to kill herself because her parents "didn't buy me a bicycle like they bought my older sister." An answer of this sort can be deceiving unless one considers the symbolic elements of rejection.

The phenomenological model can be exploited further by subdividing the information in each dimension into such categories as family, social, environmental, and personality factors. The use of these secondary categories is helpful, both in pinpointing the problems and in treatment.

In assessing the gravity of suicidal behavior, one should look for certain factors that appear to be particularly destructive: the existence of unresolvable problems, parental depression, death in the family, lack of emotional support, alienation, and excessive parental demands. To round out the picture, one must become acquainted with the family's cultural and religious background, especially with regard to death and suicide.

The utility of the phenomenological model in differentiating between serious suicidal threats and less serious ones has recently been demonstrated (Orbach, 1986). In this study, the case histories of two young girls were compared. The first was that of a twelve-year-old girl who verbally threatened that she would commit suicide and began to collect sleeping pills. She was a good pupil, but her grades had begun to slip. She was accepted socially, but she constantly denigrated herself. She was jealous of her younger sister, who, she felt, was more accepted by her parents. Her entire family lived in a confused atmosphere of constant tension and rivalry. This atmosphere grew out of the father's anxiety that his wife would leave him. He was an authoritarian but dependent man who imposed his will on the whole family and demanded submission. This family conflict affected the young girl. She suffered from the arguments and tension and feared that her parents would get divorced. She tried to deflect her parents' anger onto herself in an attempt to prevent the destructive arguments. She felt that it was her responsibility to keep the family united.

At the same time, this child was not pressured to solve an unresolvable problem, nor was she abused by either parent; and neither she nor anyone else in the family was clinically depressed. Both parents felt guilty toward her and attempted to compensate her. Above all, her maternal grandparents offered a very strong support system, and she turned to them for comfort in times of despair. When the subject of death was raised in direct discussion with her, she seemed surprised. It was almost as if the idea had never occurred to her. She did not believe in life after death and viewed death in very realistic terms. The overall impression derived from this girl's case history was that the balance of the forces leaned toward eventual survival despite her problems.

The second case, that of a seven-year-old girl, presented a higher suicide risk. The girl had never spoken of suicide and had been referred to treatment because of behavior problems. In the play therapy room, however, she revealed a romance with death through her obsessive games around the theme. The atmosphere at home was one of emotional distance, alienation, and isolation. Family relationships were exercises in intellectualization and lacked warmth. There was no vocal upheaval at home, but it was an unstable household. The parents had separated in the past; though they were now reunited, their relationship had not improved significantly. Most destructive for the young girl was her overt rejection at the hands of her mother, who had wanted a son. This rejection was augmented by conflicts stemming from the mother's own childhood. The mother's attitude was so blatant that the young girl tried to adopt the mannerisms of a boy. She would not play with girls, insisted on a very short haircut, and played boisterously and aggressively. This behavior was strongly criticized by her parents, so that the little girl was trapped in an unresolvable situation.

Furthermore, she was almost completely isolated, without any friends, support system, or sources of love. Her negativism further alienated her from her environment. She distanced herself from other people, devoting most of her time to household pets, which were her only consolation.

Discussions about death created great anxiety, yet she insisted, with a mixture of stubbornness and fear, that there was life after death and that one could bring animals back to life by feeding them. Clearly, the conversation caused her much uneasiness and disquiet, and she was clinging to her beliefs as a defense. In her fantasy about death, she imagined herself asking God to turn her into a boy because she didn't like being a girl. Apart from her pets, she had no other sources of attraction to life. Considering the relative strengths of her attitudes toward life and death, her prognosis was poor.

As these two cases demonstrate, the outward appearance of a case does not always translate into a prognosis for the future. An emphasis on the four attitudes and their delineation may redirect attention to important underlying issues and offer greater insight for subsequent preventive and therapeutic efforts.

*Treatment.* The model of attitudes toward life and death also offers a systematic approach to treatment. The therapeutic goal is to upset the destructive balance and put in its place a new balance in which the "pro-life" forces predominate. This goal involves strengthening the attraction of life and the repulsion by death and, conversely, decreasing repulsion by life and attraction to death. For example, increasing death anxiety as a defense against impulsive self-destruction has often proved effective in cases where the children were in such a mania of self-destruction that they had to be physically restrained.

This increase in anxiety can be accomplished through open, direct discussions about death. "What is death? What happens to people when they die? What will happen to you if you die? Have you ever seen a dead person?" The thrust of the discussion arouses anxiety and slowly lessens the attraction that death holds for the child. It returns him to a more realistic perception of death. A discussion of this sort is not intended to be a lecture or an explanation about the concept of death. The cases presented in Chapter Six demonstrate that even young children have a fairly good understanding of what death is. Explanations can only arouse resistance. Rather, the object is to allow the child to explore his death fantasies and realize their shortcomings. As shown earlier, distorted death concepts are very fragile defense mechanisms and cannot stand up to reality testing. Talking about death can also provide the child with an opportunity to express such feelings as anger and vengefulness. The child may derive great pleasure from the description of the pain that her death will inflict on her parents. This aggressive need is given symbolic expression during the therapeutic sessions and lessens the tendency toward destructive actions. The same process occurs when the child fantasizes about meeting a beloved person after death. Fantasizing about such an event is sufficient to provide the child with some emotional gain. Sometimes children react to such discussions with intense anxiety and request that the conversation be terminated. In the short term, this is an effective response and the subject can be broached again at a later date, when it arouses less anxiety.

Increasing the anxiety associated with death and lessening its attractiveness are merely temporary measures. They do not resolve the problem. Therapy must also confront the other attitudes held by the child. One can lessen the child's rejection of life by recognizing and dealing with the child's distress, identifying unresolvable problems, tracing problematic areas in the relations between the parents and decreasing the burdens on the child, and redefining the demands on and expectations of the child in realistic terms. Elements in the child's personality that have led to increased frustration, social isolation, poor self-esteem, and uncompromising attitudes must be recognized. At a certain point in therapy, a distinction must be drawn between the different sources of conflict, and treatment of the parents must proceed separately from that of the child. This procedure lessens the child's involvement in the parents' problems and enables both parties to confront their deepest problems more openly and honestly.

A child's attraction to life can be increased when the therapist emphasizes the child's strengths and points out the positive influence he can have on his environment—for example, in strengthening the ties between family members. This is a most important factor, since alienation is a prominent characteristic in these families. The child's unfulfilled needs—for attention, love, security, and the like—must be identified. However, it must be remembered that lack of attention does not constitute a reason for committing suicide, and giving attention does not remedy suicidal tendencies.

The theoretical principles introduced here will be further elaborated in the following chapter, which deals directly with the assessment of suicidal behavior and the practical aspects of therapy for suicidal children and their families.

# 11

# What We Can Do
# for Suicidal Children:
# Assessment and Therapy

The previous chapter concluded with a schematic application of the phenomenological model in evaluation and treatment. Although this model needs to be developed further, it can still be useful in its present form when combined with broader issues of assessment and therapy. This chapter will attempt to present some of these broader issues within the overall framework of the phenomenological approach.

### Assessment of Risk

One of the central theses in this book is that child suicide is related to certain life circumstances rather than to specific personality characteristics. These life circumstances pertain primarily to dynamics and events occurring within the family. Therefore, any assessment of risk or determination of treatment must take place within the family setting. Evaluation and treatment of the child alone would be insufficient.

Earlier discussions in this book have suggested that various sources of information must be considered in order to weigh the child's attitudes toward life and death. Other relevant features of the child's life and personality include her achievements and social satisfactions, the types of support she can draw on, her relations with adults, and her unique place in the family. In addition, one must consider her ways of coping with frustrations, impulsivity, control, emotional openness, and flexibility. Since this extensive list could include all aspects of emotional functioning, this chapter highlights those that seem to be most critical in assessing suicidal tendencies. Some of these variables address the family's life, while others deal specifically with the child.

## Assessment of the Family

*The Unresolvable Problem.* The existence of an unresolvable problem, described in detail in Chapter Nine, can be determined only through a number of therapeutic sessions with the family as a whole. Contact with the child alone may lead one to overlook the existence of a major conflict. Particular attention must be given to the manner in which the children are embroiled in the problem as well as their particular role in its resolution. As noted earlier, there are many types of unresolvable problems. Some are rooted in deep historical conflicts between parents, while others arise from their immediate relations.

*Parental Conflicts: Denial and Idealization.* Unresolvable problems are created and supported by titanic conflicts between parents. The graver the conflict and the stronger the denial that such conflict exists, the greater the likelihood that parental pressures will be focused on one particular child. Although open conflict between parents can be extremely serious, it is less likely to foster self-destructive tendencies than covert hostilities, where the parents' need to preserve an ideal but shallow façade of harmony is often met at the price of scapegoating one child. By manufacturing a problematic child, parents can maintain an image of an otherwise harmonious family. Yet for the same reason, they will resist any attempt at improvement, which would threaten their façade. The child's only escape may be to suicidal behavior. Parental conflicts leading to suicidal tendencies are not necessarily limited to any specific area of disagreement. However, one common theme is of struggle over one parent's hidden desire to leave the family. As a defensive maneuver in these instances, the parent who wants to leave will turn his dissatisfaction toward one of the children, often with the passive consent of the spouse.

Some parents who, in fact, have deep hidden conflicts may idealize their relationship. "We haven't had a fight for twenty-eight years" suggests an idyllic situation that cannot stand the test of reality. One decisive way to expose dynamics of this kind is to ask family members to act out a situation leading to a crisis and then have them switch roles. When children play the role of the parents, they often lay bare latent dynamics operating within the relationship.

These dynamics are by no means unique to suicidal behavior. Indeed, as noted earlier, they often precede a number of forms of maladjustment. Yet their presence when the child has already expressed suicidal intentions must magnify the meaning attributed to such behavior.

*Depression and Suicide Among Parents.* As described in Chapter Five, parental depression or suicidal tendencies can contribute to the growth of children's suicidal tendencies. It is therefore important for therapists to assess the emotional state of the parents. This task is not always easy or direct. However, signs of parental depression often surface in the context of discussions over experiences of loss from the recent or distant past, as well as uncompleted mourning, and in discussions that reveal anxieties about the future, one's job, current troubles, or past crises. Often, an entire family can live in the stifling atmosphere of depression without even being aware of its presence.

*The Child's Alienation from the Family and Availability of Support.* One painful result of scapegoating is the alienation and rejection of the child within the family. As the living representative of the family's difficulties, the child is alienated and isolated from parents and the other children. Assessment of alienation is crucial, since this situation increases self-destructive tendencies. Sources of support and nurturance also need to be examined. Sometimes this support comes from within the family, and sometimes it comes from a more distant relative. The absence of support in the face of mounting problems can turn a suicidal wish into a self-destructive reality.

*Extreme Symbiotic Processes in the Family.* The destructive processes associated with familial symbiosis make it a key point for assessment. As discussed in Chapters Seven and Nine, the symbiotic family has the following characteristics: lack of

boundaries between the different family members, sadomasochistic relations, neurotic exploitation of one family member by
others, exaggerated family loyalty and mock harmony, secretive
and indirect communication, lack of tolerance of separation and
independence, and lack of empathy for the child's needs.

*Permission for Emotional Expression in the Family.* Open
emotional expression within the family is another gauge of children's suicidal tendencies. Suicide threats or attempts are not as
dangerous in families where there is a willingness to accept the
expression of emotions over personal or interpersonal matters.
In the face of tensions, the freedom to express emotions defuses
destructive fury. Thus, one must evaluate families' acceptance
or rejection of the open display of anger, affection, dissatisfaction, mourning, or other feelings. Here, too, concern must be
given to particular areas of family taboo—areas that are not
open to discussion or ventilation. At times, the repression of
emotional expression is clear and apparent. For example, in one
family, the parents refused to allow their children to mourn for
a sibling who had committed suicide. In other instances, repression of emotional expression is more limited. In one therapy
session, a wife was about to broach a topic when her husband
suddenly cut her off: "You can't talk about that here, period!"

*Problem Solving in the Family.* Families with a suicidal
member often are so inflexible that they cannot arrive at even
temporary or makeshift solutions to family disputes. Indeed,
their arguments and bickering over problem resolution lead to
further escalation, without the normal emotional catharsis following conflict. Tensions rise unabated until they peak dramatically in acts of injury to self or others, destruction of property,
or permanent or temporary separation. Thus, a family's coping
mechanisms and ways of solving problems have critical bearing
on risks involved in a child's suicidal threats or attempts.

## Assessment of the Child

One further avenue for gauging the seriousness of self-
destructive behavior involves a focus on the child and his perceptions of his lot in life. This evaluation must tap a number of

facets, including the child's preoccupation with death and attitudes concerning it. It must also deal with the child's social and emotional functioning, feelings of alienation, social responsiveness, self-esteem, emotional state, and coping mechanisms.

*Obsessive Preoccupation with Death.* An obsessive preoccupation with death, discussed in Chapter Three, is one of the signal hallmarks of suicidal risk. This fact has been well documented in both clinical and research works. The nature of the preoccupation can take numerous forms in children, including an exaggerated interest in subjects related to death, continuous questions about death, or compulsive games involving death, cemeteries, funerals, or gravestones. Particularly telling are artistic works on the cycle of life or on aggression, murder, accidents, injuries, or disasters. Richman and Pfeffer (1977), for example, highlight the diagnostic importance of numerous cuts on figures the child draws as a specific sign of suicidal intent. Another specific sign is the abrupt or impulsive erasure or scratching out of figures.

Figure 5 is a highly telling portrayal by one suicidal girl, Jill. It was accompanied by a tale she invented about a second Jill, who wanted to represent her school in a local beauty contest.

> All her friends agreed that she was very pretty but doubted she would be chosen. However, Jill was sure that she was the most beautiful and that only she would win. In fact, after the first elimination, Jill was one of the ten girls remaining from the hundreds of entrants. After the second round, Jill was still in the running with four other girls. Yet in the end, Jill didn't win—she wasn't even the runner-up. Despite their disappointment, all her friends told her she had been great. Yet Jill was not satisfied. She felt that she had been the ugliest and that there was no longer any reason to live. She wanted to end her life and tried unsuccessfully to kill herself. In the end she decided not to kill herself, but continued to hate herself and her friends.

Figure 5. This drawing by a twelve-year-old girl demonstrates some of the specific signs of suicidal tendencies: the use of slashes and crossing out of the head.

Both Jill's story and her drawing are telling examples of the preoccupation with death among suicidal children. The story reveals both symbolical and direct concerns over death and suicide. In the drawing, one can see the dramatic and impulsive crossing out of the face. The story that accompanies the drawing demonstrates the validity of such drawings as a diagnostic sign of suicidal tendencies.

*Attraction to Death.* The importance of the child's attraction to death was discussed in Chapter Ten. Particularly disturbing are views of death as life under improved conditions. In a suicidal child, these rosy views of death usually reflect defensive perceptions. They are likely to facilitate a view of suicide as a method of coping. In contrast, more realistic perceptions of death, accompanied by appropriate expressions of anxiety, are evidence that the child still has no concrete plans for suicide and that the danger involved is minimal. An analysis of the child's specific fantasies about death is in itself useful, since it offers a key to understanding the distress in the child's life.

*Alienation and Social and Emotional Responsiveness.* The tendency to isolate oneself and close oneself off from others is evidence of a lack of proper and satisfying relations with the surroundings. These walls of isolation can foster negative feelings, such as low self-esteem, deprivation, despair, and hopelessness. Particularly important to diagnosis are indications that the child feels a sense of estrangement and difference from others. Alienation often leads to an experience of being a misfit and unworthy of living among others. However, the signs of this condition are camouflaged at times by an air of outer calm, self-sufficiency, or shyness.

Even when faced with a decidedly suicidal child, one can draw encouragement from certain social factors. One can be impressed favorably by the child's ability to form relationships and enjoy social encounters or to find substitute sources of support outside the family network. No less important is the child's emotional expressiveness. There is significantly less danger with a child who is capable of expressing dissatisfaction and of sharing these concerns with others. In contrast, certain emotional states and behaviors are commonly associated with suicide: depression, aggression, loss of impulse control, or signs of internal deterioration.

*Coping Patterns.* Although coping often implies successful dealing, certain patterns of coping increase self-destructive behavior. Among these problematic coping patterns, one finds escapism, withdrawal, perseveration, and a stubborn unwillingness to compromise. These patterns are related to such traits as a low frustration threshold, learned helplessness, or dichotomous thinking. These traits must be taken into consideration when one is evaluating the seriousness of self-destructive behavior. Jill's story offers a clear portrayal of the connection between dichotomous thinking, low frustration threshold, and self-destructive behavior.

## The Therapeutic Approach

The treatment of children with suicidal tendencies employs many of the same principles that are used with other forms of emotional disturbance. Nonetheless, there a few unique principles and guidelines for treating the suicidal child.

### Family Therapy

*Identifying the Unresolvable Problem.* The unresolvable problem, because of its cardinal role in child suicide, becomes a key target for the therapist. The therapist must constantly ask the following questions: What processes, situations, relations, and facts bring the child to feel that there is "no way out"? What problem does the child face and why does he feel that the only way to solve it is through self-destructive behavior? In searching for answers to these questions, the therapist must deal with the family members in different groups and combinations. When the problem hinges around the parents' relationship, the parents must be seen together. However, difficulties between a parent and one of the children are best addressed with only the involved parties present. For example, the therapist may have to reckon with the deep feelings of rejection that a mother has harbored toward her son since the day he was born. These feelings cannot be dealt with in the presence of the whole family. Similarly, an unresolvable problem may hinge on a father's negative feelings toward his daughter because she reminds him of his hated ex-wife. Here, too, the feelings cannot be clarified and dealt with in the presence of all family members.

Once the unresolvable problem has been identified, the therapist must often deal with it at multiple emotional levels matching the needs and coping abilities of the different family members. In one case, a mother—angry and humiliated because her husband had been unfaithful to her during her pregnancy— urged her daughter to commit suicide. In this case, therapy was limited to the husband and wife, since the inclusion of other family members would have been harmful. At the same time, the day-to-day manifestations of pain and anger within the wider family circle also had to be treated. The family as a whole had to learn how to handle the mother's tendency to focus all her fury on the daughter following the slightest dispute with the father.

In sum, the underlying unresolvable problem must often be clarified and initially worked through with the parents before confronting the whole family. Yet, after this preliminary groundwork, it must still be presented to the larger group in a way that the children will be capable of dealing with. The therapist should not be reluctant to conduct in-depth work with the husband and wife exclusively. The children themselves usually accept a step like this with great relief. In all cases, the process of therapy must be conducted at different depths and with different family groupings.

*Dealing with the Family's Coping and Problem-Solving Strategies.* Within the course of treatment, one focus must be on the rigid use of a highly limited group of coping strategies. These solutions often involve massive coercion of the children, since parents are unable to compromise or reduce their expectations. To lessen the danger of self-destructive behavior in the child, a therapist should encourage the parents to form less rigid coping strategies. Once they are willing to relinquish unrealistic expectations and to consider realistic compromises, they can begin to find new and more efficient means of dealing with life's problems.

Flexibility in problem solving becomes a critical goal. The

first step is to bear down on the sources of the high expectations. Here it is important to ensure that the parents' rigidity is simply a camouflage for other pressing problems. Also, since relinquishment of expectations is a form of symbolic loss, it must be handled with the same care and caution as other types of loss.

These issues arose in the family therapy of a girl who had tried several times to commit suicide. Suicide was her way of coping with her parents' expectations for academic success. This daughter was the last hope for fulfilling her parents' dreams, since her two older brothers had left school and followed other paths in life. The girl's request to go to work before completing her matriculation exams threw her parents and family into chaos. Strong and coercive pressures were wielded to change her mind and led to her acts of despair. A good part of the therapy was aimed at gradually helping the parents deal with the loss they felt as a result of their daughter's decision.

*Helping the Family Deal with Death and Other Crises.* One type of unresolvable problem involves issues of death and mourning. Children's suicide attempts often occur after a death of a family member, which the family has not yet worked through. Identifying such losses requires the active interest of the therapist, since families may not disclose them on their own accord. It should not take the therapist by surprise if parents reveal in a casual manner that, a half year before the suicidal incident, a grandfather or grandmother died. Although the parents may describe themselves as unscathed by the loss, they may describe in great detail their child's difficulties in coping with mourning.

In such cases, it is necessary to work through the parents' own experience of loss and to deal with the submerged mourning process. Different approaches may be required in therapy, depending on the nature of loss. Bereavement in the distant past or involving only one family member suggests that therapy should proceed on an individual basis with that person. However, if the loss affects the family's day-to-day life, therapy may be more appropriate within the broader family context. In the second marriage of a widower, the deceased may remain a central focus if bereavement has not taken its course. Idealizations, taboos, or continuous comparisons with the previous family life all make children's adjustment difficult. It is important to symbolically integrate the deceased into the family as a person and not as a myth. Here the question of blood relationship to the deceased is completely irrelevant.

A special type of loss that cannot be overlooked is previous suicide in the family. Past suicide can be subtly woven into the fabric of self-destruction in the present, often without the conscious awareness of those involved. Eight-year-old Ron and his family are one example. Ron had tried to throw himself out of high windows a number of times and with growing frequency. Yet his parents had turned to therapy, strangely enough, only after reports had begun to arrive about a decline in his schoolwork. Ron's parents had been married for ten years and had three children. The mother set the tone in the meetings. An impressive woman, she talked facilely and laconically, repeatedly harping on the decline in Ron's studies. Yet she showed a paradoxical calm and quiet whenever the conversation verged to the topic of Ron's self-destructive behavior. At first glance, one might have thought that she was emotionally immature and dependent. Moreover, she often took a provocative stance toward her son, which only made things worse. She freely admitted her preference for her second son, whom she showered with affection.

Ron's father was a friendly and pleasant man who watched in sorrow the destructive decline in the relationship between his wife and child. Trapped between his feelings for his wife and his pity for his child, he took no real initiative. The relations in the family slowly approached total chaos, even though glimmers could be seen of an earlier time of stability and love.

A dramatic change in the complexion of the case arose in an individual session with the mother. She recalled a few details that had slipped her memory. Three years earlier, just prior to the birth of the youngest child, the woman's own mother—with whom she had had an abusive relationship verging on physical injury—had jumped from the roof of a house. The mother recalled, matter of factly, that Ron had had a loving relationship with her mother. She only then noted the remarkable parallel between their acts of self-destruction, a realization that made tears break through her exterior calm. This confession, attained in an individual session, exposed the dramatic dynamics underlying Ron's actions. A complex picture arose involving Ron, his mother, and the grandmother. Issues of symbiosis, repressed anger, contorted identifications, and others suddenly became urgent. Each required flexible and varied therapeutic efforts within a changing family format.

The "family secret" is another facet of the unresolvable problem that requires therapeutic attention. Here a suicide or crisis is initiated by one of the parents in an attempt to avoid the disclosure of a threatening secret. For example, one couple turned in panic for counseling after their ten-year-old threatened to commit suicide for a second time. During the short therapeutic process, it became clear that the parents had recently become estranged because of the husband's suspicions that his wife was having an affair with another man. By coincidence, the mother decided at this point that her young son's suicide threats needed massive attention from the whole family. The lack of clarity over whether the child had actually threatened suicide suggested that the mother may have overreacted or even manufactured the incident in an attempt to ward off an incipient crisis with her husband. Much of the therapy had to be invested in simply uncovering the untold "secrets" that family members were afraid to bring out into the open.

*Dealing with Opposition, Aggression, and Denial.* Since suicidal behavior plays an integral role in family dynamics, it is understandable that the family will not easily relinquish its habitual coping patterns. Family members quickly manifest their opposition to therapy. For example, they may insist that the therapist is on the wrong track or that individual therapy would be preferable or that their problems are negligible or that whatever problems they had have disappeared after just a few sessions.

One common form of opposition to therapy is aggression toward the suicidal child. Spurious accusations are made, the child is denigrated, and his weaknesses are magnified against the strengths of the other children. Faced with this overt rejection of the child, the therapist must take a clear stance in defending the child from the onslaught. For instance, the therapist can actively fend off attacks on the child and clarify the child's feelings and behavior. Yet in no case does therapy require attacking the parents head on. Rather, the objective is to gradually raise the awareness of mutual despair and to relieve the underlying aggression found in the parents' guilt and the child's feelings of rejection.

Initially, the therapist may join with the attacked child in order to strengthen the child's ego and increase the child's self-esteem. Symbolically, the therapist can defend the child by sitting close to him. At times, the other children in the family can be drawn into openly supporting the suicidal child. Here the therapist's model of expressing positive feeling toward the scapegoated child can reinforce similar responses in the other children. Through the therapist's concrete example, the children come to see that it is no longer forbidden or unacceptable to aid their sibling.

Hostility and aggression are almost unavoidable characteristics of suicidal families. Richman (1979a) goes so far as to argue that intrafamily aggression by necessity must arise during therapeutic attempts to reduce the symbiosis. Any probe of intimate feelings will be met by aggressive resistance. Tension rises as the therapist and family intrude upon previously sacred grounds.

One of the features of symbiotic families is their tendency to escalate their angry feelings without cathartic relief. The unavoidable explosion of aggression strikes out in all directions—especially at the therapist, who has tried to draw out deeply recessed feelings. At this point, the therapist's role is to take advantage of the situation for positive therapeutic aims. The family must learn to sublimate and redirect these emotional energies in alternate paths in order to reach catharsis. The therapist thereby introduces into the family a new type of coping. The members learn that constructive venting of angry feelings does not threaten the family structure.

This principle of emotional reeducation is true for other feelings as well. Families characterized by self-destructive behavior have often suppressed emotions such as love or intimacy. Positive emotional expressions or attempts at rapprochement by one member are often left hanging in the air, since other members lack the ability to reciprocate. Yet these positive overtures "left hanging" refuel old angers. Richman (1979a) highlights this negativity in his description of symbiotic families and their maintenance of emotional distance in order to preserve individuality.

In the therapeutic efforts to cut away expressions of negativity, one is led to the seemingly paradoxical goal of upsetting an apparent bastion of positive strength: the parents' idealization of their relationship. At heart, this façade reflects no more than the denial of disappointments, anger, and repressed desires to keep the family together. The façade of harmony can exist simultaneously with the hidden picture of chaos in a couple who are unable to tolerate the experience of conflict. Yet it is this very ability to tolerate conflict that the therapist must instill as an overriding goal. Otherwise, couples who cannot confront conflict continue to use their child's "problematic behavior" as a protective shield. Here, too, therapeutic attempts to replace the idyllic illusion with a relatively realistic understanding can be met with resistance—especially when the confrontation is drastic or abrupt. Yet when it is handled appropriately in a gradual fashion, the parents can learn that even true conflict is not necessarily an overwhelming threat.

*Promoting Positive Family Interchanges.* Side by side with these other efforts, the therapist must not lose track of the need to promote positive interchanges between the family members and the suicidal child. One cannot remain oblivious to the child's prolonged rejection and emotional deprivation. No method or means should be cast aside in the attempt to increase pleasurable experiences and promote open expressions of affection. For similar reasons, superfluous "digging" into conflicts between the child and the parents must be avoided.

In the therapeutic process, the other children in the family must also be kept in mind. They are likely to feel that they are losing their special or even preferred place in the family because of all the changes taking place. Room must be given to them lest they choose more dramatic means of "stealing the show."

*Principles for Therapy with the Child*

Therapeutic measures directed specifically at the suicidal child are relevant whether treatment is conducted at a family level or with an individual child. The following are a number of specific principles for working with a child, derived from the literature and my own clinical practice.

*Providing Corrective Experiences.* The literature on adult suicides (Tucker and Cantor, 1975) suggests that these are people who have suffered from prolonged deprivation of basic needs and have strong yearnings for a nurturing companion and emotional dependency. Suicidal children have similar longings and will respond dramatically to physical contact, affection, and acceptance from the therapist. They are happy to form an alliance with the therapist and derive great benefit from the protection it offers them in the face of parental hostility.

When these children display destructive behavior during therapy, they receive great pleasure from the physically active stance taken by the therapist in its prevention. Many of these children do not enjoy such a response from their own parents when they threaten self-injury. Therefore, they may repeat these actions in an attempt to get a caring response from the therapist. Their behavior reflects no more than a great hunger for the gratification of emotional needs. When we consider the alienation enveloping the child's relationship with his family, this behavior is quite understandable and will not necessarily lead to an increased incidence of self-injury in the long run.

The concerned reaction of the therapist is in itself a corrective experience in the most basic sense. In treating other emotional problems, the therapist tends to avoid such a relationship with the child, but it holds great therapeutic value for the suicidal child. This is one of the differentiating points between therapy for suicidal children and others. Similar deviations from the "normal" rules of therapy occur in dealing with adult suicide. There is greater flexibility and latitude in the therapist's responsiveness to the patient's needs; choice of the time, duration, and place of therapeutic sessions; and the con-

finement of the patient to the therapeutic room. These deviations make therapy with the suicidal unique.

*Providing Alternatives to Self-Injury.* When a child starts
down the path of self-destruction, this strategy comes to domi-
nate all his problem solving. This almost automatic self-destructive response to frustration or anxiety appears quite clearly in the
therapy room. When limits are set or an apparent rejection
voiced, the child threatens suicide or self-injury. One child had a
fit of anger and started sawing the furnishings in the room during a therapeutic session. The therapist placed a limit on his behavior by telling him that he was not allowed to break or destroy the objects in the room. The boy then countered: "All
right, then I'll saw off my fingers. I don't need them anyhow."
He then proceeded to saw on them. Against a background of
tremendous internal pressures, even the smallest frustration can
set off the destructive tendency. The appearance of self-injury
is the therapist's cue for intervention. At this point, the therapist needs to help the child find alternate means of coping
with problems—through verbal expression of anger, the release
of emotions, or the clarification of the experience that has led
to the view of suicide as the sole course left open.

It is the mutual duty of both the child and the other family members to facilitate these substitute behaviors. The parents
must eventually participate in this process if the therapy is to
succeed.

*Confronting Death Fantasies.* In Chapter Ten, we emphasized the therapeutic importance of heightening the suicidal
child's anxieties regarding death by defusing the potent image
of death as a preferable alternative to present life. The depth of
the child's despair over daily reality causes her to view death as
the ideal antithesis to her life. The child attributes to death the
ability to nurture, comfort, and correct all wrongs. This idealized projection of death may be accelerated if the child has experienced a loss of someone dear to her. Longing for the deceased becomes a longing for death. In death, the child believes,
one's hopes and wishes will become reality. Good and bad become dichotomized, with death representing good and life representing evil.

Twelve-year-old Leah experienced this fantasy of death. Some years after her father's death, her mother remarried and had more children. On the surface, it seemed that family life was returning to normal. Yet Leah became the link between her dead father and the rest of the family. From a young age, she cultivated her feelings of loss and felt perpetual mourning, longing for her father and yearning for death. She idealized her father and cherished his memory.

Leah's mother unknowingly reinforced this idealization. She felt an obligation to preserve her husband's memory by maintaining a relationship with his parents. Leah was the key to this process. She spent most of her vacations with her grandparents. These vacations centered around long talks about her father, who emerged as an angelic figure, omnipotent and bursting with goodness and strength. This image deepened her feelings of loss and increased the gap between reality and imagination.

In therapy, Leah had to be helped to work through the experience of the loss; to find a realistic father figure, with weaknesses as well as strengths; and to develop realistic substitutes to fulfill her needs. Assimilating the death fantasies in the therapeutic process means to confront the idealization of death through reality testing. It is also a process of accommodation to the reality of loss and the creation of realistic alternatives. Of course, the fantasies must be confronted gradually rather than terminated abruptly.

*Examining the Choice of Suicide.* In high-risk cases of suicide, the major therapeutic breakthrough comes when the therapist participates in examining suicide as a possible solution. The patient thereby learns that simply contemplating suicide does not automatically categorize him as crazy or immoral. In discussions with the child, the therapist must listen carefully and must accept the child's experience of pain, even when it concerns the decision to inflict self-injury. The therapist must then reflect back to the child how this emotional turmoil developed into the wish for suicide. For example, when the child tells the therapist that he is bored, has nothing to do, and wants to die, the therapist can reply that when she is alone and sad she too feels there is no reason to live and would prefer death. The cardinal principle of this process is to understand and reflect on the experience of pain and the way in which it leads to a yearning for death.

At a later stage, the therapist can examine the child's beliefs about death and what he imagines will happen when he dies. What will life be like without him? What will happen to his relatives? How will they accept his death? What will the child gain? What will he lose?

After the patient's destructive impulses have subsided, the therapist can begin to reflect the person's own contributions to his suffering—sometimes by helping the patient recognize that his feelings of rejection or failure or his reactions to his parents' behavior are not always proportionate to reality. When the patient accepts these interpretations, the therapist and patient can then consider new alternatives of action and examine their efficiency.

This empathetic participation in the suicidal decision goes against the grain, since there is an automatic tendency for people to try to stop anyone who wants to end his life. However, the attempt to take away from the suicidal adult or child the only option that seems realistic to him may actually push him closer to death. This is especially true if it happens at the beginning stages, when the patient sees suicide as the only available means of action.

The passive stance that the therapist must assume demands great strength but offers great benefits. Many times, leaving the option of suicide open gives one the strength to go on living because he is free to choose death if he wishes to. A therapist who can understand the patient's feelings about suicide provides him with feelings of comradeship and mutual understanding. The therapist thereby creates a partnership where there was once only alienation and isolation.

*Splitting Between Positive and Negative Selves.* Another principle of special importance for cases where suicide is imminent is that of splitting off and nurturing the positive self. Children in immediate danger, like their elders in such circumstances, see themselves in an essentially negative light. As one adolescent remarked: "Everything good I hear about myself I turn in my head to poison." One approach to heading off this dynamic is to split between the positive and negative self-images and between desires for life and death. The therapist may slowly develop this split through his remarks to the patient: "You've got to remember you have two sides." "Even if you want to die, there is still a part of you that wants to live." "Now I'd like to talk to the good you." "That's just your self-hatred talking." In this manner, the therapist can help the patient recognize that the negative self is not the entire self and can halt the snowballing of negative energies without direct conflict. At the same time, the therapist draws attention to the patient's positive aspects, however limited.

In this dialogue, the therapist forms an alliance with the positive self. Through it, he can offer the warmth, satisfaction, assurance, and affirmation needed for the desire to live. In the course of treatment, one can see how this approach is slowly internalized. No little effort should be directed at abetting this process.

Throughout therapy, setbacks and disappointments may upset the delicate balance being formed. The positive image needs constant bolstering because of the patient's lack of internal supports. However, achieving a split between positive and negative selves must be seen as a major advance. It permits the therapist to avoid direct aggressive confrontation with the suicidal tendency, often a barren and fruitless course. Greater returns can be expected by the indirect course of splitting and bolstering self-image in order to implant the positive forces within against those of self-destruction.

## Summary

The evaluation and treatment of a child in danger of committing suicide must take place within the family context. Some of the diagnostic processes and treatment relate to family life in general, and some are specific to the destructive suicidal processes of the child himself. The central themes in assessing risk are the attraction that death holds for the child, the degree of his alienation within the family, his social status and ability to express emotions, and his ability to cope with problems. Other important aspects for diagnosis and evaluation are the parental relationship, the parents' depressions and suicidal tendencies, the child's place in the family, and the unresolvable problem.

Treatment focuses on relations between the parents and the relationship with their child in varying family settings. The specific aspects of therapy basically relate to bringing about change in destructive behavioral patterns, unraveling the unresolvable problem, providing corrective experiences, and satisfying basic needs. Distinctive principles include the examination of the death fantasy, empathetic participation in considering suicide, splitting of the self-image, and alliance with sources of strength. The common aim is to rebalance the conflict over life and death.

### Concluding Remarks

We can no longer tell ourselves reassuringly that very young children are incapable of contemplating, attempting, or actually committing suicide. Plainly, although actual instances of child suicide are relatively rare, young children do display suicidal behavior and harbor suicidal thoughts. In fact, it is striking to learn how early in life children can be devoured by feelings of hopelessness and helplessness to the point of total desperation and surrender to death.

In this book, I have taken the position that suicidal behavior in young children develops in a particular kind of family setting—namely, a setting where the child is forced to try to solve an unresolvable problem; and I have examined this problem in the framework of a broader phenomenological model with implications for evaluation, therapy, and to some extent prevention. Nevertheless, many additional questions remain about childhood suicide: Are all children affected in the same way by the devastating circumstances that lead to suicide? What other dynamic processes are involved? What, if any, is the role of genetic or social or cultural factors? Most important, how is suicidal behavior in childhood related to suicide at a later age, especially adolescence? An assumption was made in this book that the most dangerous aspect of childhood suicidal behavior is that it constitutes a nucleus for suicidal acting out in later ages. But that assumption should be further scrutinized.

One of the most important implications of the knowledge about self-destruction in children goes beyond the problem of suicide. That is, we have learned that very young children can take an existential stand with regard to issues of life and death. They do cope with death and feelings about death. Living in this world apparently poses a continuous dilemma for the young child, just as it does for adolescents and adults.

The child's deep interest in questions about life and death has been underestimated in the study of developmental psychology. If children are capable of consciously committing suicide or suicidal acts, then issues related to death must play an important role in their development. This topic deserves more attention than it has hitherto been given by psychologists and psychiatrists. In fact, the assessment of suicidal behavior should become a standard procedure in the evaluation of normal and problematic children, along with evaluation of other aspects of personality and behavior.

Many professionals who deal with children may believe that it is futile and unrewarding to attempt to treat suicidal children. I hope this book has demonstrated that such a belief is unfounded. As in all areas of therapy with young children, change and growth are frequent results of therapeutic and preventive work with suicidal children. These children are touchingly responsive to sincere, genuine, and enlightened therapeutic efforts on their behalf.

# References

Ackerly, W. C. "Latency-Age Children Who Threaten or Attempt to Kill Themselves." *Journal of the American Academy of Child Psychiatry,* 1967, *6,* 242–261.

Alexander, I. E., and Adlerstein, A. M. "Affective Responses to the Concept of Death in a Population of Children and Early Adolescents." *Journal of Genetic Psychology,* 1958, *93,* 167–177.

Ambrosini, P. J., Rabinovich, H., and Puig-Antich, J. "Biological Factors and Pharmacological Treatment in Major Depressive Disorders in Children and Adolescents." In H. S. Sudak, A. B. Ford, and N. B. Rushforth (eds.), *Suicide in the Young.* Littleton, Mass.: John Wright, 1984.

Amir, A. "Suicide Among Minors in Israel." *Israel Annals of Psychiatry and Related Disciplines,* 1973, *11,* 219–269.

Anthony, S. *The Child's Discovery of Death.* San Diego, Calif.: Harcourt Brace Jovanovich, 1940.

Anthony, S. *The Discovery of Death in Childhood and After.* New York: Basic Books, 1972.

Barraclough, B. M. "Differences Between National Suicide Rates." *British Journal of Psychiatry,* 1973, *122,* 95–96.

Beck, A. T., Rush, A. J., Show, B., and Emery, G. *Cognitive Therapy of Depression.* New York: Guilford Press, 1979.

Bemporad, J. "Psychodynamics of Depression in Children and

Adolescents." In S. Arieti and J. Bemporad (eds.), *Severe and Mild Depression.* New York: Basic Books, 1978.

Bluebond-Langner, M. *The Private World of Dying Children.* Princeton, N.J.: Princeton University Press, 1978.

Bowlby, J. *Attachment and Loss.* Vol. 1: *Attachment.* New York: Basic Books, 1969.

Bowlby, J. *Attachment and Loss.* Vol. 2: *Separation: Anxiety and Anger.* New York: Basic Books, 1973.

Bowlby, J. *Attachment and Loss.* Vol. 3: *Loss: Sadness and Depression.* New York: Basic Books, 1980.

Breed, W. "The Negro and Fatalistic Suicide." *Pacific Social Review,* 1970, *13,* 156–162.

Brent, S. B. "Puns, Metaphors and Misunderstanding in a Two-Year-Old's Conception of Death." *Omega,* 1977, *8,* 285–295.

Canon, T. J., Liebeskind, J. C., and Frenk, H. "Neural and Neurochemical Mechanisms of Pain Inhibition." In R. A. Sternbach (ed.), *The Psychology of Pain.* New York: Raven Press, 1978.

Carlson, G. A. "Depression and Suicidal Behavior in Children and Adolescents." In D. P. Cantwell and G. A. Carlson (eds.), *Affective Disorders in Childhood and Adolescence: An Update.* Jamaica, N.Y.: Spectrum Publications, 1983.

Carlson, G. A., and Cantwell, D. P. "A Survey of Depressive Symptoms in a Child and Adolescent Psychiatric Population." *Journal of the American Academy of Child Psychiatry,* 1979, *18,* 587–599.

Carlson, G. A., and Cantwell, D. P. "Unmasking Masked Depression in Children." *American Journal of Psychiatry,* 1980, *137,* 445–449.

Carlson, G. A., and Orbach, I. "Depression and Children's Attitudes Toward Death and Suicide." In *Proceedings of the American Academy of Child Psychiatry.* Washington, D.C.: American Academy of Child Psychiatry, 1982.

Chiles, J. A., Miller, M. L., and Cox, G. B. "Depression in an Adolescent Delinquent Population." *Archives of General Psychiatry,* 1980, *37,* 1179–1186.

Cohen-Sandler, R., Berman, A., and King, R. "Life Stress and Symptomatology: Determinants of Suicidal Behavior in Chil-

dren." *Journal of the American Academy of Child Psychiatry,*
1982, *21,* 178-186.

Connell, R. H. "Suicide Attempts in Childhood and Adolescence." In J. C. Howells (ed.), *Modern Perspectives in Child
Psychiatry.* London: Oliver Boyd, 1963.

Corder, B. F. "A Study of Social and Psychological Characteristics of Adolescent Suicide: Attempters in an Urban Disadvan-
taged Area." *Adolescence,* 1974, *9,* 1-6.

Crook, T., and Raskin, A. "Association of Childhood Parental
Loss with Attempted Suicide and Depression." *Journal of
Consulting and Clinical Psychology,* 1975, *43,* 277-278.

DeVos, G. A. "Ethnic Adaptation and Minority Status." *Journal of Cross-Cultural Psychology,* 1980, *11* (1), 101-104.

Dorpat, T. L., Jackson, J. K., and Ripley, H. S. "Broken Homes
and Attempted and Completed Suicide." *Archives of General
Psychiatry,* 1965, *12,* 213-216.

Durkheim, E. *Suicide: A Study in Sociology.* New York: Free
Press, 1951. (Originally published 1897.)

Farberow, N. L. "The Role of the Family in Suicide." Paper
presented at the 10th convention of the International Association of Suicide Prevention and Crisis Intervention, Paris,
July 1981.

Farberow, N. L., and Shneidman, E. S. (eds.). *The Cry for Help.*
New York: McGraw-Hill, 1965.

Fenichel, O. *The Psychoanalytic Theory of Neurosis.* New
York: Norton, 1945.

Florian, V., and Kravetz, S. "Fear of Personal Death: Attribution, Structure and Relation to Religious Belief." *Journal of
Personality and Social Psychology,* 1983, *44,* 600-607.

Florian, V., and Kravetz, S. "Children's Perception of Death: A
Cross-Cultural Study Among Muslims, Druz, Christians and
Jews in Israel." *Journal of Cross-Cultural Psychology,* 1985,
*16,* 174-189.

Frederick, C. J. "An Introduction and Overview of Youth Suicide." In M. L. Peck, N. L. Farberow, and R. E. Litman (eds.),
*Youth Suicide.* New York: Springer, 1985.

Freud, S. "The Ego and the Id." In J. Strachey (ed. and trans.),
*The Standard Edition of the Complete Psychological Works*

*of Sigmund Freud.* Vol. 19. London: Hogarth Press, 1953. (Originally published 1927.)

Furman, E. *A Child's Parent Dies.* New Haven, Conn.: Yale University Press, 1974.

Furman, E. "Some Difficulties in Assessing Depression and Suicide in Childhood." In H. S. Sudak, A. B. Ford, and N. B. Rushforth (eds.), *Suicide in the Young.* Littleton, Mass.: John Wright, 1984.

Gesell, A., and Ilg, F. L. *The Child from Five to Ten.* New York: Harper & Row, 1946.

Glaser, K. "Attempted Suicide in Children and Adolescents: Psychodynamic Observations." *American Journal of Psychotherapy,* 1965, *19,* 220–227.

Gould, R. E. "Suicide Problems in Children and Adolescents." *American Journal of Psychotherapy,* 1965, *19,* 228–246.

Green, A. H. "Self-Destructive Behavior in Battered Children." *American Journal of Psychiatry,* 1968, *135* (5), 579–581.

Grollman, E. A. (ed.). *Explaining Death to Children.* Boston: Beacon Press, 1967.

Haider, I. "Suicidal Attempts in Children and Adolescents." *British Journal of Psychiatry,* 1968, *114,* 1113–1134.

Hendin, H. "Suicide Among the Young: Psychodynamics and Demography." In M. L. Peck, N. L. Farberow, and R. E. Litman (eds.), *Youth Suicide.* New York: Springer, 1985.

Holinger, P. C., and Offer, D. "Toward the Prediction of Violent Deaths Among the Young." In H. S. Sudak, A. B. Ford, and N. B. Rushforth (eds.), *Suicide in the Young.* Littleton, Mass.: John Wright, 1984.

Hussain, S. A., and Vandiver, T. *Suicide in Children and Adolescents.* Lancaster, England: MTP Press, 1984.

Jacobs, J. *Adolescent Suicide.* New York: Wiley International, 1971.

Jaffe, Y. "Some Aspects of Childhood Depression." (In Hebrew.) *Psychology and Counseling in Education,* 1987, *1* (3), 215–225.

Jaffe, Y., Feshbach, S., and Feshbach, N. "Childhood Depression: Relationships with Self-Esteem, Aggression and Academic Achievement." Unpublished manuscript, University of California, Los Angeles, 1983.

Kane, B. "Children's Concept of Death." Unpublished doctoral dissertation, University of Cincinnati, 1978.

Kane, B. "Children's Conception of Death." *Journal of Genetic Psychology,* 1979, *134,* 141-153.

Kastenbaum, R. "The Child's Understanding of Death: How Does It Develop?" In E. A. Grollman (ed.), *Explaining Death to Children.* Boston: Beacon Press, 1967.

Kastenbaum, R. *Death, Society and Human Experience.* St. Louis: Mosby, 1977.

Kastenbaum, R., and Aisenberg, R. *The Psychology of Death.* New York: Springer, 1972.

Kazdin, A. E. "Assessment Techniques for Childhood Depression: An Empirical Appraisal." *Journal of the American Academy of Child Psychiatry,* 1981, *20,* 358-375.

Kazdin, A. E., and others. "Hopelessness, Depression and Suicidal Intent Among Psychiatrically Disturbed Inpatient Children." *Journal of Consulting and Clinical Psychology,* 1983, *5* (4), 504-510.

Kellerman, J., Zeltzer, L., Ellenberg, L., and Rigler, D. "Psychological Effects of Illness in Adolescence." *Journal of Pediatrics,* 1980, *97,* 126-131.

Klein, M. "A Contribution to the Theory of Anxiety and Guilt." *International Journal of Psychoanalysis,* 1948, *29,* 114-123.

Koocher, G. "Talking with Children About Death." *American Journal of Orthopsychiatry,* 1974, *44,* 404-411.

Kosky, R. "Childhood Suicidal Behavior." *Journal of Child Psychology and Psychiatry,* 1983, *24* (3), 457-468.

Kovacs, M., and Beck, A. T. "An Empirical-Clinical Approach Toward a Definition of Childhood Depression." In J. G. Schulterbrandt and A. Raskin (eds.), *Depression in Childhood: Diagnosis, Treatment and Conceptual Models.* New York: Raven Press, 1977a.

Kovacs, M., and Beck, A. T. "The Wish to Die and the Wish to Live in Attempted Suicide." *Journal of Clinical Psychology,* 1977b, *33,* 361-365.

Lefkowitz, M. M., and Burton, N. "Childhood Depression: A Critique of the Concept." *Psychological Bulletin,* 1978, *85,* 716-726.

Leon, G. R., Kendall, P. C., and Garber, J. "Depression in Children: Parent, Teacher, and Child Perspectives." *Journal of Abnormal Child Psychology,* 1980, *8,* 221-235.

Levi, I. D., Fales, C. H., Stein, M., and Sharp, L. H. "Separation and Attempted Suicide." *Archives of General Psychiatry,* 1966, *12,* 213-216.

Leviton, O. "Life and Death Attitudes of Parents of Children with Problems." *Omega,* 1971, *8,* 333-357.

Lonetto, R. *Children's Conception of Death.* New York: Springer, 1980.

McCarthy, J. B. *Death Anxiety: The Loss of the Self.* New York: Gardner Press, 1980.

McWhirter, L., Young, V., and Mazury, Y. "Belfast Children's Awareness of Violent Death." *British Journal of Social Psychology,* 1983, *22,* 81-92.

Maris, R. M. *Pathways to Suicide: A Survey of Self-Destructive Behavior.* Baltimore: Johns Hopkins University Press, 1981.

Marx, P. A., and Heller, D. L. "Now I Lay Down for Keeps: A Study of Adolescent Suicide Attempts." *Journal of Clinical Psychology,* 1977, *33,* 390-400.

Mattson, A., Seese, L. R., and Hawkins, J. W. "Suicidal Behavior as a Child Psychiatric Emergency." *Archives of General Psychiatry,* 1969, *20,* 100-109.

Maurer, A. "Maturation of Concepts of Death." *British Journal of Medicine and Psychology,* 1960, *39,* 35-41.

Maurer, A. "Adolescent Attitudes Toward Death." *Journal of Genetic Psychology,* 1964, *105,* 75-90.

Melear, J. "Children's Conception of Death." *Journal of Genetic Psychology,* 1972, *123,* 359-360.

Menninger, K. *Man Against Himself.* San Diego, Calif.: Harcourt Brace Jovanovich, 1938.

Mitchell, M. C. *The Child's Attitude to Death.* New York: Schocken Books, 1967.

Motto, J. A. "Treatment Concerns in Preventing Youth Suicide." In M. L. Peck, N. L. Farberow, and R. E. Litman (eds.), *Youth Suicide.* New York: Springer, 1985.

Nagy, M. "The Child's View of Death." *Journal of Genetic Psychology,* 1948, *73,* 3-27.

Neubower, D. N. "Suicide in Children: An Analysis of 31 Cases."

Paper presented at the 139th annual meeting of the American Psychiatric Association, Washington, D.C., May 10–16, 1986.

Neuringer, C. "Changes in Attitudes Toward Life and Death During a Serious Suicidal Attempt." *Omega,* 1970, *1,* 301–309.

Novic, J. "Attempted Suicide in Adolescents: The Suicidal Sequence." In H. S. Sudak, A. B. Ford, and N. B. Rushforth (eds.), *Suicide in the Young.* Littleton, Mass.: John Wright, 1984.

Orbach, I. "Suicidal Behavior in Young Children." Paper presented at the 11th convention of the International Association for Suicide Prevention and Crisis Intervention, Paris, Aug. 1981.

Orbach, I. "Personality Characteristics, Life Circumstances and Dynamics of Suicidal Children." *Death Education,* 1984 (Supp.), pp. 37–52.

Orbach, I. "Assessment of Suicidal Behavior in Young Children: Case Demonstration." In R.F.W. Diekstra (ed.), *Suicidal Behavior Among Adolescents.* Amsterdam: Martinus Nijhoff, 1986.

Orbach, I., Bar-Yosef, H., and Dror, J. "Problem-Solving Strategies Among Suicidal Individuals." Unpublished manuscript, Bar-Ilan University, Ramat Gan, Israel, 1987.

Orbach, I., Feshbach, S., Carlson, G., and Ellenberg, L. "Attitudes Towards Life and Death in Suicidal, Normal, and Chronically Ill Children: An Extended Replication." *Journal of Consulting and Clinical Psychology,* 1984, *52,* 1020–1027.

Orbach, I., and Florian, V. "Attitudes Toward Life and Death in Religious and Nonreligious Boys and Girls." Unpublished manuscript, Bar-Ilan University, Ramat Gan, Israel, 1986.

Orbach, I., and Glaubman, H. "Suicidal, Aggressive and Normal Children's Perception of Personal and Impersonal Death." *Journal of Clinical Psychology,* 1978, *34,* 850–857.

Orbach, I., and Glaubman, H. "Children's Perception of Death as a Defensive Process." *Journal of Abnormal Psychology,* 1979a, *88* (6), 671–674.

Orbach, I., and Glaubman, H. "The Concept of Death and Suicidal Behavior in Young Children." *Journal of the American Academy of Child Psychiatry,* 1979b, *18* (4), 668–678.

Orbach, I., Gross, Y., and Glaubman, H. "Some Common Characteristics of Latency Age Suicidal Children: A Tentative Model Based on a Case Study Analysis." *Suicide and Life-Threatening Behavior,* 1981, *4,* 180-190.

Orbach, I., Gross, Y., Glaubman, H., and Berman, D. "Children's Perception of Death in Humans and Animals as a Function of Age, Anxiety and Cognitive Ability." *Journal of Child Psychology and Psychiatry,* 1985, *26,* 453-463.

Orbach, I., Rosenheim, E., and Hary, E. "Some Aspects of Cognitive Functioning in Suicidal, Chronically Ill, and Normal Children." *Journal of the American Academy of Child and Adolescent Psychiatry,* 1987, *26,* 181-185.

Orbach, I., Talmom, O., Kedem, P., and Har-Even, D. "Sequential Patterns of the Death Concepts in Children." *Journal of the American Academy of Child and Adolescent Psychiatry,* 1987, *26,* 578-582.

Orbach, I., and others. "Attraction and Repulsion by Life and Death in Suicidal and Normal Children." *Journal of Consulting and Clinical Psychology,* 1983, *51,* 661-670.

Otto, U. "Suicidal Acts by Children and Adolescents: A Follow-Up Study." *Acta Psychiatrica Scandinavica,* 1977 (Supp.), pp. 5-123.

Paulson, M. J., Stone, D., and Sposto, R. "Suicide Potential and Behavior in Children Ages 4 to 12." *Suicide and Life-Threatening Behavior,* 1978, *8* (4), 225-242.

Peck, M. "Youth Suicide." *Death Education,* 1982, *6,* 29-42.

Petti, T. A. "Depression in Hospitalized Child Psychiatry Patients: Approaches to Measuring Depression." *Journal of the American Academy of Child Psychiatry,* 1978, *17,* 49-59.

Pfeffer, C. R. "The Family System of Suicidal Children." *American Journal of Psychotherapy,* 1981a, *35,* 330-341.

Pfeffer, C. R. "Suicidal Behavior of Children: A Review with Implications for Research and Practice." *American Journal of Psychiatry,* 1981b, *138* (2), 154-159.

Pfeffer, C. R., Conte, H. R., Plutchik, R., and Jerrett, I. "Suicidal Behavior in Latency Age Children: An Empirical Study." *Journal of the American Academy of Child Psychiatry,* 1979, *18,* 679-692.

Pfeffer, C. R., Conte, H. R., Plutchik, R., and Jerrett, I. "Suicidal Behavior in Latency Age Children: An Outpatient Population." *Journal of the American Academy of Child Psychiatry,* 1980, *19,* 703–710.

Pfeffer, C. R., Plutchik, R., and Mizruchi, M. S. "Suicidal and Assaultive Behavior in Children: Classification, Measurement and Interrelations." *American Journal of Psychiatry,* 1983, *140,* 154–157.

Pfeffer, C. R., Zuckerman, S., Plutchik, R., and Mizruchi, M. S. "Suicidal Behavior in Normal School Children: A Comparison with Child Psychiatric Inpatients." *Journal of the American Academy of Child Psychiatry,* 1984, *23,* 416–423.

Phillips, D. P., and Carstensen, L. L. "Clustering of Teenage Suicide After Television News Stories About Suicide." *New England Journal of Medicine,* 1986, *315* (11), 685–689.

Piaget, J. *The Construction of Reality in the Child.* New York: International Universities Press, 1954.

Puig-Antich, J. "Major Depression and Conduct Disorders in Prepuberty." *Journal of the American Academy of Child Psychiatry,* 1982, *21,* 118–128.

Puig-Antich, J. "Affective Disorders." In H. I. Kaplan and B. J. Sadock (eds.), *Comprehensive Textbook of Psychiatry.* (4th ed.) Vol. 2. Baltimore: Williams & Wilkins, 1985.

Puig-Antich, J., Chambers, W. J., and Tabrizi, M. A. "The Clinical Assessment of Current Depressive Episodes in Children and Adolescents: Interviews with Parents and Children." In D. P. Cantwell and G. A. Carlson (eds.), *Affective Disorders in Childhood and Adolescence: An Update.* Jamaica, N.Y.: Spectrum Publications, 1983.

Reilly, T. P., Hasazi, E. J., and Bond, L. A. "Children's Conception of Death and Personal Mortality." *Journal of Pediatric Psychology,* 1983, *8,* 21–31.

Reiner, J. D. "Genetic Factors in Depression." *American Journal of Psychotherapy,* 1984, *38,* 329–340.

Richman, J. "Family Determinants of Suicide Potential." In D. B. Anderson and L. J. McLean (eds.), *Identifying Suicide Potential.* New York: Human Sciences Press, 1971.

Richman, J. "Symbiosis, Empathy, Suicidal Behavior and the

Family." *Suicide and Life-Threatening Behavior,* 1978, *8* (3), 139-149.

Richman, J. "Family Therapy of Attempted Suicide." *Family Process,* 1979a, *18,* 131-142.

Richman, J. "Suicide and the Closed Family System." Paper presented at the 10th International Congress for Suicide Prevention and Crisis Intervention, Ottawa, Canada, June 1979b.

Richman, J. "The Family Therapy of Suicidal Adolescents: Promises and Pitfalls." In H. S. Sudak, A. B. Ford, and N. B. Rushforth (eds.), *Suicide in the Young.* Littleton, Mass.: John Wright, 1984.

Richman, J., and Pfeffer, C. "Figure Drawings for the Assessment of Suicide Potential in Children." Paper presented at the 9th International Congress for Suicide Prevention and Crisis Intervention, Helsinki, Finland, 1977.

Rie, H. E. "Depression in Childhood: A Survey of Some Pertinent Contributions." *Journal of the American Academy of Child Psychiatry,* 1966, *5,* 653-685.

Rochlin, G. "The Loss Complex: A Contribution to the Etiology of Depression." *Journal of the American Psychoanalytic Association,* 1959, *7,* 299-316.

Rochlin, G. "How Younger Children View Death and Themselves." In E. A. Grollman (ed.), *Explaining Death to Children.* Boston: Beacon Press, 1967.

Rosenthal, P. A., and Rosenthal, S. "Suicidal Behaviors by Preschool Children." *American Journal of Psychiatry,* 1984, *141* (4), 520-525.

Ross, C. "Teaching Children the Facts of Life and Death." In M. L. Peck, N. L. Farberow, and R. E. Litman (eds.), *Youth Suicide.* New York: Springer, 1985.

Roy, A. "Family History of Suicide." *Archives of General Psychiatry,* 1983, *40,* 971-974.

Sabbath, J. C. "The Suicidal Adolescent—The Expendable Child." *Journal of the American Academy of Child Psychiatry,* 1969, *38,* 211-220.

Salk, L., and others. "Relationship of Maternal and Prenatal Conditions to Eventual Adolescent Suicide." *Lancet,* 1985, *16,* 624-627.

Scharl, A. E. "Regression and Restitution to Object Loss." *Journal of the Psychoanalytic Study of the Child*, 1961, *16*, 451–470.

Schechter, D. M. "The Recognition and Treatment of Suicide in Children." In E. S. Shneidman and N. L. Farberow (eds.), *Clues to Suicide*. New York: McGraw-Hill, 1957.

Schilder, P., and Wechsler, D. "The Attitudes of Children Toward Death." *Journal of Genetic Psychology*, 1934, *45*, 405–451.

Schotte, E. D., and Clum, A. G. "Suicidal Ideation in a College Population: A Test of a Model." *Journal of Consulting and Clinical Psychology*, 1982, *50*, 690–696.

Shaffer, D. "Suicide in Childhood and Early Adolescence." *Journal of Child Psychology and Psychiatry*, 1974, *15*, 275–291.

Shaffer, D., and Fisher, P. "The Epidemiology of Suicide in Children and Young Adolescents." *Journal of the American Academy of Child Psychiatry*, 1981, *20*, 545–565.

Shafii, M., and others. "Psychological Restructuring of Completed Suicide in Childhood and Adolescence." In H. S. Sudak, A. B. Ford, and N. B. Rushforth (eds.), *Suicide in the Young*. Littleton, Mass.: John Wright, 1984.

Shaw, G. R., and Scheklum, R. F. "Suicidal Behavior in Children." *Psychiatry*, 1965, *28* (2), 157–168.

Shneidman, E. *Voices of Death*. New York: Harper & Row, 1982.

Shneidman, E. *The Definition of Suicide*. New York: Wiley, 1985.

Smith, K. "An Ego Vulnerability Approach to Suicide Assessment." Paper presented at meeting of the Society for Personality Assessment, San Diego, Calif., March 1983.

Smith, K. "An Ego Vulnerability Approach to Suicide." Paper presented at a seminar on suicide in adolescents, Karl Menninger Institute, Topeka, Kans., 1984.

Speece, M. W. "Research Plan: Preliminary Investigation—A Study of Young Children's Death and Death-Related Experiences." Unpublished manuscript, Wayne State University, 1982.

Speece, M. W., and Brent, S. B. "Children's Understanding of

Death: A Review of Three Components of the Death Concept." *Child Development*, 1984, *55*, 1671-1686.

Spitz, R. A. *The First Year of Life*. New York: International Universities Press, 1965.

Stanley, E. J., and Barter, J. T. "Adolescent Suicidal Behavior." *American Journal of Orthopsychiatry*, 1970, *40* (1), 87-96.

Teicher, J. D., and Jacobs, J. "Adolescents Who Attempt Suicide." *American Journal of Psychiatry*, 1966, *122*, 1248-1257.

Tishler, C. L. "Intentional Self-Destructive Behavior in Children Under Age Ten." *Clinical Pediatrics*, 1980, *19* (7), 451-453.

Toolan, J. M. "Suicide and Suicidal Attempts in Children and Adolescents." *American Journal of Psychiatry*, 1962, *118*, 719-724.

Toolan, J. M. "Suicide in Children and Adolescents." *American Journal of Psychotherapy*, 1975, *29*, 339-344.

Topol, P., and Reznik, M. "Perceived Peer and Family Relationship, Hopelessness, and Locus of Control as Factors in Adolescent Suicide." *Suicide and Life-Threatening Behavior*, 1982, *12* (3), 141-150.

Tucker, S., and Cantor, P. "Personality and Status Profiles of Peer Counselors and Suicide Attempters." *Journal of Consulting Psychology*, 1975, *22*, 423-430.

Van Hellmuth, E. "The Child's Concept of Death." *Psychoanalytic Quarterly*, 1965, *34*, 499-516.

Van Praag, H. M. "Biological Suicide Research: Outcome and Limitations." *Biological Psychiatry*, 1986, *21*, 1305-1323.

Weinberg, W. A. "Depression in Children Referred to an Educational Diagnostic Center: Diagnosis and Treatment." *Journal of Pediatrics*, 1972, *83*, 1065-1072.

Weller, A., Florian, V., and Tenenbaum, R. "The Concept of Death—Masculine and Feminine Attributes." *Omega*, forthcoming.

Worden, W. J. *Grief Counseling and Grief Therapy*. New York: Springer, 1986.

Yalom, I. D. *Existential Psychotherapy*. New York: Basic Books, 1980.

Zeligs, R. *Children's Experience with Death*. Springfield, Ill.: Thomas, 1974.

# Index